Making Sense of the Multilevel Governance of Migration

Tiziana Caponio

Making Sense of the Multilevel Governance of Migration

City Networks Facing Global Mobility Challenges

Tiziana Caponio
Department of Cultures, Politics
and Society
University of Turin, and Collegio
Carlo Alberto
Turin, Italy

ISBN 978-3-030-82550-8 ISBN 978-3-030-82551-5 (eBook)
https://doi.org/10.1007/978-3-030-82551-5

This Palgrave Macmillan imprint is published by the registered company Springer Nature Switzerland AG
The registered company address is: Gewerbestrasse 11, 6330 Cham, Switzerland

To Chloe and Fabio, for always supporting me…

Preface

A buzzword, a compelling metaphor or a major theoretical breakthrough, multilevel governance (MLG) is certainly one of the concepts in political science that scholars cannot completely ignore. In this book I engage with the MLG perspective from a specific angle that might seem narrow in many respects: city networks (CNs) mobilised on migration and mobility issues. However, it is precisely by anchoring a rather vague concept to a concrete research puzzle that I aim to contribute more generally to pushing forward theorisation on what MLG is and how it works.

Since my Ph.D. in 2003, the importance of cities as the locus where migration and migrant integration policies concretely take shape has always been very clear to me. In 2008–2010 I had the opportunity to be directly involved in the *European Network of Cities for Local Integration Policies for Migrants* (CLIP, https://www.eurofound.europa.eu/about-clip). The network was founded in 2006 by the Congress of Local and Regional Authorities of the Council of Europe, the City of Stuttgart and Eurofound, the European Foundation for the Improvement of Living and Working Conditions (EUROFOUND). The aim was to support a learning process shared among the participating cities with the support of a group of expert European research centres. As a member of one of these centres, i.e. FIERI (the Forum for International and European Research on Immigration), I found myself in the privileged position of having direct access to rich first-hand material on 30 different European cities' integration policies and, most importantly, of observing their interactions and relations with one another and with various institutions and organisations in the European migration policy arena.

What intrigued me most about that experience was precisely the idea, conveyed by the leaders of the network and also by some—but not all—member cities, of being involved in a unique MLG policy process. In the end, this seemed to me very similar to what academics and scholars do all the time: travel, attend conferences, chat during coffee breaks and establish new relationships. Was all this social relations work really contributing to shaping the emergence of a new MLG of migration policy in Europe?

Looking at that experience ten years later in a completely different context might lead me to incline towards a pessimistic view. In fact, while writing this book in 2020 and 2021, hopes of a new age of migration MLG appeared vain as never before. Dramatic events like the 2015 'European refugee crisis' followed by the outbreak of the COVID-19 pandemic seem to have spearheaded an unprecedented era of revamped nationalism. Combined with the rise of populist parties and the spread of anti-immigration attitudes, migration policy in the dawn of the 2020s resembles more a case of multilevel crisis than multilevel governance. How has it come about that the great expectations of CLIP and other CNs in the EU supranational system are confronted with such a gloomy picture?

It was with this question in mind and with the memory of my enthusiastic engagement with the CLIP network that in 2014 I started to collect material on migration CNs in Europe. In 2018, I could finally start a research project on the topic, MiNMUS, 'Migration Policy in Multilevel Political Settings. City Networks in Europe and North America,' with the support of a Marie Curie fellowship awarded me by the European Union. This book is the result of this research journey on CNs and MLG, which has also brought me to question the supposed particularity of city engagement in the EU supranational system. To this end, I explored the experience of two CNs in the United States, which, as in Europe, were confronted in the 2010s with a perception of a mounting 'migration crisis.' As I will show, similarities in patterns of city mobilisation and networking on migration on the two sides of the Atlantic, which are certainly more than I originally expected, have led me to (re)think MLG in a non-EU-centric manner, as a configuration of policymaking which can find fertile ground in different multilevel political systems.

Therefore, going back to my direct experience in the CLIP network, I now have no doubt that I had been involved in an MLG project which succeeded in bringing together many different policymakers and stakeholders, even if without it eventually leading to a radical change in the usual state-based modes of making migration policy in the EU. The capacity of cities to rule the world, to borrow the words from Benjamin Barber's famous essay, is still an open question. This book takes a rather critical and sceptical view of such high expectations. Nevertheless, I remain convinced that cities and local communities are the fundamental contexts where many 'crises' can find a real resolution.

Tiziana Caponio
Department of Cultures, Politics
and Society
University of Turin, and Collegio
Carlo Alberto
Turin, Italy

Acknowledgements

As mentioned in the Preface, this study was realised in the context of the MInMUS project, 'Migration Policies in Multi-level Political Settings. City Networks in Europe and North America,' funded by the EU Marie Curie Fellowship programme (Standard Fellowships, Grant Agreement No. 794012). I would like to thank the Migration Policy Centre at the EUI for hosting the project, and more specifically its Director, Andrew Geddes, for all his support during my stay in Fiesole. Special thanks go to Martin Ruhs, Leila Hadj-Abdou, Andrea Pettrachin, Leiza Brumat, Lenka Dražanová, Sergio Carrera and all my MPC colleagues for their useful comments and many insightful conversations.

Since this book is the result of a long research process that started as early as 2014, I should probably thank more people than the space allows me. I will mention just a few. First of all, the FIERI group, and in particular Giovanna Zincone, Ferruccio Pastore and Irene Ponzo, with whom I worked in the CLIP project, and many more. The Department of Cultures, Politics and Society of the University of Turin and the Collegio Carlo Alberto, which provided me not only with the material resources to carry out the research but more importantly with a stimulating work environment and great colleagues with whom to exchange views and ideas.

I would also like to thank the many colleagues and friends in Europe and in the US with whom I shared ideas and insights on the MiNMUS Project. Again, the list would be too long for the publisher to accept.

However, I would like to mention at least the IMISCOE Standing Committee on the Multilevel Governance of Migration and Immigrant Policies, and more specifically Rinus Penninx, with whom I started to engage in IMISCOE, and then Peter Scholten and Ricard Zapata-Barrero, who shared the chair of the Standing Committee with me from 2013. On the other side of the Atlantic, special thanks go to Michael Jones-Correa, who generously helped me to better understand the role of cities in US migration policies, and to Els de Graaw, Meghan Benton and Philip Connor for contacts with and interesting conversations on mayors, cities and migration politics in the US. I would also like to mention the group at the Cornell Institute for European Studies which hosted me in April–June 2017, providing me with a unique opportunity to discuss my research ideas and collect background data.

In a final note, I would also like to thank the many interviewee partners that dedicated their precious time and attention (an anonymised list can be found in the Appendix). Thank you also to David Barnes for having copy-edited the manuscript and to Francesco Bagnardi and Yassin Dia for having helped me in the final stages of the book's preparation to put my chaotic sources and references in order. And, of course, special thanks go to my parents, Fabio and Chloe for their patience and support.

Contents

List of Figures

List of Tables

CHAPTER 1

Introduction

Abstract This introduction provides an overview of the theoretical and research puzzle underlying this book, which is the nexus between CNs and MLG on highly salient migration and mobility issues in the EU and US multilevel political settings. These are 'wicked' or 'intractable' policy issues for local authorities which are traditionally in the remit of national governments and dealt with in a top-down manner. The emergence of CN organisations has been interpreted by scholars, especially in the EU context, as indicative of a new MLG turn. However, we still lack a real understanding of the factors and mechanisms that can lead to the emergence of MLG policymaking on these issues. The research design presented in this chapter, which is based on a combination of transatlantic comparison, case study research and causal process tracing, has precisely the aim of contributing in this direction and pushing forward theorisation of the CN-MLG nexus in the migration policy field.

1.1 Migration and Mobility: What Challenges for Cities?

If at the beginning of 2000 the 'mobility turn' in the social sciences (Urry, 2000) had normalised the idea of a world on the move, not even two decades later the power of the state to determine who can move, under which conditions and how has re-emerged in all its strength. On the one hand, the refugee crises of 2015 in Europe and of 2017–2018 in the US

T. Caponio, *Making Sense of the Multilevel Governance of Migration*,
https://doi.org/10.1007/978-3-030-82551-5_1

(the so-called Central American Migrant Caravans) clearly brought to the fore that not everyone's movement is welcome and that states can effectively constrain what they see as the problematic movement of the poor and needy. On the other hand, at the beginning of 2020 the outbreak of the coronavirus pandemic unfolded an unprecedented mobility crisis, with people forcibly asked to stay put within the borders of their countries, regions and even cities of residence.

In a world that for decades had nurtured great expectations of the capacity of international and regional supranational organisations to coordinate states' responses to global challenges, withdrawal to the nationalism of old times indeed sounds like defeat. This book deals with exactly one of these great coordination challenges: that of cities coordinating through voluntary networks on matters of mobility and migration. While writing this book in summer and fall 2020, cities were confronted at the same time with the pandemic and new arrivals of migrants from areas of humanitarian crisis. This complex context notwithstanding, CNs both in Europe and in the US seemed no less convinced of their capacity to bring about change and deliver a better world:

> As the European Commission and member states are stepping up efforts to tackle the public health emergency, city governments are acting locally to protect people and business. And across Europe, our cities are collaborating to urgently learn from each other's responses and deal with the crisis in the most effective way. (*Eurocities' reaction to the Covid-19 Emergency*, March 2020)
>
> As the COVID-19 virus spreads across the nation and world, [...] Welcoming communities can and will play an important role, modelling how our values drive the decisions we make going forward, and we applaud the leadership already being demonstrated by so many on the local level in this moment. When certain groups are prevented from fully participating in the solution, communities risk the health and safety of all people. The uncertainties of COVID-19, our susceptibility to bias, and the impact of isolation will make it all the more important that we use our voice and power to maintain norms of cohesion and cooperation, especially across lines of difference. (Rachel Paric, Welcoming America, *Statement on the Covid-19 situation*, 13 March 2020, https://www.welcomingamerica.org/about/blog/covid19)

The statements reported above are testimony to the faith of cities in local thinking even in a context of unprecedented nationalist revival. The aim of this book, however, is not to celebrate cities' activism. That has already been done by influential policy analysts and political thinkers (for a liberal pragmatic perspective, see Barber, 2013; and for a review of the more critical neo-municipalism stream of thought, see Thompson, 2020). My aim is instead to sharpen and enrich our understanding of what really happens in city networking beyond official statements. Why do cities in different multilevel political contexts get together to coordinate their efforts and policies on typical matters of state sovereignty such as migration and mobility? And how? But most of all, are these coordination efforts from below leading to the emergence of a new multilevel governance of migration?

To answer these questions, in this book I take an original transatlantic comparative research approach which aims to go beyond an understanding of MLG as being intimately linked to the study of the EU sui-generis polity. While applying the MLG concept beyond Europe is certainly not new (for a review, see Agranoff, 2018; Alcantara et al., 2016), comparative studies are less common. For instance, Ongaro et al. (2010, p. 2) note that different research traditions, based on intergovernmental relations (IGR) theories in the US and MLG in the EU, reflect radical differences between the two political systems. However, other scholars regard this debate as somewhat obsolete. Behnke et al. (2019, p. 4), for instance, suggest employing Lowi's (1972) 'policy determines politics' perspective to understand how MLG policymaking can actually take place in different policy domains independently of the institutional context. MLG is therefore conceptualised as an instance of policymaking the occurrence of which in specific contexts and situations is a matter for empirical analysis. Building on these premises, transatlantic comparison is not only possible but extremely useful in order to theorise on MLG policymaking factors and mechanisms.

A transatlantic comparative perspective becomes even more important when considering the relation between CNs and MLG on matters of migration and mobility. As will be illustrated in this book, throughout the 2000s cities in both the EU and the US became increasingly involved in migration issues, leading to a lively debate on the local dimension of migration policy in the respective scholarly communities and, more recently, also to some trans-Atlantic comparative studies (see, e.g., de Graauw & Vermeulen, 2016). At the same time, migration CNs have been mushrooming, even though this development has only recently attracted scholarly attention (Lacroix, 2021). Most existing studies focus on European cases and take an EU-centred system approach to MLG, therefore implicitly assuming a strong causal link between the EU's supranational institutional opportunity structure and city mobilisation (Penninx, 2015). On the other hand, research studies on migration CNs on the other side of the Atlantic, even though they do not explicitly engage with the MLG approach, still unravel the complex multilevel political dynamics underlying their emergence (see, e.g., Huang & Liu, 2018; Housel et al., 2018; McDaniel et al., 2019).

Hence, the CN-MLG nexus, while it is often assumed to be a key development in policymaking in the context of increasing global interdependence and state authority dispersion (Agranoff, 2018, p. 45), is actually a missing link. Systematic research on why, how and with what effect CNs mobilise in the multilevel politics of migration and mobility is still scarce and falls short of advancing our understanding of MLG policymaking. This book, by proposing a comparative study on the nexus between migration CNs and MLG in the very different EU and US multi-layered institutional contexts, aims to fill this gap. In other words, the ambition is not only to produce more systematic empirical knowledge on a still under-researched phenomenon; instead, I aim to contribute to broadening our understanding of the role of CNs in MLG policy-making by pushing forward theorisation on the factors and mechanisms that account for the emergence of a nexus between them.

To this end, however, a preliminary clarification of how CN organisations and MLG are understood in this study is in order. This is precisely the aim of the Sects. 1.1 and 1.2 of this introduction. In Sect. 1.3 I present the case studies in the EU and the US and introduce the methodological approach underlying my empirical research on the CNs-MLG nexus, while Sect. 1.5 provides an outline and a brief illustration of the contents of the chapters of this book.

1.2 City Networks in Migration Policymaking. Assumptions and Open Questions

CNs can be defined as organisations that gather local authorities together on a voluntary basis in order to pursue some kind of perceived collective interest or purpose and therefore present established patterns of communication, policymaking and exchange (Acuto & Rayner, 2016, p. 1149).

In many cases, CNs link cities across different countries, therefore representing instances of transnational city networking (Flamant et al., 2021; Huggins, 2018). This book deals with the more encompassing category of CNs to include initiatives that, while based in specific countries, still pursue the aim of raising cities' approaches to migration beyond city and national walls and to this end establish links and connections with similar organisations in other countries and regions.

Compared with other policy areas like sustainability and environmental issues (Kern & Bulkeley, 2009), economic development (Herrschel & Newman, 2017), social cohesion and urban regeneration (Brenner, 2004), on which CNs started to mobilise in the early 1990s, city mobilisation on matters of mobility and migration in Europe and beyond is a recent phenomenon that started to take place in the early 2000s (on Europe, see Penninx, 2015; on the US and Canada, see Filomeno, 2017). This reflects the fact that states have always been reluctant to devolve control on an issue that touches on sensitive matters of sovereignty and national identity (Boswell & Geddes, 2011). However, throughout the 1990s states' responsibilities for migration started to gradually shift up to international and supra-national institutions, out to non-public actors and down to local-level authorities (Guiraudon & Lahav, 2000, p. 164). In this process of pluralisation of the migration policy arena, local authorities soon emerged to the fore as key players, not only in implementing national migration policies but also in actively shaping them from below (see, e.g., Penninx & Martiniello, 2004, pp. 139–141).

This local turn in research on migration policy resonates with more general discourses and analyses that emphasise the role of the city and urban governance in addressing the downfall of globalisation and exploiting the opportunities in global competition (Clarke, 2006; Hambleton & Simone Gross, 2007; Pierre, 2016). Migration policy scholars like Penninx (2015, p. 106) have stressed that "At the city level, the confrontation with the day to day consequences of immigration is far more direct ... European cities are increasingly aware that they need long-term, consistent integration policies in order to preserve their viability as communities and their liveability for all residents." For Thouez (2020, p. 651), "Facing the challenges of migration remains a non-choice for cities ... [Mayors and their administrations] are keenly aware that as their citizenry becomes more socially and economically diverse, they must find ways to govern that are both pragmatic and inclusive of all city residents."

As is clear, these statements rest on the assumption that CNs, by articulating the voice of cities in MLG policymaking, can concretely contribute to the adoption of more legitimate and effective policy solutions or, in other words, of policies that reflect the 'real' needs of local citizens and successfully address problematic issues at the grassroots level. However, evidence from empirical research does not fully support this thesis and poses a series of caveats that call for the problematisation of the role of CNs in MLG policymaking.

First of all, scholars have shown that local policymakers can well aim to exclude migrants rather than integrating them in the local community (for Europe, see, e.g., Mahnig, 2004; Ambrosini, 2013, 2020; for the US, Ramakrishnan & Wong, 2010; Varsanyi, 2010). What a 'pragmatic solution' is cannot be easily established a priori but will depend on (local) policymakers' interests, perceptions and definitions of the situation. Second, research on city international mobilisation shows that this is usually undertaken by politically sympathetic and/or well-organised pioneer cities (see, e.g., Kern & Bulkeley, 2009 on climate change mitigation), whereas in general a pattern of 'passivism' (Fourot et al., 2021, p. 2) will prevail because of a lack of either political interest in CNs or of resources to go international. It follows that the policies promoted by CNs will most probably reflect the situations and interests of pioneer cities and in any case will remain too general to respond to specific local situations in terms of migration pressure, the composition of the migrant population, structural conditions of the labour market, etc. It should come as no surprise if policies formally agreed on and officially supported by CNs are often disregarded by their members (Bansard et al., 2017, p. 230).

Building on these critiques, in this book I conceive of CNs as *arenas*, i.e. as organisations where different categories of actors with specific interests and views contribute to shaping internal strategies and agendas. In other words, CN engagement in MLG policymaking does not reflect cities' preferences or searches for pragmatic policy, but instead depends on the political strategies and agendas of network organisations. Having clarified my approach to CNs, below I introduce my perspective on the analysis of MLG.

1.3 Conceptualising MLG and the CN-MLG Nexus. An Actor-Centred and Relational Approach

The debate on the concept of MLG is apparently never-ending. What is worse, rather than contributing to clarification, ongoing discussions seem to have fuelled increasing definitional murkiness (Tortola, 2017, p. 234). To engage once more with this perspective might sound like a sterile if not useless exercise.

However, this criticism notwithstanding, there are at least two good reasons for undertaking systematic research on the CN-MLG nexus on highly pitched migration and mobility issues. First of all, both objects of analysis, i.e. CNs and MLG, have taken on strong normative connotations in policy discourses on migration. As mentioned above, pragmatic cities are depicted as key actors in promoting attempts to solve problems rather than just talking about them. Hence, from a policy perspective, research is needed in order to understand if and how such great expectations actually translate into concrete practices of MLG, and what the limits of CN action in different multilevel political contexts are.

Second, and from a more scientific point of view, conceptual disputes do not per se undermine the theoretical validity of concepts since such disputes are quite common in political science and in the social sciences more generally. What seems particular about MLG is the poor elaboration of causal explanations. To this end, it seems crucial to take a position in the debate and clarify how this study defines MLG and conceives the CN-MLG nexus.

For the purpose of this introduction (for a more detailed state-of-the-art review, see Chapter 2), I identify four main different uses of the term MLG that can be ordered along a classical Sartori abstraction ladder (Sartori, 1970). Whereas more abstract and general definitions are characterised by low intension, i.e. few and general defining attributes, and high extension, and therefore cover an ample range of empirical phenomena, constraining definitions based on the specification of key defining features apply to a more limited number of empirical referents.

At a very general and descriptive level, MLG is often used to allude to processes of dispersion of state power leading to increasing multilevelness and complexity in contemporary political systems. In this rather unspecified meaning, MLG is actually synonymous with multilevel politics (Scholten, 2013, p. 2015) and has often been the object of sharp criticism. As Peters and Pierre (2004, p. 88) sentence, “any complex and multi-faceted political process can be referred to as multi-level governance."

Down the ladder towards the middle we find a series of definitions which are revealing of a holistic 'system(s) approach' to MLG (Alcantara et al., 2016, p. 5). A clear case in point is the distinction between Type I and Type II MLG proposed by Hooghe and Marks (2003) in 2003. We will come back to this distinction in Chapter 2. For the time being, it suffices to note that, as underlined by Alcantara et al. (2016, p. 5) "the differentiation of subtypes suggests that MLG is an all-encompassing phenomenon that manifests itself in various forms," federalism included, to which Type I MLG actually corresponds (see also Curry, 2016, 2018). A less encompassing version of the system approach can be found in the original use of MLG by Gary Marks (1993, p. 402) in 1993 to characterise the European Community as a system of "continuous negotiation among nested governments at different territorial tiers."

At the bottom of the ladder can be found definitions of MLG as a specific *instance* of multilevel policymaking along with other possible instances like intergovernmental relations (IGR) (Alcantara et al., 2016; see also Scholten, 2013 for a similar approach). This is exactly the approach underlying this study. More specifically, Piattoni (2010, p. 83) indicates three criteria to understand whether a given policymaking process is or is not an instance of MLG: (1) different levels of government are simultaneously involved; (2) non-governmental actors at different levels are also involved; (3) relationships defy existing hierarchies and take the form of non-hierarchical networks. Similarly, Caponio and Jones-Correa (2018, p. 1999) propose a definition of MLG as a specific type of policy arrangement which presents three characteristics: (1) it challenges vertical state-centred hierarchies of distribution of power and responsibility and state/society boundaries; (2) actors are interdependent, in the sense that a certain policy cannot be carried out by just one level of government but the involvement of other tiers and non-public actors is required; and (3) interactions are based on cooperation and negotiation. Hence, a CN-MLG is only established when there is evidence of CN participation and engagement in a structure or process of policymaking that can be characterised as an instance of MLG along the lines defined above.

Even though literature is still scarce, as we will see in more depth in Chapter 2, some hypotheses or heuristic interpretations of the CN-MLG nexus can be distilled. More specifically, current debates underline the importance of three factors: (1) the particular EU institutional opportunity structure; (2) the pressure problem and increased interdependence created by new global challenges; and (3) CN leaders' policy agendas, e.g. mayors, city officials, CN staff officers, etc. Research in the migration policy field has focused on the first two factors. On the one hand, Penninx (2015) has shown that in the early 2000s the specific programmes and funding provided by the European Commission were crucial in sustaining the emergence of organisations representing the interests of cities and regions beyond their states of belonging. On the other hand, Scholten et al. (2018) emphasise "the 'bottom-up' coordinated efforts by local governments" (p. 2031) in triggering the establishment of MLG arrangements on the topic of CEE migrants' access to welfare services in the Netherlands.

In this book I build on these hypotheses but I aim to go beyond by proposing a more encompassing actor-centred and relational interpretative framework. As I will argue in Chapter 3, I see the engagement of CNs in MLG, and therefore the emergence of a nexus, as the result of the interaction between the demand side and the supply side of multilevel policymaking processes on migration. The demand side regards CN goals and strategies that are the results of internal political processes of agenda-setting engaging CN leaders/activists and (different categories of) members more generally. These agendas can be more or less favourable to pursuing collaborative policymaking relationships with other stakeholders and public authorities at different territorial levels. On the supply side instead, the institutional structure determines which actors and institutions, among the plethora of policymakers and stakeholders that can have an interest in mobilising on migration, represent the key gatekeepers that can provide CNs with important material and symbolic resources for participation in policymaking or simply deny any access. In the section below I briefly present my research strategy and anticipate some of the key results of this study.

1.4 Analysing and Theorising the CN-MLG Nexus. Towards a Research Strategy

To push forward our understanding of the CNs-MLG nexus, and theorise about the mechanisms and factors that account for its emergence, in this book I present an explorative in-depth study of four migration CNs, two in Europe and two in the US. Hence, the objects of this study are not cities but their network organisations. More specifically, the aim is to trace CNs' prevailing modes of policymaking and their eventual engagement in MLG-like decision-making arrangements in order to unravel the specific conditions under which a CN-MLG nexus is more likely to occur in the contentious migration policy field, how it works and what its impact on migration policy is.

To this end, I propose a research design based on a combination of comparative case studies and causal process tracing. Following Kay and Baker (2015, p. 3), such a research design is particularly well suited to dealing with the theoretical pluralism characterising research in public policy. On the one hand, it enables a comparative assessment of middle-range theoretical propositions; on the other, it allows for identification of other possible explanatory mechanisms and factors not considered in the literature.

In the context of this research strategy, as is clear, case selection is of paramount importance in order to set the empirical boundaries of the validity of the proposed theory on the causal factors and mechanism(s) linking X to Y, i.e. in our case CNs to MLG policymaking. To this end, I follow the diverse-case method, which, according to Gerring (2017, p. 98), has the aim of achieving maximum variance among the dimensions that are deemed relevant in the analysis. More specifically, as mentioned above, on the basis of the literature (for a more extensive review, see Chapter 3), two dimensions appear particularly relevant in accounting for the emergence of a CN-MLG nexus: the presence/absence of a supranational multilevel polity, which can offer specific opportunities for cities to establish and/or join migration CNs; and the type of network (see also Lacroix, 2021), to distinguish organisations directly promoted by cities to pursue their interests and approaches to migration from organisations established by external actors, like, for instance, an international organisation or an NGO, which will presumably have a different agenda from that of cities. Figure 1.1 presents the four cases which have been selected at the intersection of these two dimensions.

More specifically, in the EU supranational context the Eurocities Working Group on Migration and Integration (WGM&I) represents a case of transnational mobilisation directly promoted by municipalities, while the Intercultural Cities Programme (ICC), in contrast, is more of an externally promoted initiative since it was set up in 2008 by the Council of Europe with the support of the European Commission. Similarly, in the US Cities4Action (C4A) is a case of direct city mobilisation, while the

		Supranational level	
		Yes (EU)	No (US)
Mode of mobilisation	Directly promoted by cities	1) Working Group on Migration and Integration (WGM&I)	2) Cities for Action (C4A)
	Promoted by external actors	3) Intercultural Cities Programme (ICC)	4) Welcoming America (WA)

Fig. 1.1 Case selection

mobilisation of Welcoming America (WA) was undertaken by an NGO, and therefore it has an external origin.

Following the process tracing method, for each of the four CNs the study seeks to systematically investigate traces of within-case causal mechanisms and configurations of factors accounting for their engagement in MLG policymaking (for details on the methodology and data sources, see Sect. 3.4). A key result of the analysis carried out in this book is that the CN-MLG nexus is by no means a specificity of the EU context, since traces of such collaborative relationships can also be found in the US and, in the least likely case of WA, can be based on external mobilisation of cities by an NGO. The emergence of a CN-MLG nexus instead seems more linked to national governments' migration politics and interest in city mobilisation. Therefore, the in-depth reconstruction of the configuration of factors and causal mechanisms underpinning the involvement of migration CNs in MLG challenges the hypotheses suggested in the literature, while it draws attention to national governments' migration politics. Rather than being prompted by a bottom-up activation of cities, MLG is a product of the will of national governments and reflects their political orientations towards the issue.

This does not mean that CNs do not attempt to exert their influence in migration and mobility policymaking. Quite the contrary, they are often successful in putting pressure on specific aspects of national policy on the matter, as will be demonstrated. Nevertheless, successful lobbying or pressure does not seem to be linked to the emergence of cooperative modes of policymaking involving all the main stakeholders in the migration policy field. As I demonstrate in this book, instances of MLG policymaking, understood as a mode of governing migration based on cooperation between public and non-public actors operating on different territorial scales, not only are rare but are also underpinned by deeply rooted power and political dynamics.

1.5 Book Outline

This introduction has provided an overview of my theoretical and research puzzle, which is the nexus between CNs and MLG on highly salient migration and mobility issues. These are 'wicked' or 'intractable' policy issues for local authorities, traditionally in the remit of national governments and dealt with in a top-down manner. The study presented in this book aims to throw light on the emergence of CN organisations, which are often regarded by scholars, especially in the EU context, as indicative of a new MLG policy turn. However, we still lack a real understanding of the factors and mechanisms that can lead to the emergence of modes of non-hierarchical collaborative policymaking on the highly contentious migration issue.

To investigate this puzzle, in Chapter 2 I delve into scholarly debates on MLG and CNs in more depth to identify key perspectives, promising research avenues and also pitfalls and limitations. In the second part of the chapter, I build on this literature to propose a new conceptual and analytical framework that explicitly addresses the theorisation of the factors and mechanisms underlying the emergence of a CN-MLG nexus. This framework rests on two key premises: (1) a conceptualisation of MLG as a specific *instance* or mode of policymaking; and (2) an understanding of CNs as *arenas*, i.e. as organisations shaped by actors' different agendas and perspectives. Taken together, these two premises constitute the background against which I argue for a need to take an actor-centred relational approach to the analysis of the CN-MLG nexus.

Chapter 3 is dedicated to a discussion of the migration studies literature, which has addressed from different perspectives—i.e. EU policymaking, paradiplomacy and urban policy—the emergence of a CN-MLG link. More specifically, I review the scholarly debate on the local dimension of migration policy by first considering literature that focuses on policy outputs (3.2) and then studies that conceptualise policy as processes (3.3), therefore taking a more encompassing perspective that aims to contribute to the literature on multilevel policymaking dynamics beyond the specialist field of migration. In Sect. 3.4 I further develop my theoretical framework by first discussing the main hypotheses on the migration CN-MLG nexus that can be drawn from the literature and then presenting an actor-centred relational interpretative framework. In the concluding section I provide details of the methodology and data sources for my empirical study of migration CNs in the EU and the US.

Chapter 4 presents the research findings on the two Europe-based CNs, i.e. the WGM&I and the ICC Programme, through the use of structured narratives. Furthermore, following the causal process tracing methodology, for each case I provide a map of the sequence of events leading to the engagement of CNs in MLG. In a similar manner, Chapter 5 provides structured narratives on the two US-based networks, i.e. WA and C4A, together with maps of the sequences of events. At the end of each chapter, a cross-case comparative assessment of the CN-MLG nexus in each multilevel political context is provided.

In Chapter 6, I engage in a transatlantic cross-case comparison in order to assess the validity of the interpretations presented in the literature and draw conclusions on the explanatory leverage of the actor-centred and relational interpretative framework for the CN-MLG nexus. On this basis, I discuss the contribution of my study to ongoing debates on MLG (6.3) and on the role of CNs in the governance of global challenges (6.4). I finally identify perspectives and challenges for future developments in research on MLG, cities and migration in the context of the (post) COVID-19 pandemic.

References

Acuto, M., & Rayner, S. (2016). City networks: Breaking gridlocks or forging (new) lock-ins? *International Affairs, 92*, 1147–1166. https://doi.org/10.1111/1468-2346.12700

Agranoff, R. (2018). *Local governments in multilevel governance: The administrative dimension*. Lexington Books.

Alcantara, C., Broschek, J., & Nelles, J. (2016). Rethinking multilevel governance as an instance of multilevel politics: A conceptual strategy. *Territory, Politics, Governance, 4*, 33–51. https://doi.org/10.1080/21622671.2015.1047897

Ambrosini, M. (2013). 'We are against a multi-ethnic society': Policies of exclusion at the urban level in Italy. *Ethnic and Racial Studies, 36*, 136–155. https://doi.org/10.1080/01419870.2011.644312

Ambrosini, M. (2020). The local governance of immigration and Asylum: Policies of exclusion as a battleground. In M. Ambrosini, M. Cinalli, & D. Jacobson (Eds.), *Migration, border and citizenship: Between policy and public spheres* (pp. 195–215). Palgrave Macmillan.

Bansard, J. S., Pattberg, P. H., & Widerberg, O. (2017). Cities to the rescue? Assessing the performance of transnational municipal networks in global climate governance. *International Environmental Agreements, 17*, 229–246. https://doi.org/10.1007/s10784-016-9318-9

Barber, B. R. (2013). *If mayors ruled the world: Dysfunctional nations*. Yale University Press, New Haven.

Behnke, N., Broschek, J., & Sonnicksen, J. (2019). *Configurations, dynamics and mechanisms of multilevel governance*. Palgrave Macmillan.

Boswell, C., & Geddes, A. (2011). *Migration and mobility in the European Union*. Palgrave Macmillan.

Brenner, N. (2004). *New state spaces: Urban governance and the rescaling of statehood*. Oxford University Press.

Caponio, T., & Jones-Correa, M. (2018). Theorising migration policy in multilevel states: The multilevel governance perspective. *Journal of Ethnic and Migration Studies, 44*, 1995–2010. https://doi.org/10.1080/1369183X.2017.1341705

Clarke, S. E. (2006). Globalisation and the study of local politics: Is the study of local politics meaningful in the global age? In H. Baldershein & H. Wollman (Eds.), *The comparative study of local government and politics: Overview and synthesis* (pp. 33–65). Barbara Budrich Publishers.

Curry, D. (2016). The question of EU legitimacy in the social OMC peer review process. *Journal of European Social Policy, 26*, 168–182. https://doi.org/10.1177/0958928716637141

Curry, D. (2018). Intra-European movement: Multi-level or mismatched governance? In P. Scholten, M. van Ostaijen (Eds.), *Between mobility and migration: The multi-level governance of intra-European movement* (pp. 141–160). SpringerOpen.

de Graauw, E., & Vermeulen, F. (2016). Cities and the politics of immigrant integration: A comparison of Berlin, Amsterdam, New York City, and San Francisco. *Journal of Ethnic and Migration Studies, 42*, 989–1012. https://doi.org/10.1080/1369183X.2015.1126089

Filomeno, F. A. (2017). *Theories of local immigration policy*. Palgrave Macmillan.

Flamant, A., Fourot, A.-C., & Healy, A. (2021). At the interplay of subnationalization and supranationalization: City networks activism in the governance of immigration. *Local Government Studies* forthcoming.

Fourot, A.-C., Healy, A., & Flamant, A. (2021). French participation in transnational migration networks: Understanding city (dis)involvement and "passivism." *Local Government Studies*, 1–23. https://doi.org/10.1080/03003930.2020.1857246

Gerring, J. (2017). *Case study research: Principles and practices* (2nd ed.). Cambridge University Press.

Guiraudon, V., & Lahav, G. (2000). A reappraisal of the state sovereignty debate: The case of migration control. *Comparative Political Studies, 33*, 163–195. https://doi.org/10.1177/0010414000033002001

Hambleton, R., & Simone Gross, J. (2007). *Governing cities in a global era: Urban innovation, competition and democratic reform*. Palgrave Macmillan.

Herrschel, T., & Newman, P. (Eds.) (2017). *Cities as international actors: Urban and regional governance beyond the nation state*. Palgrave Macmillan.

Hooghe, L., & Marks, G. (2003). Unraveling the central state, but how? Types of multi-level governance. *American Political Science Review, 97*, 233–243. https://doi.org/10.1017/S0003055403000649

Housel, J., Saxen, C., & Wahlrab, T. (2018). Experiencing intentional recognition: Welcoming immigrants in Dayton, Ohio. *Urban Studies, 55*, 384–405. https://doi.org/10.1177/0042098016653724

Huang, X., & Liu, C. Y. (2018). Welcoming cities: Immigration policy at the local government level. *Urban Affairs Review, 54*, 3–32. https://doi.org/10.1177/1078087416678999

Huggins, C. (2018). Subnational transnational networking and the continuing process of local-level Europeanization. *European Urban and Regional Studies, 25*, 206–227. https://doi.org/10.1177/0969776417691564

Kay, A., & Baker, P. (2015). What can causal process tracing offer to policy studies? A review of the literature. *Policy Studies Journal, 43*, 1–21. https://doi.org/10.1111/psj.12092

Kern, K., & Bulkeley, H. (2009). Cities, Europeanization and multi-level governance: Governing climate change through transnational municipal networks. *JCMS: Journal of Common Market Studies*, 47, 309–332. https://doi.org/10.1111/j.1468-5965.2009.00806.x

Lacroix, T. (2021). Migration related city networks: A global overview. *Local Government Studies*. https://doi.org/10.1080/03003930.2021.1938553

Lowi, T. J. (1972). Four systems of policy, politics and choice. *Public Administration Review, 32*, 298–310.

Mahnig, H. (2004). The politics of minority-majority relations: How immigrant policies developed in Paris, Berlin, Zurich. In R. Penninx, K. Kraal, M. Matiniello, & S. Vertovec (Eds.), *Citizenship in European Cities: Immigrants, local politics and integration policies* (pp. 17–37). Ashgate.

Marks, G. (1993). Structural policy and multilevel governance in the EC. In A. Cafruny & G. G. Rosenthal (Eds.), The Maastricht debates and beyond. The state of the European community (Vol. 2, pp. 391–410). Lynne Rienner.

McDaniel, P. N., Rodriguez, D. X., & Wang, Q. (2019). Immigrant integration and receptivity policy formation in welcoming cities. *Journal of Urban Affairs, 41*, 1142–1166. https://doi.org/10.1080/07352166.2019.1572456

Ongaro, E., Massey, A., Holzer, M., & Wayenberg, E. (Eds.). (2010). *Governance and intergovernmental relations in the European Union and the United States*. Edward Elgar.

Penninx, R. (2015). European cities in search of knowledge for their integration policies. In P. Scholten, H. Entzinger, R. Penninx, & S. Verbeek (Eds.), *Integrating immigrants in Europe: Research-policy dialogues* (pp. 99–115). Springer International Publishing.

Penninx, R., & Martiniello, M. (2004). Integration policies and processes: State of the art and lessons. In R. Penninx, K. Kraal, M. Martiniello, & S. Vertovec (Eds.), *Citizenship in European cities: Immigrants, local politics and integration policies* (pp. 139–163). Ashgate.

Peters, G. B., & Pierre, J. (2004). Multi-level governance and democracy: A Faustian bargain? In I. Bache & M. Flinders (Eds.), *Multi-level Governance* (pp. 75–89). Oxford University Press.

Piattoni, S. (2010). *The theory of multi-level governance: Conceptual, empirical, and normative challenges*. Oxford University Press.

Pierre, J. (2016). Urban and regional governance. In C. Ansell & J. Torfing (Eds.), *Handbook on theories of governance* (pp. 477–485). Edward Elgar Publishing.

Ramakrishnan, K., & Wong, T. (2010). Partisanship, not Spanish: Explaining municipal ordinance affecting undocumented immigrants. In M. W. Varsanyi (Ed.), *Taking local control: Immigration policy activism in U.S. cities and states* (pp. 74–96). Stranford University Press, Stanford.

Sartori, G. (1970). Concept misformation in comparative politics. *The American Political Science Review, 64*, 1033–1053. https://doi.org/10.2307/1958356

Scholten, P., Engbersen, G., van Ostaijen, M., & Snel, E. (2018). Multilevel governance from below: How Dutch cities respond to intra-EU mobility. *Journal of Ethnic and Migration Studies, 44*, 2011–2033. https://doi.org/10.1080/1369183X.2017.1341707

Scholten, P. W. A. (2013). Agenda dynamics and the multi-level governance of intractable policy controversies: The case of migrant integration policies in the Netherlands. *Policy Sciences, 46*, 217–236. https://doi.org/10.1007/s11077-012-9170-x

Thompson, M. (2020). What's so new about New Municipalism? *Progress in Human Geography*. https://doi.org/10.1177/0309132520909480

Thouez, C. (2020). Cities as emergent international actors in the field of migration: Evidence from the lead-up and adoption of the UN global compacts on migration and refugees. *Global Governance: A Review of Multilateralism and International Organizations, 26*, 650–672. https://doi.org/10.1163/19426720-02604007

Tortola, P. D. (2017). Clarifying multilevel governance. *European Journal of Political Research, 56*, 234–250. https://doi.org/10.1111/1475-6765.12180

Urry, J. (2000). Mobile sociology. *The British Journal of Sociology, 52*, 185–203. https://doi.org/10.1111/j.1468-4446.2009.01249.x

Varsanyi, M. W. (2010). *Taking local control: Immigration policy activism in U.S. cities and states*. Stranford University Press.

CHAPTER 2

Multilevel Governance and City Networks. Theorising the Missing Link

Abstract In this chapter, I delve into scholarly debates on MLG and CNs in more depth to identify key perspectives, promising research avenues and also pitfalls and limitations. In the second part, I build on this literature to propose a new conceptual and analytical framework for the theorisation of the factors and mechanisms underlying the emergence of a CN-MLG nexus. This framework rests on two key premises: (1) a conceptualisation of MLG as a specific *instance* or mode of policymaking; and (2) an understanding of the city as an *arena* and of CNs as organisations shaped by actors' different agendas and perspectives. Taken together, these two premises constitute the background against which I argue for a need to take an actor-centred and relational approach to the analysis of the CN-MLG nexus.

2.1 Unpacking the Puzzle. The CN-MLG Nexus Questioned

As I argued in Chapter 1, the existing literature tends to assume the presence of a virtuous nexus between CNs and MLG: through their network organisations, cities are able to contribute to the emergence of new modes of policymaking based on collaboration with public authorities and non-public actors operating on different territorial scales. However, evidence is still scarce and in the end contradictory. CNs are found

T. Caponio, *Making Sense of the Multilevel Governance of Migration*,
https://doi.org/10.1007/978-3-030-82551-5_2

to perform different functions and can assume different roles in policymaking processes (see, e.g., Kern & Bulkeley, 2009; Oomen, 2020). MLG does not seem to emerge as a priority for CNs, especially in the contentious migration policy field.

In this chapter, I argue that to push forward our understanding of the CN-MLG nexus we first need to problematise it. The thesis of cities as 'entrepreneurs of MLG' is just one possible scenario. *How* the CN-MLG nexus actually works and *which factors* and *mechanisms* account for its emergence are the key questions that we need to address in order to build the theoretical framework that will guide our empirical exploration on the involvement of CNs in—politically sensitive—migration policymaking. To this end, we first need to unpack our core concepts, i.e. CNs and MLG, in order to clarify how they have been understood in the relevant literatures.

As a matter of fact, scholars working on CNs with different disciplinary perspectives, e.g. critical political geography, urban economy, sociology and international relations, have often borrowed the concept of MLG without clearly specifying it. To complicate things further, different literatures have developed in isolation with almost no dialogue between them. Whereas for some scholars, like those working on city paradiplomacy, CNs are key actors in the emergence of a new MLG-like system of global governance (see, e.g., Curtis, 2014, pp. 2–10), for others, like critical political geographers, CNs are the product of the complex interdependencies underlying the dynamics of state power rescaling in the context of the neoliberal global economy (Brenner, 2004). In both literatures, however, the nexus with MLG policymaking remains foggy and under-specified.

To throw light on this nexus, in this chapter I propose a new conceptual and analytical framework that has the explicit aim of addressing the theorisation of the factors and mechanisms underlying the emergence of a CN-MLG nexus. This framework rests on two key premises: (1) a conceptualisation of MLG as an *instance* of policymaking; and (2) an understanding of CNs as arenas, that is as organisations shaped by actors' different agendas and perspectives. In the first part of this chapter, I discuss these two theoretical premises by grounding them in scholarly debates on MLG and CNs. Taken together, these premises constitute the background against which it is possible to formulate an explanatory framework of the CN-MLG nexus and to move the research agenda on MLG forward. To illustrate this framework is exactly the aim of the second part of the chapter.

2.2 Debating Multilevel Governance. From European Integration to the Local Turn

Very generally, and following the two main proponents of the term, i.e. Gary Marks and Lisbet Hooghe, MLG can be defined as the process of dispersion of authority away from the nation state across interdependent and yet autonomous public authorities and non-public organisations at different levels of government (Hooghe & Marks, 2001, p. xi). However, as I already pointed out in Sect. 1.3, at least four variants of the MLG concept can be found in political science, ranging from very general abstract understandings to more specific constraining ones. The concomitant presence of these different definitions in the literature greatly contributes to the ambiguity of the concept, which is often—implicitly—defined in different ways by scholars working in different research traditions and contributing to different debates. Below I discuss the variants of MLG underlying the political science literature to turn, in the second part of the section, to building an analytical framework for the analysis of MLG as an *instance* of policymaking that does not, however, renounce the ambition of the MLG literature to push forward theorisation on state authority restructuring in the age of globalisation.

2.2.1 *Variants of MLG: Systems and Instances of Multilevel Policymaking*

Of the four variants of MLG I identified in Sect. 1.3, three are the more common ones in the political science literature, i.e. variants 2, 3 and 4. These seem to correspond to three waves of conceptualisation that emanate from different—and yet often concomitant—debates: European integration; state authority dispersion or the unravelling of the nation state; and local policymaking and regulatory processes. More specifically, these debates—and the corresponding variants of MLG—differ along three key dimensions: (1) the prevailing analytic/explanatory or prescriptive/normative approach to theorisation; (2) the definition of governance; and (3) the type of actors and policymaking relations actually considered: whether they are limited to intergovernmental vertical relations or extended to horizontal relations with non-public actors.

The last two of these dimensions are particularly relevant since they regard the different theories of governance implied by MLG scholars. Governance is in itself a highly debated concept: some authors use it in a broad or encompassing sense to mean political steering and social regulation, including 'market' and 'hierarchy' as opposed ideal types (Keating, 2008, p. 76); others prefer a restricted use to indicate a specific mode of policymaking based on coordination and negotiation (see also Héritier, 2002, pp. 185–186; Treib et al., 2007, p. 4). Furthermore, whereas some scholars privilege a perspective focused on the vertical dimension of governing or intergovernmental relations, others link the concept to the emergence of new configurations of relations between public and non-public actors in the horizontal state-society dimension. Authors like Klijn and Koppenjan (2016, p. 11), for instance, use the expression 'network governance' to describe "public policymaking, implementation and service delivery through a web of relationships between autonomous yet interdependent government, business and civil society actors" (see also: Ansell & Gash, 2008).

Table 2.1 presents an analytical map of the different waves of conceptualisation of MLG along the three dimensions specified above, i.e. the theoretical approach, the definition of governance and the type of relationships.

The first wave of conceptualisation of MLG took place in the context of debates on European integration processes and the *sui generis* EU polity of the early-mid-1990s. Marks (1993, 1996) introduced the concept for analytical/explanatory purposes in order to make sense of unexpected developments in the building of the European Community and more specifically of structural and regional policies that established direct links

Table 2.1 Variants of MLG: theoretical debates

	Debate	*Theoretical approach*	*Definition of governance*	*Type of relationships*
EU sui generis system	European integration (early 1990s)	Descriptive-explanatory	Broad/encompassing	Vertical
System(s) approach	Optimal allocation of state power; federalism	Normative-prescriptive	Broad/encompassing	Primarily vertical
Instance of policy-making	Public policy, NPM and local government studies	Normative-prescriptive	Specific	Vertical and horizontal

between subnational governments and the European Commission for the first time. In terms of theories of governance, Marks's work explored the emergence of new forms of EU-centred modes of governing (Bache et al., 2016, p. 487) and therefore viewed governance essentially as intergovernmental vertical relations (see also: Stephenson 2013).

The second wave of conceptualisation of MLG draws on Hooghe and Marks's (Hooghe & Marks, 2003, 2004; Marks & Hooghe, 2000) co-authored works of the early 2000s and is aimed at contributing to normative/prescriptive theoretical debates on the optimal allocation of state authority, especially in federalist systems (see, e.g., Scharpf, 1997, 2001). Governance is understood as social and political regulation in a broad sense and can take different forms, as is pointed out by the identification of two sub-types of MLG characterised by different constitutional designs and legal jurisdictions (Hooghe & Marks, 2003, see also Sect. 1.3). Whereas type I MLG mirrors federalism and describes a governing arrangement based on a limited number of clearly defined non-overlapping territorial jurisdictions, each with a 'bundle' of functions, type II MLG is defined as a more anarchical order of single-purpose or task-specific jurisdictions with overlapping memberships. Although in principle Hooghe and Marks (2001) also mention the importance of processes of re-distribution of authority to non-public organisations operating at different levels of government, the role of non-governmental actors in the two types of MLG remains unspecified (Tortola, 2017, p. 4).

The re-conceptualisation of MLG as a system of state power allocation has favoured its application beyond the original domain of EU integration theory to a multiplicity of national, transnational and international political settings. More specifically, MLG has become increasingly debated in the context of globalisation studies as a benchmark to assess global governance structures (Zürn, 2011) and in the literature on problem-solving in federalist polities and in the EU (Benz, 2000; Scharpf, 1997, 2001). In this latter respect, scholars have emphasised the capacity of MLG systems to produce coordinated policy outputs in order to solve shared problems. Other authors (see: Heinelt & Niederhafner, 2008; Papadopoulos, 2007, 2010; Peters & Pierre, 2004), however, have highlighted the potential trade-off between problem-solving and democratic accountability in MLG systems (see also, Bache et al., 2016, p. 488). Maggetti and Trein (2019, p. 356), for instance, propose an assessment of type I and type II MLG in the EU in terms of both their problem-solving capacities and problem-generating potentials: whereas type I systems generate conflicts between jurisdictions on competences, funding and/or implementation practices, type II systems are likely to raise disputes on matters of legitimacy, democratic accountability and decision-making transparency.

The third and last wave of conceptualisation of MLG lies at the intersection between public policy analysis, new public management (NPM) and local government studies. Whereas debates on European integration and on state authority redefinition viewed MLG as a new emerging *system* of authority and power allocation, the third wave is characterised by a focus on the relations taking place in the context of processes of policymaking around specific issues. It is therefore an intrinsically relational perspective and looks at MLG as an *instance* or configuration of multilevel politics coexisting with other possible instances like intergovernmental relations (Alcantara et al., 2016, p. 36).

Similarly to the second wave described above, this third wave also shows a prevailing normative/prescriptive approach to theorisation. Scholten (2013, p. 230), for instance, emphasises the link between MLG and policy convergence across levels of government, a convergence that is regarded as preferable to risks of inconsistency and decoupling between national and local policies on migration. Other authors, however, also integrate in their theorisation efforts the horizontal dimension of state-society relations. A case in point is Agranoff's (2018) analysis of local governments in MLG policymaking. Somewhat echoing the New Public Management scholarly tradition, Agranoff (2018) takes a problem-solving perspective: in a scenario characterised by the intersection of complex vertical intergovernmental relations and horizontal partnership networks, MLG structures emerge at a subnational level to connect different public and private actors engaged in finding solutions to a specific policy issue. Alcantara and Nelles (2014, p. 192), on the other hand, put more stress on issues of accountability and participation, suggesting an understanding of MLG in terms of a "negotiated order" among public and non-public actors. For these authors, whose analysis develops in the context of the literature on (Canadian) federalism, the distinctive feature of MLG policymaking is interdependence, in the sense that "non-governmental actors cannot be effectively excluded from direct participation in policy processes as their collaboration is required for the success of the process."

Hence, the European integration-centred definition of MLG which had earmarked the origins of the concept appears to have been turned upside down by the focus of more recent literature on local governments. Whereas studies on European integration have looked at the mobilisation of subnational authorities linked to the new opportunity structure created by European policies, scholars in the third wave pay greater attention to local governments' agency and autonomous mobilisation beyond the EU and more specifically in different world regions and even at the global level (Agranoff, 2018; Herrschel & Newman, 2017). Below I take this local government perspective to elaborate a typology of possible instances or modes of policymaking in multilevel political settings.

2.2.2 *Instances of Policymaking in Multilevel Political Settings*

Existing definitions of MLG as a specific *instance* or configuration of policymaking in multilevel political settings (Alcantara et al., 2016; Caponio & Jones-Correa, 2018; Piattoni, 2010; Scholten, 2013) converge in identifying three key features: (1) different levels of government are simultaneously involved; (2) non-governmental actors at different levels are also involved; and (3) relationships between different levels of government and with non-governmental actors take the form of non-hierarchical networks based on cooperation and consensus building.

Whereas criterion 2 clearly asserts that instances of MLG do not have to be confused with instances of intergovernmental relations (Alcantara & Nelles, 2014), criterion 3 draws attention to the type of relationships that characterise MLG as a specific mode of policymaking, i.e. non-hierarchical and cooperative relations *in both* the intergovernmental/vertical and the state-society/horizontal dimensions. As such, MLG is likely to coexist with other possible modes of policymaking characterised by different levels of cooperation (or a lack thereof) in the vertical and/or horizontal dimensions.

Figure 2.1 presents a conceptual map of possible ideal types of modes of making policy in multilevel settings where policy is understood as the authoritative allocation of values (Easton, 1965), therefore implying some political steering on the part of one or more government authorities.[1] Taking a local government perspective, different configurations

[1] From the map are excluded forms of advocacy and (interest) group politics that, while targeting governmental authorities, do not imply the establishment of a relationship in the policymaking process. This is the case, for instance, of demonstrations and protests by social movements and also of lobbying activities through which interest groups attempt to promote their positions on specific policy issues.

		Horizontal dimension - Collaboration with stakeholders	
		+ High	Low -
Vertical dimension – Intergovernmental collaboration	+ High	MLG	IGR Collaboration *Venue shopping*
	- Low	Network governance	*Lobbying* *Peer-to-peer network* Hierarchical relations

Fig. 2.1 Typology: modes of multilevel policymaking from a local government perspective

of policymaking are defined by the intersection of two continua representing levels of collaboration in the vertical dimension, i.e. with other government authorities, and in the horizontal dimension, i.e. with non-public actors and civil society organisations. Following Ansell and Gash (2008) collaboration implies ongoing interaction to negotiate interests and build consensus on shared strategies and goals. Hence, levels of collaboration are established on the basis of two criteria: inclusiveness and intensity (Bache et al., 2016; Schiller, 2019). A high degree of collaboration implies that almost all the relevant actors in the vertical and/or horizontal dimension are actively included and participate in the policy process, and that interaction is regular rather than sporadic and ad hoc; on the contrary, low collaboration is characterised by the participation of a limited number of stakeholders and by irregular or occasional interaction.

Hence, consistently with this conceptual space, *MLG* is defined as inclusive and intense collaboration *in both* the vertical and horizontal dimensions in which local governments interact with all the relevant actors concerned with or having an interest in a specific issue on a constant and regular basis. When such intense collaboration only takes place in the vertical dimension, i.e. between local governments and other public authorities on different territorial scales, we have an instance of *intergovernmental collaborative relation*. This mode of policymaking reflects the operation of so-called "co-operative federalism" (Spiro, 2001) but it can also be found in unitary systems when intergovernmental platforms are established in order to achieve coordination between the policies and programmes on a certain issue promoted by different governmental authorities (Peters, 1998). Conversely, when high collaborative relations link local governments with non-public actors engaged on a certain policy issue, then we have an instance of *network governance*, understood as a mode of policymaking that challenges the separation between public and non-public actors in decision-making and/or the implementation of a specific policy (see also: Ansell & Torfing, 2015). Last but not least, in their pure form *hierarchical instances* of policymaking will follow a traditional state-based division of powers and competences on a specific issue. On the vertical dimension, local governments will simply comply with commands from above, while on the horizontal dimension relations with non-public stakeholders will be limited to the contracting out of services, but no collaboration will be pursued.

Hence, as is clear, collaboration is the very hallmark of MLG, in which coordination between different public and non-public actors is not achieved through top-down hierarchical commands but rather through voluntary engagement on a specific issue of common interest. In fact, as Peters (1998) suggests, coordination understood as an end state in which policies and programmes are characterised by "minimal redundancy, incoherence and lacunae" (p. 296) can be a product of "hierarchy, markets and networks" (p. 297). MLG is clearly a mode of policymaking where coordination is achieved through network patterns of interaction based on collaboration on—at least some—shared aims.

To resist coordination imposed from above through hierarchical relations, local authorities can undertake various strategies of alliance and collaboration on the vertical and/or horizontal dimensions. These are represented in Fig. 2.1 in italics. *Lobbying* and *venue shopping* are cases in point. In the former, local authorities will seek collaboration with non-public actors and/or other subnational authorities in order to put pressure on higher levels of governments for the adoption of a specific measure or policy. In the latter, instead, subnational authorities will seek to collaborate with the level of government that is more favourable to their cause (Baumgartner & Jones, 1993). Collaboration is usually limited to the venue 'shopped,' e.g. the EU, while venues that are regarded as hostile or not interested in the issue are excluded (see also Scholten, 2013, p. 238).

Another mode of collaborative interaction particularly relevant for local authorities is *peer-to-peer networking*. In this case, collaboration takes place only with peers, i.e. subnational authorities, while there is no remarkable engagement with public authorities at other territorial scales in the vertical dimension, or with civil society organisations in the horizontal dimension. Municipalities exchange practices and share experiences among each other forming a sort of 'community of practice,' implying according to Wenger (2000, p. 226), (1) an ongoing mutual engagement; (2) a sense of joint enterprise and a shared domain of interest; and (3) a shared repertoire of knowledge and practices. These type of networks rely upon mechanisms of peer accountability, whereby "network participants become primarily accountable to their network partners in soft and horizontal accountability relations" (Papadopoulos, 2010, p. 1040).

The conceptual space presented in Fig. 2.1 has to be understood as an analytical tool aimed at enabling the identification of configurations of policymaking that approximate ideal types. What is more important is that thinking in terms of a conceptual space containing continua rather than dichotomous yes/no variables allows MLG and hierarchy to be considered two distinct yet not totally mutually exclusive configurations of policymaking in which local governments are likely to be involved. In other words, this analytic and realistic approach allows the link between MLG and 'good governance' that underlies much literature to be broken. The search for instances of ideal–typical or 'true' MLG becomes less relevant, while unanswered questions about the factors and mechanisms accounting for the emergence of MLG-like policymaking can finally be brought to the fore. I posit that this is a key paradigmatic shift in order to move our theoretical comprehension of MLG forward from a meso-perspective, i.e. as a specific mode of policymaking, and from a macro-perspective, i.e. as a more general process of restructuring state authority.

CNs are part and parcel of such processes of state authority transformation. For the burgeoning CN-enthusiastic literature, these organisations contribute to a deep restructuring of the nation state by putting cities to the fore and making pressure for the establishment of MLG policymaking venues and arrangements. However, as was noted in Chapter 1, there are several caveats to this argument that deserve close empirical scrutiny. Hence, below I turn my attention to the CN literature to see how the nexus with MLG has been actually conceptualised and understood.

2.3 Cities and the CN-MLG Nexus. Competing Approaches

The role of subnational governments and CNs in the context of processes of dispersion of state authority and globalisation has been the object of a lively debate in different disciplines and research strands since the late 1990s. Critical political geography, urban economy, European integration studies, international relations, public policy analysis, and urban and political sociology have all contributed to illuminating specific aspects of state-city relations (Pinson, 2019). It is at the crossroad of these different literatures, which are only partially in dialogue with each other, that I situate the emergence of a corpus of research studies on the nexus between CNs and MLG.

Table 2.2 presents the different interpretations of the role of CNs in processes of (international) policymaking and multilevel governance that can be found in the literature. Each interpretation links to a specific conceptualisation of cities. Ljungkvist (2014) identifies two main approaches: cities as *sites* undergoing processes of economic and political globalisation, which prevails among political geographers and urban economists; and cities as *agents* that pursue strategic goals and actively engage in addressing the challenges of globalisation, which underlies the international relations literature on paradiplomacy. A third approach can be added reflecting research on local government and urban governance, i.e. cities as *arenas* where different institutions, actors and organisations

Table 2.2 Conceptualisations of cities and CNs in the literature

Cities	*Research streams*	*CNs*	*Understanding of MLG*
Sites	New economy of scale, new municipalism	Outcome of neoliberal globalisation and state rescaling	MLG as complex interdependence
Agents	Paradiplomacy, Europeanisation	New actors in the EU/global political sphere	MLG as complex interdependence MLG as a system
Arenas	Public policy and urban policy studies	Internally plural organisations	MLG as a system (MLG as an instance)

concretely take part in the shaping of local policies on specific issues (Le Galès, 2002).

In the remainder of this section, I review the contribution of the different approaches identified in Table 2.2 to the analysis and understanding of the CNs-MLG nexus. Without claiming to be exhaustive, this state-of-the-art review brings to light different research traditions that often remain implicit in much research on migration CNs, therefore generating considerable confusion over the factors and mechanisms leading to the emergence of a nexus with MLG policymaking.

2.3.1 Cities as Sites

In the first perspective, cities are understood as strategic geographical areas within processes of economic globalisation and re-shaping of political authority in the EU and at the global level. In this context, CNs represent a response to dynamics of MLG understood as increasing global interdependence. Hence, the CN-MLG nexus is essentially considered from a macro-perspective and remains quite opaque in its concrete functioning.

A key reference in this debate is Harvey's (1989) analysis of urban governance transition from an era of 'managerialism' to one of 'entrepreneurialism.' Whereas in the context of welfare state policies local authorities essentially had the goal of organising and managing public services, in the post-Keynesian scenario of budget cuts and service retrenchment local governments started to be increasingly involved in economic development activities to attract and support private investments. The 'new economy of scale' (Jessop, 2016) interprets this shift as reflecting processes of downscaling of state authority whereby the decentralisation or devolution of regulatory tasks to subnational tiers of government does not imply a demise or erosion of national statehood but instead its spatial reconfiguration. In other words, as put by Brenner (2004, p. 4), state institutions remain "major animateurs and mediators of political-economic restructuring at all geographical scales" (see also Brenner & Theodore, 2002, p. 344).

In this literature, CNs take a highly ambivalent role. On the one hand, they are regarded as organisations that by enhancing the international profile of cities and, in the European context, enabling access to EU programmes and funding, reinforce—rather than contrasting—the competition-driven logic underlying neoliberal policies (Brenner, 2004;

Lauermann, 2018; Leitner & Sheppard, 1999). On the other hand, however, CNs have also been being recognised as promoting a progressive agenda in a globalising world, one which emphasises the democratisation of the economy and the empowering of civil society (Leitner & Sheppard, 2002, p. 501). This progressive view animates recent debates on 'new municipalism,' a research strand somewhat lying between analytical and militant approaches to urban policy. Whereas historical accounts of international city networking emphasised its 'apolitical' connotation (Saunier, 2002, p. 508), the novelty of new municipalism "resides in a newly-politicised and radical-reformist orientation towards the (local) state, in imagining new institutional formations that embody *urban* rather than state logics" (Thompson, 2020, p. 2). A case in point is identified by Thompson (2020, p. 3) in the *Fearless Cities* movement, which is described as a "radical-democratic and transformative response to urban-capitalist crises." These kinds of politically militant networks seem to differ considerably from 'traditional' network organisations like Eurocities, which, according to Brenner (2004), have instead the function of helping to mitigate the most polarising and disruptive effects of neoliberal policies.

Similarly to the 'new economy of scale,' also in the social movement-like approach underlying the 'new municipalism' literature MLG remains somewhat in the background, reflecting conditions of increasing complexity in a globalised world. In fact, the radical political agenda inspiring this movement, which upholds the democratic autonomy of municipalities over political and economic life vis-à-vis the state (Russell, 2019), does not seem to allow pursuing cooperative modes of policymaking in the intergovernmental vertical dimension. Studies have focused more on relations with NGOs and civil society organisations in a conceptualisation of transnationalism which is grounded on grassroots cooperation and counterhegemonic political discourses.

2.3.2 Cities as Agents

To the somewhat passive or reactive understanding of cities in dynamics of state rescaling underlying the critical approaches reviewed above, studies on European integration and international relations oppose the image of cities as *agents*. By mobilising internationally and transnationally, cities understood as municipal/metropolitan governments pursue strategic goals that do not necessarily correspond to those of their national governments. In these literatures, CNs are organisations that articulate city agency in multilevel political systems, i.e. the EU supranational polity in the debate on the Europeanisation of subnational authorities (SNAs) and the global system in international relations studies on city paradiplomacy.

As regards the first research stream, following the reform of cohesion policy and structural funds in 1986, attention was initially devoted to how European policies had affected intergovernmental relations and territorial restructuring within member states (see, e.g., Goldsmith, 1993; Hooghe, 1996), with a primary focus on the role of the regions. However, building on a conceptualisation of European policies as a new opportunity structure for SNAs (Keating, 1999), the first studies on networking between cities in cross-border regions (Church & Reid, 1996, 1999; Perkmann, 1999) noted the importance of transnational collaboration in securing access to EU funding and the capacity to lobby European institutions. In other words, using the terms of Schultze (2003, p. 121), transnational CNs have allowed subnational authorities to shift from 'policy takers' to 'policy makers,' implying direct engagement and involvement in influencing decision-making processes (see also, Heinelt & Niederhafner, 2008, p. 175).

In this perspective, CNs understood as 'transnational municipal networks,' i.e. organisations formed first and foremost by municipal governments that join on a voluntary basis (Kern & Bulkeley, 2009, p. 309), have been conceptualised as a specific development of Europeanisation processes and part of the multilevel European governance (Dossi, 2017; Huggins, 2018a, 2018b; Nadalutti, 2013). More specifically, CNs contribute to redefining relations in the vertical dimension, favouring the emergence of direct EU-local authority relations beyond and above the national state. Less attention is devoted, however, to the horizontal state-society dimension of MLG, which, when considered, usually refers to city-to-city relations and only marginally takes into account non-governmental actors.

In parallel with the debate on the Europeanisation of local authorities, seminal work on the economic and political power of 'global cities' (Castells, 1996; Sassen, 1991) has brought into the debate the topic of the agency of cities in the global system. Since the late 1990s, international relations scholars have been paying increasing attention to the mobilisation of cities in the international arena and to their paradiplomacy

(Aldecoa & Keating, 1999; Lecours, 2002; Tavares, 2016). This literature assumes that cities are somewhat unitary actors embodying a specific political willingness and pursuing strategic goals. In this perspective, CNs reflect and are the outcome of processes of empowerment of cities in the post-Cold war international context characterised by the weakening of the role of states and the emergence of global governance understood as a system of complex and multilevel interdependency (Curtis, 2014).

2.3.3 Cities as Arenas

Between the two rather opposed views illustrated above, the approach that looks at cities as political *arenas* (Kaufmann & Sidney, 2020; Magnusson, 2014; Pinson & Vion, 2000) conceptualises urban agency not simply as reflecting the agendas of elected governments and/or mayors but in a more pluralist way (Bassens et al., 2019), i.e. as forged by coalitions and alliances between a wide range of public and private actors. Following on from these premises, research on CNs primarily takes a city perspective in order to investigate the factors and actors accounting for the international mobilisation and engagement of cities in CNs (see, e.g., Mocca, 2017, 2019).

Starting from an understanding of MLG as the system of governing relations characterising the EU institutional setting, Mocca (2019) criticises this perspective for being 'unhistorical, descriptive and normative' and therefore unfit to yield a critical analysis of cities' engagement in CNs. To this end, an urban-centric approach is suggested as a more appropriate and useful analytical framework to unravel "the place-specific economic, political and institutional urban structures and the instrumental expectations of local political élites that exploit networks to obtain collective and selective benefits" (Mocca, 2019, p. 280). However, other scholars looking at CNs as organisations where different categories of actors with specific interests and views contribute to shaping internal strategies and agendas (the *arenas* approach) have more fruitfully conceptualised MLG as a specific instance or mode of policymaking that CNs can eventually pursue along with other modes of policymaking (see, e.g., Scholten et al. 2018). The puzzle then is to understand why and how CNs get involved in instances—rather than systems—of MLG policymaking.

In the next section, I build on these insights to further elaborate on the analytical framework of MLG *instances* discussed in Sect. 2.2.2 and graphically presented in Fig. 2.1. First, I identify the main hypotheses regarding the causal factors underlying the CN-MLG nexus that can be derived from the literature on CNs and then I move forward by proposing an actor-centred and relational approach to make sense of the mechanisms that can lead to the emergence of the nexus.

2.4 Towards a Causal Understanding of the CN-MLG Nexus. Factors and Mechanisms in Instances of MLG

From the—still scarce—literature addressing the CN-MLG nexus analysed above, three explanatory hypotheses can be derived: (1) an institutional hypothesis, which highlights the particular EU institutional opportunity structure; (2) an external pressure hypothesis, which emphasises the increased interdependence created by new global challenges; and (3) a leadership hypothesis, which concerns the policy agendas pursued by CN leaders, e.g. mayors, city officials, CN staff officers, etc.

The first hypothesis underlies research studies that conceive CNs as a result of bottom-up mobilisation by subnational authorities to engage in EU policymaking beyond national government structures (Benz et al., 2015). As was pointed out above, the interaction between processes of Europeanisation and subnationalisation was the primary focus of early MLG studies (Hooghe, 1996). In this context, CNs started to be regarded as part and parcel of the EU multilevel system (Giest & Howlett, 2013; Heinelt & Niederhafner, 2008). Regarding migration policy, Penninx (2015, p. 107) notices the importance of funding provided by the European Commission (EC) in stimulating the setting up of organisations representing cities and regions vis-à-vis EU institutions. The CN-MLG nexus is therefore the outcome of the particular opportunity structure underlying EU policymaking and dynamics of subnationalisation.

The second hypothesis draws attention to how new global challenges, from climate change mitigation to migration, lead to an increasing centrality of local governments in establishing systems of relations with other levels of government and with multiple non-governmental actors (Agranoff, 2018, p. 143). In this perspective, the mobilisation of CNs reflects the key role assumed by municipalities in ensuring effective policy responses to global challenges independently of the opportunities—or lack of them—offered by the surrounding institutional system.

This approach underlies international relations research on city mobilisation in transnational networks operating in the global MLG system (see, e.g., Betsill & Bulkeley, 2006; Stürner & Bendel, 2019).

The third hypothesis is linked to the entrepreneurial role and policy agendas of decision-makers. It resonates with the cities as *arenas* approach illustrated above in which CNs are complex organisations where different actors' views and strategies are at play. A case in point is that of mayors, who have been depicted as strategic actors deliberately pursuing internationalisation strategies in order to build political legitimacy in the eyes of the local electorate and to seek resources for policy solutions to urban problems (Beal & Pinson, 2014). In a similar vein, Scholten et al. (2018) highlight the importance of the aldermen of Rotterdam and The Hague in establishing structures for institutional multilevel cooperation on the locally salient issue of EEC citizens' access to welfare services. Other scholars (see, e.g., Payre, 2010 on Eurocities), however, contend that CN leaders and officers enjoy non-negligible autonomy in decisions regarding strategic goals and governance relationships. Hence, in this latter perspective MLG policymaking will only be pursued insofar as it is considered by CN leaders a valuable strategic option to reach the organisation's goals.

Hence, the three hypotheses identified above enable the identification of a number of explanatory factors to be operationalised and then tested on evidence gathered through empirical research, with the ultimate aim of identifying the causal factor that has the greater explanatory leverage. However, such a procedure takes the emergence of a CN-MLG nexus for granted while leaving its concrete functioning obscure, as is shown in Fig. 2.2. More specifically, the hypotheses drawn from the literature do not provide a full picture of *why* and *how* CNs get engaged in MLG.

However, as was mentioned at the beginning of this chapter, if we are to understand the CN-MLG nexus, this has to be questioned in the first

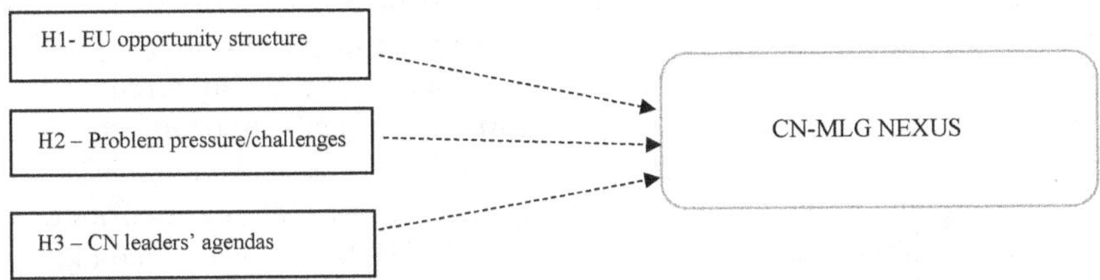

Fig. 2.2 Explaining the CN-MLG nexus

place. In fact, local governments are likely to be found in different policymaking configurations and so are CNs, the engagement of which in MLG can occur along with other modes of political mobilisation as was shown in Fig. 2.1. CNs can be engaged in intergovernmental relations, which seem to be particularly important in the European studies literature, or in network governance configurations when relations with NGOs and/or private companies assume key relevance in achieving CN goals. Even hierarchy cannot be completely ruled out. On the one hand, at least in hypothetical terms, CNs can be directly engaged in the implementation of policies that have been decided elsewhere by higher tiers of government, reflecting the argument that in the EU multilevel system policy networks usually take place in the 'shadow of supranational hierarchy' (Börzel, 2010, p. 210). On the other hand, critical approaches to city internationalisation alert us to the capacity of states to reconfigure their power through processes of political rescaling in order to more effectively pursue strategies of neoliberal economic accumulation (Brenner, 2004).

Hence, if we are to push forward our understanding of the CN-MLG nexus, answering *why* questions in a canonical hypothesis-testing sense does not seem sufficient. *How* questions appear far more important and crucial in order to make sense of processes that are shaped by complex multilevel political dynamics. In other words, following Payre (2010), the CN-MLG nexus is a product of complex political work that still needs to be fully unravelled and accounted for.

To this end, a focus on the causal mechanisms accounting for CNs engagement in MLG policymaking, rather than on causal factors, appears more appropriate. In this respect, I posit that actors and their agendas are crucial. However, such agendas do not form in a void but are shaped and influenced by the contexts in which CN policymakers deploy their action. Furthermore, leaders' agendas are not necessarily geared towards MLG policymaking. This may be part of the CN official and rhetorical discourse, yet concrete practices may go in different directions, like lobbying, network governance or intergovernmental relations (IGR). The point then, as is shown in Fig. 2.3, is to understand the concrete political work that can lead CNs to be engaged in and/or actively promote MLG policymaking.

As we shall see in the next chapter, the big blue arrow identified in Fig. 2.3, with few exceptions (Scholten et al., 2018), has remained almost unexplored in the literature. To understand and make sense of what is still a question mark, I posit the necessity of taking an actor-centred

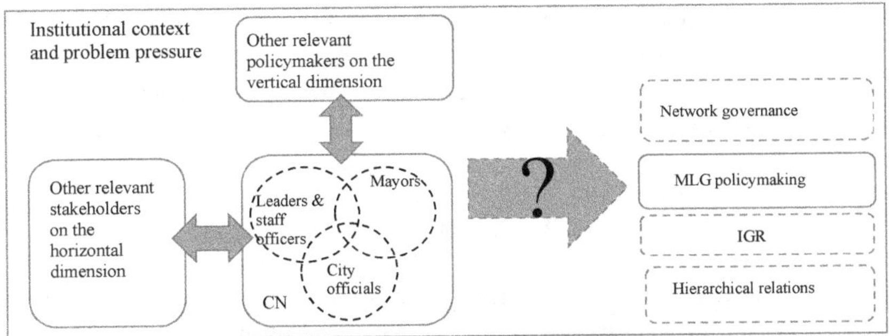

Fig. 2.3 Understanding the CN-MLG nexus

and relational approach. The goal is that of unravelling the practices and relations that are concretely established by different categories of policy actors both within CNs and outside, with the other relevant policymakers and stakeholders mobilised on the vertical and horizontal dimensions of policymaking processes on a specific issue. It is through these multiple practices and relationships that MLG eventually comes into play.

2.5 The CN-MLG Nexus in Processes of State Power Restructuring. A Synthesis

Current debates on MLG have identified two directions of theoretical development: MLG as a theory of public policy, on the one hand, and MLG as a theory of state power restructuring, on the other (Tortola, 2017). In this respect, the analysis of the CN-MLG nexus delineated in this chapter goes in the direction of contributing to the theorisation of public policy, and more specifically to the understanding and explanation of decision making and implementation processes in multi-layered political settings. By aiming to broaden our understanding of the complex 'political work' that underlies CN engagement in MLG policymaking, this book clearly takes a meso-level perspective and engages primarily with scholarly work on MLG as an instance or mode of policymaking vis-à-vis other possible types of instances (Alcantara et al., 2016; Scholten, 2013).

However, unlike Tortola (2017), I do not conceive the two theoretical developments of MLG as non-communicating routes, building on different research interests and in dialogue with different literatures. This approach seems to fall short of recognising the very originality of MLG as a heuristic concept, i.e. its ambition to link together theoretical reflections on the transformation of policymaking processes and state authority structures. In fact, by analysing the meso-level factors and mechanisms that can lead to the emergence of a CN-MLG nexus, this research study intends to also contribute to illuminating how macro-level processes of state authority dispersion and/or restructuring concretely take place. The engagement, or lack of engagement, of CNs in policymaking relations on the vertical and the horizontal dimensions of migration policymaking clearly reveals how states deal with or avoid dealing with the issue.

In other words, researching policies is a fundamental step in order to theorise on processes of—presumed—shifting state powers down to local authorities, up to supranational authorities and out to civil society and private interests (Guiraudon & Lahav, 2000). MLG policymaking can be regarded as a possible outcome of such processes, taking the form of collaborative problem-solving relations among the different policymakers and stakeholders interested in a certain policy issue. However, its practice very often appears underpinned by mundane political dilemmas regarding unequal distributions of power and resources (Alcantara & Morden, 2019; Bache, 2010; Papadopoulos, 2007, 2010), with state level authorities certainly having the upper hand when it comes to determining the direction and modes of delegation of power, and therefore, in the very end, also how and to what extent to engage in MLG policymaking. Problem-solving endeavours are usually riddled with problem-generating implications (Maggetti & Trein, 2019, p. 358), highlighting the deep intricacies of governance, politics and power that underpin processes of state power transformation in the context of globalisation.

Hence, seen from a macro-perspective, the puzzle underlying this book is that of understanding if and to what extent MLG takes place 'in the shadow of hierarchy' and, above all, of which hierarchy. Whereas Börzel (2010, p. 210) underlines the key relevance of the EU supranational authorities in setting the institutional framework for the development of new (MLG) policy networks, I contend that, especially when highly pitched political issues like migration are at stake, the 'shadow of hierarchy' is more likely to be that of the nation state. In other words, rather than emerging from below, MLG can well be the result of an initiative starting from above and of which the modes of functioning and impact are constrained by state will. The MLG of migration is therefore more likely to reflect the persistent strength of state power rather than its weakening.

With these caveats in mind, in the following chapters I take a meso-level policy studies perspective in the analysis of the CN-MLG nexus in the migration policy field to contribute to scholarship on MLG policy-making and to broader debates in international relations on the role of cities in the system of multilevel interdependency characterising global governance (Curtis, 2014). As pointed out above, studies on paradiplomacy (Acuto, 2014; Aldecoa & Keating, 1999; Tavares, 2016) have conceptualised cities as unitary actors embodying a specific political will and pursuing strategic goals. Evidence of CN activism and mobilisation has often been interpreted as reflecting processes of city empowerment and the capacity of cities to claim and obtain a seat in an increasingly dispersed international arena. However, if the rise of CNs, together with that of (some) cities and their mayors as global actors is actually a fact, if (and how) this has led to a re-shaping of policies on specific globalisation challenges and, in the end, to a weakening of the role and prerogatives of states on these issues is still an open matter.

Therefore, through a systematic analysis of policymaking relationships engaging CNs, state authorities and civil society organisations around the controversial migration issue, I aim to reconcile the two directions of theorisation on MLG mentioned above and bring them into conversation with each other. This appears to be a key and unavoidable step in order to move beyond a silo-like approach to MLG theorisation and to contribute to making sense of broader patterns of complexification of cities and CN engagement in multilevel and multi-actor policymaking processes.

References

Acuto, M. (2014). An urban affair. How mayors shape cities for world politics. In S. Curtis (Ed.), *The power of cities in international relations* (pp. 69–87). Routledge.

Agranoff, R. (2018). *Local governments in multilevel governance: The administrative dimension*. Lexington Books.

Alcantara, C., Broschek, J., & Nelles, J. (2016). Rethinking multilevel governance as an instance of multilevel politics: A conceptual strategy. *Territory, Politics, Governance, 4*, 33–51. https://doi.org/10.1080/21622671.2015.1047897

Alcantara, C., & Morden, M. (2019). Indigenous multilevel governance and power relations. *Territory, Politics, Governance, 7*, 250–264. https://doi.org/10.1080/21622671.2017.1360197

Alcantara, C., & Nelles, J. (2014). Indigenous peoples and the state in settler societies: Toward a more robust definition of multilevel governance. *Publius, 44*, 183–204. https://doi.org/10.1093/publius/pjt013

Aldecoa, F., & Keating, M. (Eds.). (1999). *Paradiplomacy in action: The foreign relations of subnational governments*. Frank Cass Publishers.

Ansell, C., & Gash, A. (2008). Collaborative governance in theory and practice. *Journal of Public Administration Research and Theory, 18*, 543–571. https://doi.org/10.1093/jopart/mum032

Ansell, C., & Torfing, J. (2015). How does collaborative governance scale? *Policy & Politics, 43*(3), 315–329. https://doi.org/10.1332/030557315X14353344872935

Bache, I. (2010). Partnership as an EU policy instrument: A political history. *West European Politics, 33*, 58–74. https://doi.org/10.1080/01402380903354080

Bache, I., Bartle, I., & Flinders, M. (2016). Multi-level governance. In C. Ansell & J. Torfing (Eds.), *Handbook on theories of governance* (pp. 486–498). Edward Elgar.

Bassens, D., Beeckmans, L., Derudder, B., & Oosterlynck, S. (2019). An urban studies take on global urban political agency. In S. Oosterlynck, L. Beeckmans & D. Bassens (Eds.), *The city as a global political actor*. Routledge.

Baumgartner, F., & Jones B. D. (1993). *Agendas and instability in American politics*. University of Chicago Press.

Beal, V., & Pinson, G. (2014). When mayors go global: International strategies, urban governance and leadership. *International Journal of Urban and Regional Research, 38*, 302–317. https://doi.org/10.1111/1468-2427.12018

Benz, A. (2000). Two types of multi-level governance: Intergovernmental relations in German and EU regional policy. *Regional & Federal Studies, 10*, 21–44. https://doi.org/10.1080/13597560008421130

Benz, A., Kemmerzell, J., Knodt, M., & Tews, A. (2015). The trans-local dimension of local climate policy. Sustaining and transforming local knowledge orders through trans-local action in three German cities. *Urban Research & Practice, 8*, 319–335. https://doi.org/10.1080/17535069.2015.1051380

Betsill, M. M., & Bulkeley, H. (2006). Cities and the multilevel governance of global climate change. *Global Governance, 12*, 141–159.

Börzel, T. (2010). European governance: Negotiation and competition in the shadow of hierarchy. *JCMS: Journal of Common Market Studies, 48*, 191–219. https://doi.org/10.1111/j.1468-5965.2009.02049.x

Brenner, N. (2004). *New state spaces: Urban governance and the rescaling of statehood*. Oxford University Press.

Brenner, N., & Theodore, N. (2002). Preface: From the "new localism" to the spaces of neoliberalism. *Antipode, 34*, 341–347. https://doi.org/10.1111/1467-8330.00245

Caponio, T., & Jones-Correa, M. (2018). Theorising migration policy in multilevel states: The multilevel governance perspective. *Journal of Ethnic and Migration Studies, 44*, 1995–2010. https://doi.org/10.1080/1369183X.2017.1341705

Castells, M. (1996). *The rise of the network society*. Blackwell.

Church, A., & Reid, P. (1996). Urban power, international networks and competition: The example of cross-border cooperation. *Urban Studies*. https://doi.org/10.1080/0042098966664

Church, A., & Reid, P. (1999). Cross-border co-operation, institutionalization and political space across the english channel. *Regional Studies, 33*, 643–655. https://doi.org/10.1080/00343409950078684

Curtis, S. (2014). Introduction: Empowering cities. In S. Curtis (Ed.), *The power of cities in international relations* (pp. 1–15). Routledge.

Dossi, S. (2017). *Cities and the European Union: Mechanisms and Modes of Europeanisation*. Rowman & Littlefield and ECPR Press.

Easton, D. (1965). *A systems analysis of political life*. John Wiley.

Giest, S., & Howlett, M. (2013). Comparative climate change governance: Lessons from European transnational municipal network management efforts. *Environmental Policy and Governance, 23*, 341–353. https://doi.org/10.1002/eet.1628

Goldsmith, M. (1993). The Europeanisation of local government. *Urban studies, 30*, 683–699. https://doi.org/10.1080/00420989320081871

Guiraudon, V., & Lahav, G. (2000). A reappraisal of the state sovereignty debate: The case of migration control. *Comparative Political Studies, 33*, 163–195. https://doi.org/10.1177/0010414000033002001

Harvey, D. (1989). From managerialism to entrepreneurialism: The transformation in urban governance in late capitalism. *Geografiska Annaler, 71*(B), 3–17

Heinelt, H., & Niederhafner, S. (2008). Cities and organized interest intermediation in the EU multi-level system. *European Urban and Regional Studies, 15*, 173–187. https://doi.org/10.1177/0969776408090023

Héritier, A. (2002). Public-interest services revisited. *Journal of European Public Policy, 9*, 995–1019. https://doi.org/10.1080/1350176022000046463

Herrschel, T., & Newman, P. (Eds.). (2017). *Cities as international actors: Urban and regional governance beyond the nation state*. Palgrave Macmillan.

Hooghe, L. (1996). *Cohesion policy and European integration: Building multilevel governance*. Oxford University Press.

Hooghe, L., & Marks, G. (2001). *Multi-level governance and european integration*. Rowman & Littlefield.

Hooghe, L., & Marks, G. (2003). Unraveling the central state, but how? Types of multi-level governance. *American Political Science Review, 97*, 233–243. https://doi.org/10.1017/S0003055403000649

Hooghe, L., & Marks, G. (2004). Does identity or economic rationality drive public opinion on European integration? *PS: Political Science & Politics, 37*, 415–420. https://doi.org/10.1017/S1049096504004585

Huggins, C. (2018a). Subnational transnational networking and the continuing process of local-level Europeanization. *European Urban and Regional Studies 25*, 206–227. https://doi.org/10.1177/0969776417691564

Huggins, C. (2018b). Subnational government and transnational networking: The rationalist logic of local level Europeanization. *JCMS: Journal of Common Market Studies. 56*, 1263–1282. https://doi.org/10.1111/jcms.12740

Jessop, B. (2016). Territory, politics, governance and multispatial metagovernance. *Territory, Politics, Governance, 4*, 8–32. https://doi.org/10.1080/21622671.2015.1123173

Kaufmann, D., & Sidney, M. (2020). Toward an urban policy analysis: Incorporating participation, multilevel governance, and "seeing like a city." *PS: Political Science & Politics, 53*, 1–5. https://doi.org/10.1017/S1049096519001380

Keating, M. (1999). Regions and international affairs: Motives, opportunities and strategies. *Regional & Federal Studies, 9*, 1–16. https://doi.org/10.1080/13597569908421068

Keating, M. (2008). Thirty years of territorial politics. *West European Politics, 31*, 60–81. https://doi.org/10.1080/01402380701833723

Kern, K., & Bulkeley, H. (2009). Cities, Europeanization and multi-level governance: Governing climate change through transnational municipal networks. *JCMS: Journal of Common Market Studies, 47*, 309–332. https://doi.org/10.1111/j.1468-5965.2009.00806.x

Klijn, E. H., & Koppenjan, J. (2016). *Governance networks in the public sector*. Routledge.

Lauermann, J. (2018). Municipal statecraft: Revisiting the geographies of the entrepreneurial city. *Progress in Human Geography, 42*, 205–224. https://doi.org/10.1177/0309132516673240

Le Galès, P. (2002). *European cities. Social conflicts and governance*. Oxford University Press.

Lecours, A. (2002). Paradiplomacy: Reflections on the foreign policy and International relations of regions. *International Negotiation, 7*, 91–114. https://doi.org/10.1163/157180602401262456

Leitner, H., & Sheppard, E. (1999). Transcending interurban competition: Conceptual issues and policy alternatives in the European Union. In A. Jonas & D. Wilson (Eds.), *The growth machine: Critical perspectives twenty years later* (pp. 227–246). State University of New York Press.

Leitner, H., & Sheppard, E. (2002). "The city is dead, long live the net": Harnessing European interurban networks for a neoliberal agenda. *Antipode, 34*, 495–518. https://doi.org/10.1111/1467-8330.00252

Ljungkvist, K. (2014). The global city. From strategic site to global actor. In S. Curtis (Ed.), *The power of cities in international relations* (pp. 32–56). Routledge.

Maggetti, M., & Trein, P. (2019). Multilevel governance and problem-solving: Towards a dynamic theory of multilevel policy-making? *Public Administration, 97*, 355–369. https://doi.org/10.1111/padm.12573

Magnusson, W. (2014). The symbiosis of the urban and the political. *International Journal of Urban and Regional Research, 38*, 1561–1575. https://doi.org/10.1111/1468-2427.12144

Marks, G. (1993). Structural policy and multilevel governance in the EC. In A. Cafruny & G. G. Rosenthal (Eds.), *The Maastricht debates and beyond. The state of the European Community* (Vol. 2, pp. 391–410). Lynne Rienner.

Marks, G. (1996). An actor-centred approach to multi-level governance. *Regional & Federal Studies, 6*, 20–38. https://doi.org/10.1080/13597569608420966

Marks, G., & Hooghe, L. (2000). Optimality and authority: A critique of neoclassical theory. *JCMS: Journal of Common Market Studies, 38*, 795–816. https://doi.org/10.1111/1468-5965.00265

Mocca, E. (2017). City networks for sustainability in Europe: An urban-level analysis. *Journal of Urban Affairs, 39*, 691–710. https://doi.org/10.1080/07352166.2017.1282769

Mocca, E. (2019). The ubiquity of the level: The multi-level governance approach to the analysis of transnational municipal networks. *Journal of Contemporary European Research, 15*, 269–283. https://doi.org/10.30950/jcer.v15i3.960

Nadalutti, E. (2013). Does the 'European grouping of territorial co-operation' promote multi-level governance within the European union? *JCMS: Journal of Common Market Studies, 51*, 756–771. https://doi.org/10.1111/jcms.12014

Oomen, B. (2020). Decoupling and teaming up: The rise and proliferation of transnational municipal networks in the field of migration. *International Migration Review, 54*, 913–939. https://doi.org/10.1177/0197918319881118

Papadopoulos, Y. (2007). Problems of democratic accountability in network and multilevel governance. *European Law Journal, 13*, 469–486. https://doi.org/10.1111/j.1468-0386.2007.00379.x

Papadopoulos, Y. (2010). Accountability and multi-level governance: More accountability, less democracy? *West European Politics, 33*, 1030–1049. https://doi.org/10.1080/01402382.2010.486126

Payre, R. (2010). The importance of being connected. City networks and urban government: Lyon and eurocities (1990–2005). *International Journal of Urban and Regional Research, 34*, 260–280. https://doi.org/10.1111/j.1468-2427.2010.00937.x

Penninx, R. (2015). European cities in search of knowledge for their integration policies. In P. Scholten, H. Entzinger, R. Penninx, & S. Verbeek (Eds.), *Integrating immigrants in Europe: Research-policy dialogues* (pp. 99–115). Springer International Publishing.

Perkmann, M. (1999). Building governance institutions across European borders. *Regional Studies, 33*, 657–667. https://doi.org/10.1080/00343409950078693

Peters, B. G. (1998). Managing horizontal government: The politics of co-ordination. *Public Administration, 76*, 295–311. https://doi.org/10.1111/1467-9299.00102

Peters, G. B., & Pierre, J. (2004). Multi-level governance and democracy: A Faustian bargain? In I. Bache & M. Flinders (Eds.), *Multi-level governance* (pp. 75–89). Oxford University Press.

Piattoni, S. (2010). *The theory of multi-level governance: Conceptual, empirical, and normative challenges*. Oxford University Press.

Pinson, G., et al. (2019). Voracious cities and obstructing states? In S. Oosterlynck, L. Beeckmans, & D. Bassens (Eds.), *The city as a global political actor* (pp. 60–85). Routledge.

Pinson, G., & Vion, A. (2000). L'internationalisation des villes comme objet d'expertise. *Pôle Sud, 13*, 85–102. https://doi.org/10.3406/pole.2000.1088

Russell, B. (2019). Beyond the local trap: New municipalism and the rise of the fearless cities. *Antipode, 51*, 989–1010. https://doi.org/10.1111/anti.12520

Sassen, S. (1991). *The global city: New York, London, Tokio*. Princeton University Press.

Saunier, P.-Y. (2002). Taking up the bet on connections: A municipal contribution. *Contemporary European History, 11*, 507–527. https://doi.org/10.1017/S0960777302004010

Scharpf, F. W. (1997). *Games real actors play: Actor-centered institutionalism in policy research*. Westview Press.

Scharpf, F. W. (2001). Notes toward a theory of multilevel governing in Europe. *Scandinavian Political Studies, 24*, 1–26.

Schiller, M. (2019). The local governance of migration-based diversity in Europe: The state of the art and a conceptual model for future research. In T. Caponio, P. Scholten, & R. Zapata-Barrero (Eds.), *The Routledge handbook of the governance of migration and diversity in cities* (pp. 204–215). Routledge.

Scholten, PWA. (2013). Agenda dynamics and the multi-level governance of intractable policy controversies: The case of migrant integration policies in the Netherlands. *Policy Sciences, 46*, 217–236. https://doi.org/10.1007/s11077-012-9170-x

Scholten, P., Engbersen, G., van Ostaijen, M., & Snel, E. (2018). Multilevel governance from below: How Dutch cities respond to intra-EU mobility. *Journal of Ethnic and Migration Studies, 44*, 2011–2033. https://doi.org/10.1080/1369183X.2017.1341707

Schultze, C. J. (2003). Cities and EU governance: Policy-Takers or policy-makers? *Regional & Federal Studies, 13*, 121–147. https://doi.org/10.1080/714004785

Spiro, P. J. (2001). Federalism and immigration: Models and trends. *International Social Science Journal, 53*, 67–73. https://doi.org/10.1111/1468-2451.00294

Stürner, J., & Bendel, P. (2019). The Two-way 'glocalisation' of human rights or: How cities become international agents in migration governance. *Peace Human Rights Governance, 3*, 215–240. https://doi.org/10.14658/pupj-phrg-2019-2-3

Tavares, R. (2016). *Paradiplomacy—Cities and states as global players*. Oxford University Press.

Thompson, M. (2020). What's so new about New Municipalism? *Progress in Human Geography*. https://doi.org/10.1177/0309132520909480

Tortola, P. D. (2017). Clarifying multilevel governance. *European Journal of Political Research, 56*, 234–250. https://doi.org/10.1111/1475-6765.12180

Treib, O., Bähr, H., & Falkner, G. (2007). Modes of governance: Towards a conceptual clarification. *Journal of European Public Policy, 14*, 1–20. https://doi.org/10.1080/13501760601071406

Wenger, E. (2000). Communities of practice and social learning systems. *Organization, 7*, 225–246. https://doi.org/10.1177/135050840072002

Zürn, M. (2011). Global governance as multi-level governance. In H. Enderlein, S. Wälti, & M. Zürn (Eds.), *Handbook on multi-level governance* (pp. 80–99). Edward Elgar Publishing.

CHAPTER 3

City Networks in Multilevel Policymaking on Migration. A Least-Likely Case for MLG?

Abstract This chapter is dedicated to a discussion of the migration studies literature that has addressed from different perspectives—i.e. EU policymaking, paradiplomacy and urban policy—the emergence of a CN-MLG link. More specifically, I review the scholarly debate on the local dimension of migration policy by first considering literature that focuses on policy outputs (3.2) and then studies that conceptualise policy as processes and look at cities in the context of multilevel policymaking dynamics. In the fourth section I further develop my theoretical framework by first discussing the main hypotheses on the migration CN-MLG nexus that can be drawn from the—scarce—existing literature and then building an actor-centred and relational interpretative framework. In Sect. 3.5 I provide details of the methodology and data sources for my empirical study of migration CNs in the EU and the US, and I introduce the CNs I have observed.

3.1 Setting the Scene. Cities Facing 'Wicked' Migration and Mobility Issues

Migration policy has for a long time been considered a 'high' state politics affair touching on vital issues of sovereignty like entry controls (Freeman, 1995), national identity and citizenship rights (Bauböck, 2006; Joppke, 2007). However, notwithstanding the traditional reluctance of nation states to devolve and/or share competences and responsibilities on such

T. Caponio, *Making Sense of the Multilevel Governance of Migration*, https://doi.org/10.1007/978-3-030-82551-5_3

a sensitive issue (Boswell & Geddes, 2011, p. 36), in the 1990s a shifting of state responsibilities up to international and supra-national institutions, out to non-public actors and down to local level authorities was observed (Guiraudon & Lahav, 2000, p. 164). In this context, cities, rather than being simply in charge of the implementation of national policies, started to emerge as key actors in the multilevel policymaking processes leading to the definition of migration and mobility policies (Zapata-Barrero et al., 2017, p. 243).

Scholars in Europe have often observed a pragmatic orientation of local policies on migration-related issues (Moore, 2004; Penninx & Martiniello, 2004; Poppelaars & Scholten, 2008; Scholten, 2013). According to what can be called the 'pragmatism thesis,' since local governments have to face the situation 'as it is' and cope with 'concrete problems,' they have no choice but to take a pragmatic problem-solving approach. Hence, local migration policy is conceived as ontologically different to national politics. Whereas the latter is informed by abstract ideas and paradigms, the former is developed in close contact with the local population and under the pressure of concrete situations. In this perspective, pragmatism results in 'accommodative' policy solutions that take into account the needs of both migrants and national residents (see, e.g., Penninx & Martiniello, 2004, pp. 144–145).

However, the pragmatism thesis is controversial. In fact, research on local migration policy and policymaking in Europe (see e.g., Ambrosini, 2013; Ambrosini & Boccagni, 2015; Mahnig, 2004) and North America (Mitnik & Halpern-Finnerty, 2010; Steil & Vasi, 2014; Varsanyi, 2008) has shown that pragmatic attitudes and accommodative solutions are just as likely as decisions aiming to exclude migrants. Furthermore, what a 'pragmatic solution' is cannot easily be established a priori but will depend on policymakers' interests, perceptions and definitions of situations. With respect to the reception of asylum seekers for instance, ignoring the issue can represent a perfectly pragmatic decision for local authorities, especially when they perceive prevailing negative attitudes to migrants in the resident population (Pettrachin, 2019).

Hence, not unlike what happens at the national level, migration and mobility can represent 'wicked' or intractable policy issues (Alford & Head, 2017) for local authorities: not only is the situation far from being clear but also the possible solutions are debatable, since public officials and stakeholders' interests and views can be fragmented and conflicting with each other. Furthermore, like other global challenges such as climate change mitigation, migration and mobility are likely to face local authorities with additional specific challenges that can be ascribed to the category of 'super wicked' problems (Levin et al., 2012, p. 124; Kemmerzell, 2019, p. 156), i.e. mismatches in local politics/policy timing, contradictory roles of cities and complex interdependency.

First of all, researchers have observed a mismatch in timing between local policy and politics. Whereas climate change mitigation requires immediate actions the impact of which is likely to be dispersed temporally and spatially, politics follows the logic of electoral cycles and is prone to privilege actions that have an immediate or short-term return. In a similar vein, the effects of policies dealing with the challenges of migration and mobility like social integration can only be appreciated in the long term, and therefore are hardly compatible with the limited horizon of a political mandate (Penninx & Martiniello, 2004, p. 143). Symbolic policies (Edelman 1985) and quick fixes are likely to be preferred, with a risk, however, of producing negligible if not negative effects. Reception measures for asylum seekers are a case in point: while using a restored military base or abandoned plant might seem pragmatic solutions to solve the immediate necessity of providing housing without putting local finances under strain, this type of quick fix will most probably result in segregation and marginalisation.

Second, not unlike what is observed in the environmental sector, cities experience both the benefits and pitfalls of migration. Cities have been traditional magnets of migration inflows benefitting from the presence of different types of migrants, both highly and poorly qualified, with the latter massively employed in low-wage and highly flexible jobs in the vital tertiary sector (Sassen, 1991). However, cities also have to face the potential negative consequences of the overlap between social disadvantage and cultural difference, as is evident from the emergence of segregated neighbourhoods and ethnic ghettos. This dilemma favours political immobilism and a blind-eye approach, as is eloquently shown by the case of undocumented migrants (Spencer, 2018).

Last but not least, similarly to environmental issues, also migration phenomena have global and local implications at the same time. More specifically regarding climate policies, cities are described by Kemmerzell (2019, p. 158) as part of a system characterised by a lack of central authority and complex interdependency in which the decisions taken at different levels of government depend on the actions of other, mostly unrelated, actors. At first sight, migration and mobility might look like the opposite case: authority undoubtedly lies in the hands of national governments, as was mentioned above. However, this does not rule out the complex interdependency which is created both by processes of devolution of state responsibilities and competences and by the complex nature of migration challenges. While national governments (seem to) struggle to control entries and admissions for work purposes, arrivals for family reunion, asylum and even more through irregular channels respond to different humanitarian and social network logics (Massey et al., 1993). Hence, cities represent transit and/or final hubs in migratory movements that are well beyond their capacity to control, and often even beyond that of the states they belong to.

The mismatch between the formal primacy of state authority and the—concrete—multilevel interdependence underlying migration and mobility issues creates an additional layer of 'super-wickedness': contentiousness and politicisation. In fact, not only are interests fragmented but they are likely to be underpinned by political conflicts due to the different party affiliations and ideological orientations of governments at different territorial levels. Furthermore, political divisions and power relations are also likely to permeate state-society relations on different territorial scales. The 2015 European asylum crisis, for instance, was underpinned by the mobilisation of social movements and NGOs, sometimes supported by local authorities, against restrictive state policies (Della Porta, 2018). Scholten (2020) defines this deeply entrenched conflictual character of migration and mobility as 'political alienation,' understood as the "estrangement of complexification driven by the reproduction of structural inequalities and conflict. Rather than coming to terms with complexity, political alienation involves interest-driven and selective ways of denying or reducing complexity" (p. 120).

To contrast these tendencies, Scholten (2020) calls for reflexive policy dialogues and a 'mainstreaming' of migration, which should be treated as a 'whole-of-society' issue and not as a 'stand-alone' problem. MLG policymaking would represent the ideal institutional solution to set in motion such a complex, and at the same time cross-sectoral and cross-level, reflexive approach to migration. With the caveat, however, that 'flash and blood' actors from cities, national governments, NGOs, etc., usually engage in policy processes from their differently biased or 'alienated' political perspectives. This may challenge reflexive MLG policymaking in at least two ways. First, *ex-ante*, not all policymakers and stakeholders will be interested or willing to engage in MLG, while at the same time not all actors will be invited to participate. Second, *ex-post*, the outcomes of MLG-like actions, e.g. specific policy measures and general statements, can always be contested or simply not implemented by the actors participating and/or by actors that have not taken part in the arrangement.

These observations point to the intricacies of governance and power in MLG policymaking (see, e.g., Bache, 2004; Papadopoulos, 2007; Stoker, 2019), or, as put by Maggetti and Trein (2019, p. 355), to the 'problem-generating' implications of MLG as a problem-solving strategy. Participation and effectiveness represent key challenges for MLG input and output legitimacy (Piattoni, 2010, pp. 343–345) which have to be acknowledged and duly accounted for when considering 'super-wicked' migration and mobility issues. Why and how cities get engaged in instances of MLG policymaking notwithstanding the highly contested character of migration-related issues is a puzzle that has so far received only partial and unsatisfactory solutions.

In the next two sections I review the scholarly debate on the local dimension of migration policy by considering first literature that focuses on policy outputs (3.2) and then research that conceptualises policy as processes (3.3), therefore taking a more encompassing perspective that aims to contribute to the literature on multilevel policymaking dynamics beyond the specialistic field of migration. Against this background, in Sect. 3.4 I further develop my actor-centred and relational approach to the analysis of the CN-MLG link on migration introduced in Chapter 2. In the concluding section I provide details of the methodology and data sources for my empirical study of migration CNs in the EU and the US.

3.2 Explaining Local Migration Policy Outputs. Localist and Relational Approaches

Since the very outset, research on the local dimension of migration has been almost exclusively concerned with policy outputs, i.e. with describing and explaining the emergence of specific local measures and their variation across different localities. In other words, the focus appears to be on the 'products' of policymaking rather than on the processes leading to such products. In the long run, this research agenda seems to have confined studies on local migration policy within the boundaries of specialist migration literature, limiting dialogue with more general literatures on multilevel governance and urban governance. In this section, in order to go beyond these limits, I argue for a second-generation agenda centred on a change of research paradigm from explaining policy outputs to making sense of policy processes.

The first-generation agenda appears to be profoundly shaped by the national/local dualism underlying the development of migration policy studies more generally (Filomeno, 2017; Scholten & Penninx, 2016). Early research on local policies can be regarded as an attempt to remedy the 'methodological nationalism' of mainstream literature (Wimmer & Glick-Schiller, 2003) and therefore had a highly localist connotation. In this perspective, migration policies were conceptualised as the product of the specific local configuration of a series of factors, i.e. the problem pressure, the local power structure (in terms of party politics, local leadership, etc.) and the institutional setting underlying policymaking in a certain city (Alexander, 2007; Dekker et al., 2015; Filomeno, 2017). Whereas, as mentioned above, some scholars have emphasised the pragmatism and problem-solving orientation of local policies (Jørgensen, 2012; Penninx et al., 2004; Poppelaars & Scholten, 2008), bringing to light cases of local/national policy decoupling (Scholten, 2013; Spencer, 2018), others have shown that city policies can also be restrictive (Ambrosini, 2013; Mahnig, 2004), sometimes even more than those promoted by national governments (Varsanyi, 2008; see, e.g., in the case of the US, Mitnik & Halpern-Finnerty, 2010).

According to Filomeno (2017, p. 7), the localist perspective has "ontological, theoretical and methodological limitations." The point is the insensitivity of this approach to the multiple interdependences that underlie local migration policy. Far from being simply results of the actions taken by local actors under local conditions, the decisions of local authorities are part of broader policymaking processes that risk being obscured by an exclusive focus on local conditions and factors. To the 'methodological localism' underlying early studies, Filomeno (2017, p. 8) opposes a relational mode of explanation, i.e. one that focuses on the relational dimension of local migration policy and interprets it as the product of broader processes "that encompass, link and cut across multiple localities, generating interdependencies." Two types of relational arguments are identified, i.e. vertical and horizontal arguments. Whereas the former focus on top-down, bottom-up and two-way intergovernmental processes, the latter look at processes of inter-city competition and/or cooperation and at the spillover of pro- and anti-immigrant social mobilisation (Filomeno, 2017, p. 66).

A relational approach along the lines suggested by Filomeno (2017; see also Dekker et al., 2015) is certainly important to complement the understanding of local migration policy outputs as part and parcel of broader economic, institutional and political puzzles. It integrates key insights from macro-structural theories of state re-scaling (see, e.g., Light, 2006) with a meso-level analytical perspective emphasising institutional state-periphery relations (see, e.g., Spiro, 2001 and the literature on federalism). However, the relational approach too shows limitations. First, it often conceives of cities as *sites* (see Sect. 2.3) for processes and dynamics operating on other scales, indicating a quite passive understanding of their role in migration policymaking. In other words, this approach risks disregarding the autonomous agency of the multiplicity of stakeholders engaged in local policymaking processes. Quite paradoxically, the relational approach does not seem to recognise the intrinsically relational nature of cities.

Second, while claiming to analyse processes, the relational approach actually focuses on policy outputs, leaving the mechanisms that link the two in a black box. For instance, even when using concepts such as policy networks or policy diffusion (Filomeno, 2017, p. 77), attention is not on why and how policy networks or processes of diffusion actually take place in local policymaking around migration but on the outputs of such processes in order to explain policy convergence/divergence across localities. Processes are treated as independent variables the impact of which on policy is often investigated—not unlike localist studies—with single case or small-N comparative studies.

Explaining migration policy outputs is indeed important, and contributes to ongoing debates in migration studies on the redefinition of immigrant integration models in Europe (Jørgensen, 2012; Schiller, 2016) and on municipal responses to undocumented migrants and refugees in the US (de Graauw, 2014; Gulasekaram & Ramakrishnan, 2015; Ramakrishnan & Wong, 2010; Steil & Vasi, 2014). However, what seems lacking in this perspective is the recognition of migration policy as part and parcel of broader puzzles in contemporary politics that concern the reconfiguration of state powers and modes of governing vis-à-vis the challenges of globalisation. In other words, migration policy research, even when borrowing concepts from mainstream political science like policy networks or policy diffusion, somehow adopts an 'inward-looking approach,' i.e. one that focuses exclusively on theorising (local) migration policy in its own right. This risks remaining a self-referential exercise which takes for granted that the specificity of the migration issue requires a specific—relational rather than localist—theory of migration policy of hardly any relevance for other domains.

However, facts tell a different story: state competences and powers have been in a state of flux for at least four decades now, while cities have been organising and networking on a multiplicity of issues, with migration actually being—as mentioned in Chapter 1—a latecomer topic in this respect. To understand local migration policy, and even more cross-city collaboration on the issue, I argue for an 'outward-looking' second-generation agenda, i.e. one that aims to theorise local migration policy in the context of broader multilevel political dynamics and policymaking processes triggered by globalisation.

To this end, in the next section I discuss the main contributions that take a policy process perspective to analyse the role of cities in multilevel political dynamics around migration issues. I consider both top-down and bottom-up approaches. Whereas the former thematise processes of state authority dispersion, the latter instead aim to make sense of cities' entrepreneurial role in response to external problem pressure. It is exactly at the crossroads of institutional and problem pressure dynamics that city networking around migration takes shape.

3.3 Cities in Multilevel Policymaking Dynamics on Migration. A State of the Art

The existing literature on multilevel policymaking dynamics around migration-related issues has looked at the role of cities either from a top-down or a bottom-up perspective. In the first perspective, cities are analysed in the context of processes of decentralisation and devolution of nation state responsibilities and competences on the migration issue. Studies have been carried out mainly on a national/regional basis, with a focus on Europe and overseas main destination countries like Canada, the US and, to a more limited extent, Australia (see, e.g., Paquet, 2017). In the second perspective, instead, the attention focuses on cities' mobilisation from below vis-à-vis migration challenges. While the first perspective is primarily concerned with intergovernmental relations, the second has shown greater attention to network relations with non-public organisations. Table 3.1 provides an overview of the existing literature on multilevel policymaking dynamics on migration, also specifying the implications in terms of conceptualisation of the CN-MLG nexus.

Table 3.1 Multilevel policymaking dynamics on migration. A map of the literature

Approach	*Theoretical foci*	*Empirical focus*	*CNs-MLG nexus*
Top-down	State dispersion of authority/institutional (re)structuring	Regional/national institutional systems and intergovernmental relations	Institutional opportunity structure
Bottom-up	Urban and local governance	Cities in one or more countries	Urban actors' agendas and interests
		City networks	City leadership and agendas vs leadership and agendas in CN organisations

3.3.1 *The Top-Down Perspective*

In a top-down perspective, multilevel policymaking dynamics around migration are analysed essentially as part of systems of intergovernmental relations. It follows that city mobilisation, and the eventual emergence of migration CNs, is understood as reflecting specific institutional configurations of opportunities and constraints on the action of local authorities.

More specifically, with respect to the European context, policymaking processes on migration have been described as two 'reversed pyramids' (Adam & Caponio, 2019, p. 28): whereas interactions on immigration control and admission policies take place primarily in upper governmental tiers, namely between the EU, international organisations and the state, those regarding immigrant integration are mostly situated at lower tiers of government, namely between the state and local authorities and/or regions.

In this latter stream of literature, studies have analysed the role of municipalities in the implementation of integration policies, therefore focusing on policymaking relations with regional levels of government, which appear particularly crucial in federalist and regionalised countries (Hepburn & Zapata-Barrero, 2014). Relations with civil society organisations and NGOs have been essentially considered in relation to the provision of integration services established by national laws, such as civic integration and language courses (see, e.g., Caponio et al., 2016; Schiller, 2016).

Looking more specifically at city networking, Penninx (2015) has noted the key role played by the European Commission in favouring the emergence of migration CNs through the provision of specific financial resources supporting local authorities' integration projects (see also Sect. 4.1). These developments seem to disclose the emergence of "new coalitions in the multi-level governance of migration and integration in Europe" (Penninx, 2015, p. 105). However, other scholars have shown that state-led civic integration programmes have significantly affected cities' autonomy with respect to integration policy and brought the state back in, therefore challenging the very idea of the emergence of new MLG coalitions in Europe (Emilsson, 2015; Gebhardt, 2016).

With respect to the cases of Canada and the US, the top-down perspective on the study of multilevel policymaking dynamics around migration has typically adopted the lens of studies on federalism and intergovernmental relations (see, e.g., Spiro, 2001; Varsanyi et al., 2012; Paquet, 2017). Canada has been described as the most decentralised immigration and reception regime of all the liberal democracies (Banting, 2012, p. 80), since its 1867 constitution already defined immigration as an area of 'shared federal-provincial jurisdiction' (Schertzer et al., 2016, p. 16). Provincial involvement became more and more relevant after 1991, when the Canada-Quebec Accord assigned to the francophone province the ability to directly select economic migrants and full autonomy in the management of federal funds allocated to welcoming and integration (Paquet, 2014). Since then, the other provinces have started to negotiate bilateral agreements with the federal government (Schertzer et al., 2016; Seidle, 2010). As a consequence, much of the existing research on multilevel policymaking dynamics in Canada focuses on relations between provincial authorities and the plethora of actors engaged in the implementation of reception policies, including municipalities and NGOs. Leo and August (2009), for instance, contrast the case of British Columbia, based on market-oriented and public choice principles, with that of Manitoba, where provincial authorities engaged in building a system of multilevel governance relations tailored to meet the specific requirements of different local communities. Bradford and Andrew (2011), on the other hand, have analysed the case of Ontario, focusing on the role of the province in promoting so-called 'Local Integration Partnerships' (LIPs), which are described as "a *living experiment* in the new public governance – embracing collaboration, responding to community rhythms, and forging relationships across levels of government and public, private and voluntary sectors" (Bradford & Andrew, 2011, p. 3).

Regarding the United States, the top-down perspective can be identified in studies on intergovernmental relations and political conflicts between jurisdictions on issues of immigration control (see, e.g., Newton, 2018 on municipal ID cards). Although migration control and admission policies are in the exclusive hands of the federal government, collaboration with state and city authorities is fundamental to ensure law enforcement (Gulasekaram & Ramakrishnan, 2015; Varsanyi, 2010). The emergence of sanctuary cities, which openly challenge federal policies by offering protection to undocumented migrants (de Graauw, 2014; Kaufmann, 2019), has been interpreted as a consequence of such contentious policymaking dynamics (Lacroix, 2021), as we will see more in-depth in Sect. 5.1.

3.3.2 *The Bottom-Up Perspective*

The bottom-up perspective on the analysis of policymaking dynamics around migration adopts the theoretical lens of local and urban governance to make sense of processes of city mobilisation in response to specific local challenges. Relations with other levels of government and with non-public actors are thematised not so much in relation to the formal structure of division of competences but instead in the context of governance relations that can extend well beyond the city boundaries.

It is in the context of studies adopting such a perspective that migration CNs have—recently—become objects of a burgeoning debate.

Most existing research has taken a city perspective with the aim of understanding municipalities' strategies of engagement and disengagement from migration CNs (see, e.g., Fourot et al., 2021 on French cities; Caponio 2018 on Italian cities). Some scholars have observed the importance of city marketing strategies (Hadj-Abdou, 2014; Jørgensen, 2012), whereas others have noticed the key role played by civil society organisations and NGOs in sustaining municipal efforts to participate in international networks (Caponio and Clément, 2021; Rodriguez et al., 2018) and to establish transnational relations with other cities (Scholten et al., 2018).

Still from a bottom-up perspective on the study of policymaking dynamics around migration, scholars have recently started to investigate CN organisations and how they engage in processes of international and global migration governance. A case in point is a study by Oomen (2020), which builds on a database on the 20 most important transnational municipal networks in refugee and migrant welcoming and integration in Europe, and shows how by 'teaming up' cities develop narratives on migration that counter national restrictive discourses and contribute to 'decoupling' local from national migration governance. In a similar vein, Stürner and Bendel (2019) look at cities and their networks as key agents in the global governance of migration since they engage in creating soft laws that ensure that local reception policies are grounded in fundamental international and European rights. Heimann et al. (2019), on the other hand, focus on the notion of solidarity vis-à-vis the refugee issue in Europe and investigate how this is re-interpreted in a trans-municipal perspective.

As is clear, these studies link to debates on paradiplomacy and cities in international relations (see Sect. 3.3) and conceptualise cities, and more specifically municipal governments, as unitary actors pursuing strategies that aim to challenge state-based policies and modes of regulating migration from below. However, other scholars take a more critical perspective on the mobilisation of CNs in international migration policymaking dynamics. Cianetti (2018, p. 13), for instance, shows how European CN discourses on diversity represent a—quite contradictory—'pragmatic-adaptive' response to a context characterised by shrinking financial resources, in which "cities are incentivised to change and/or reframe existing policy approaches, in a combination of accommodation of and resistance to antimulticulturalist and austerity imperatives." Lacroix (2021), on the other hand, interprets the recent surge in the number of migration CNs in the context of the 2015 European 'migration crisis' as a result of the top-down influence of international organisations such as the EU and the bottom-up reaction of municipalities facing growing contradictions between their welcoming responsibilities and national security policies. City agency is therefore problematised vis-à-vis the multiple and contradictory pressures that lead to mobilisation in CNs.

However, also in this more critical perspective, CNs are conceptualised as unitary actors that somehow embody the cities' point of view on migration issues vis-à-vis national governments and international institutions. Other studies taking a more actor-centred approach show that CNs can be more realistically conceptualised as arenas where different actors take part in the shaping of the policy agenda. More specifically, Flamant (2017) and Gebhardt and Güntner (2021) analyse relationships among different categories of policymakers in the Eurocities Working Group on Migration and Integration. Whereas the first study focuses on city officers' different frames of immigrant integration, the second aims to understand how the interactions between city officers and the network secretariat have produced entrepreneurial capacities with regard to mutual learning and influencing EU policies.

Hence, as is clear, the burgeoning research on migration CNs somewhat complements more established mainstream literature on migration policymaking in the EU and migration federalism and intergovernmental relations in North America, contributing to illuminating migration policymaking from a different explanatory perspective, i.e. that of the mobilisation and agency of CNs.

3.3.3 *Implications in Terms of Analysing the CN-MLG Nexus*

From the literature review above we can draw some implications for the analysis of the CN-MLG nexus on migration-related issues, and more specifically in terms of identifying the relevant factors driving the emergence of this nexus.

The top-down approach to the study of multilevel policymaking dynamics on migration emphasises the key importance of institutional structures. Two conclusions can be drawn from this research stream. First, MLG is only possible when institutional centre-periphery relations are characterised by collaboration, as in the EU and the Canadian cases, whereas it will be difficult to achieve when conflicts between jurisdictions prevail, as can be seen in US scholarly works. Second, the involvement of cities and their networks will depend on 'metagovernace' (Jessop, 2004) or on the concrete rules underlying policymaking relations. Whereas in the EU at the beginning of the 2000s funding and policy actions deployed by the European Commission (EC) on matters of migration favoured mobilisation by cities (see also Sect. 4.1 below), in the Canadian system collaboration has been centred around the federal government/provinces axis de facto assigning a subordinate role to cities. Hence, from a top-down perspective, the CN-MLG nexus on migration is the specific and somewhat unique outcome of the EU *sui generis* supra-national system, and of the alliance with cities promoted by the EC in order to circumvent member state ideological approaches and contain the politicisation of the immigrant integration issue (Penninx, 2015).

The bottom-up approach, on the other hand, emphasises the mobilisation of cities from below, in which CNs respond to problem pressure, interests and their members' definitions of migration challenges. However, two different perspectives can be identified in the—still scarce—research on CNs engagement in migration policymaking: a unitary perspective that conceives of CNs as agents pursuing a pragmatic agenda on migration and therefore contradicting ideologically-driven national government agendas (Oomen, 2020; Stürner & Bendel, 2019; Thouez, 2020); and a pluralistic perspective that regards CN organisations as arenas where different categories of actors—e.g. politicians, staff officers, etc.—mobilise to pursue their respective agendas.

The first perspective essentially looks at CNs as organisations promoting the international mobilisation of municipal governments and/or their mayors *vis-à-vis* specific problems. According to Stürner and Bendel (2019, p. 233), expertise in local migration issues strengthens cities' self-confidence and supports their demands for political authority: "In this context, the retranslation of cities' local practices into international and European human rights discourses enables local authorities to become active agents in migration governance." Hence, by setting standards for migrant welcoming and integration in a horizontal way, i.e. standards which are agreed on and actively monitored by member cities, CNs engage in 'glocalising' international norms and in turn influence international processes of standard-setting by adding specific contents to rights (Oomen, 2020). In this literature, MLG is usually evoked as the more general context in which cities deploy their agency in global policymaking on migration.

The pluralistic *arena* perspective, instead, rather than assuming a distinctive 'city' international agenda, by taking an actor-centred approach aims to identify who mobilises within CNs and why. In other words, this research stream unravels the agendas pursued by the different actors involved in processes of city internationalisation. It is in this second perspective that the political work underlying the CN-MLG nexus can be better brought to the fore, as we will see in more depth below.

3.4 Migration City Networks as Agents of MLG? An Actor-Centred and Relational Interpretative Framework

The arguments proposed in this book have been developing in concentric circles, from the more general plan of defining MLG policymaking and conceptualising the CN-MLG nexus in Chapter 2 to the more specific arguments introduced above on multilevel policymaking dynamics around migration issues and the mobilisation of migration CNs. Hence, in this section I further elaborate on my approach to the analysis of the CN-MLG nexus by applying it to the specific dilemmas raised by the 'super-wicked' migration policy issue.

To this end, below I first attempt to better operationalise the nexus, i.e. to specify what it should look like or, in other words, how it can be detected empirically. In fact, even though CNs often present a discourse emphasising interaction and collaboration in multilevel decision-making processes, a nexus with MLG is only established when there is evidence of participation and engagement in a structure or process of policymaking that can be characterised as an instance of MLG. As was already discussed in Sect. 2.2, in this study instances of MLG are defined by the concomitant presence of three elements: (1) different levels of government are simultaneously involved; (2) non-government actors at different levels are also involved; and (3) relationships between different levels of government and with non-governmental actors take the form of non-hierarchical networks based on cooperation and consensus-building.

As was already argued, I see the engagement of CNs in MLG, and therefore the emergence of a nexus, as the product of a complex political work that engages on the one hand CN leaders/activists and on the other the potentially ample plethora of policymakers and stakeholders mobilised on the migration policy issue on different territorial scales. Such political work takes place in the context of specific configurations of opportunities and constraints in terms of: (1) the institutional structure underlying the making of migration policies; and (2) pressure problems and specific migration challenges.

More specifically, the institutional structure defines the formal role of each actor and the power structure underlying policymaking relations on migration. In other words, policymakers and stakeholders engage in policymaking from different institutional positions and have different resources in terms of power and influence in the decision-making process.

The problem pressure, on the other hand, regards the overall evolution of migratory phenomena in a certain context, which is, however, actively defined and interpreted by policymakers and stakeholders engaged in policymaking processes on migration.

It is in this complex context characterised by different frames of migration challenges and problem pressure, institutional roles and power structures that the interaction between the demand side and the supply side of multilevel migration policymaking takes place. As is graphically shown in Fig. 3.1, the demand side concerns CN goals and strategies that are the results of internal political processes of agenda-setting engaging CN leaders/activists and (different categories of) members more generally. These agendas can be more or less favourable for pursuing collaborative policymaking relationships with other stakeholders and public authorities at different territorial levels. In other words, a quest for engagement in MLG policymaking on the part of CNs should not be taken for granted, since they might well be interested in engaging in other modes of—collaborative or contentious—intergovernmental relations like intergovernmental collaboration (IGC), lobbying or venue shopping, and/or in collaborating with non-public actors through horizontal networks (HN). CNs can therefore pursue either inclusive or selective policymaking interactions.

Fig. 3.1 An actor-centred interpretative framework of CNs modes of policymaking

As for the supply side, this involves the mobilisation of policymakers and stakeholders on the vertical and horizontal dimensions of migration policymaking. However, as mentioned above, the institutional structure assigns different roles and power resources to these actors. More specifically, supranational and international organisations, on the one hand, and national governmental authorities, on the other, represent key gatekeepers that can either provide CNs with important material and symbolic resources for participation in migration policymaking or simply deny any possibility of access, eventually leading to the prevalence of traditional hierarchical relations (HR).

Hence, as is clear, CNs' openness and availability to engage in collaborative policymaking relationships, while necessary, does not represent a sufficient condition for the establishment of MLG-like arrangements. This will also require a willingness to enter into such collaborative interactions on the part of those actors that have more power in the making of migration policy and that, as is the case of national governments in particular, have a clear stake in the issue, given the implications of migration in terms of state sovereignty. Hence, departing from the general mechanisms underlying modes of policymaking illustrated in Figs. 3.1 and 3.2 further specifies the causal factors and mechanism that I expect to lead to the emergence of a CN-MLG nexus in the migration policy field.

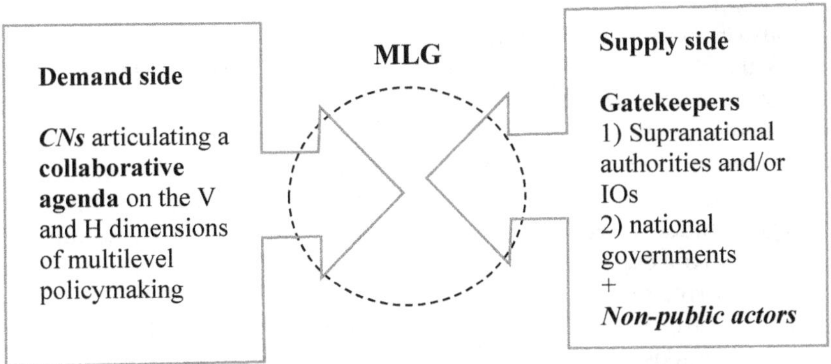

Fig. 3.2 An actor-centred interpretative framework of the CNs-MLG nexus

As is shown in the figure, MLG as a specific policymaking arrangement implies collaboration *on both* the horizontal and vertical dimensions, and therefore an attempt to pursue coordination among all the key actors in a certain policy field through collaboration on shared goals. Drawing on these premises, I argue that MLG is not a politics-free mode of governing migration but is instead politics-dependent. In other words, the key factors and mechanisms linking CNs to MLG are primarily of a political kind, and regard: (1) migration CN internal processes of agenda setting, which should lead to the emergence of a collaborative agenda; and (2) the political willingness of national governments to engage in cooperative multilevel policymaking processes on the sensitive migration issue.

The interpretative framework presented above challenges the understanding of MLG as a 'top-down move' by EU institutions to build new policymaking alliances aimed at bypassing member states' restrictive migration policies (Penninx, 2015). This mode of policymaking appears somewhat a type of intergovernmental cooperation based on a bilateral partnership between local and supra-national governments and excluding the direct engagement of NGOs.

At the same time, the actor-centred and relational interpretative framework does not imply a diametrically opposed 'bottom-up' view of MLG, as is suggested in Scholten et al.'s (2018) study on Dutch city mobilisation on the issue of CEE citizens' access to welfare services. According to this study, "a nascent multi-level governance structure on 'intra-EU movement' was not so much established top-down by European institutions or member states, but rather 'bottom-up' by coordinated efforts by local governments" (Scholten et al., 2018, p. 2031). However, the authors also note that vertical interaction between levels of government and increasing awareness and engagement on the part of the European Commission were facilitated by the politicisation of intra-EU movement by populist and mainstream political parties. In other words, cooperative intergovernmental relations appear to have been the result of a contingent process of converging interests and views between political actors, with a prominent role of national governments.

The actor-centred and relational interpretative framework proposed in this book builds on both top-down and bottom-up accounts of cooperative intergovernmental relations on migration-related issues, and yet it aims to go beyond them in at least two respects. First of all, it seeks to understand the role of NGOs and non-public actors in these relations. In fact, existing empirical accounts of the CN-MLG nexus on migration often appear limited to instances of intergovernmental relations. However, given the importance of non-public organisations in the provision of different types of services to migrants, especially at the local level, their role in MLG policymaking should be given greater attention. Second, it looks at CNs not simply as reflecting member cities' interests and approaches to migration, but as complex organisations or arenas where different categories of actors interact in the setting of internal policy agendas which can be more or less conducive to MLG.

The interpretative framework presented in Fig. 3.2 takes these caveats seriously and aims to overcome them through an in-depth analysis of CNs' modes of policymaking and the—eventual—emergence of MLG arrangements in the context of different institutional multilevel systems, i.e. the EU supranational and the US federal systems, and on a highly controversial policy issue like migration. Below I illustrate and further specify the research design and methodological approach underlying this book, which was already introduced in Sect. 1.4.

3.5 The Migration CN-MLG Nexus in Practice. Research Design and Methodology

Three research questions underlie this book. Why do cities get together to coordinate their efforts and policies on typical matters of state sovereignty such as migration and mobility? Are these coordination efforts from below leading to the emergence of a new multilevel governance of migration? And, in the affirmative, which are the key factors and mechanisms accounting for the emergence of a CN-MLG nexus?

To answer these questions, this study focuses on CN organisations—rather than on cities—and proposes a research design based on a combination of a transatlantic comparative case-study method and causal process tracing. This method enables critical assessment of normative statements on the capacity of cities 'to rule' migration challenges through engagement in MLG networks. At the same time, it allows empirical research on MLG policymaking to move forward by unravelling the factors and mechanisms underlying the emergence of vertical and horizontal collaborative policymaking relations on the highly contentious migration issue. As is clear, this study aims to contribute to the literature by pursuing theory-building (see also Sect. 1.4), that is, by illuminating the possible under-explored causal factors and mechanisms that can underpin the emergence of a CN-MLG nexus in different multilevel institutional contexts.

3.5.1 A Theory-Building Approach to Process Tracing

Beach and Pedersen (2019, pp. 10–11) define theory-building process-tracing as a creative iterative process of moving back and forth between empirical probing and theorisation in which inference is based on cross-case comparison of within-case causal mechanisms and configurations of factors. The final result of such a research process should be a theorised mechanism that sheds light on how a cause or set of causes (C) contribute to producing an outcome (O). To this end, they suggest selecting cases where both C and O are present, and therefore the hypothesised mechanism should at least in principle also be present.

However, given the still very scarce research on the CN-MLG nexus, in this study I take a more explorative approach, i.e. one that focuses on different cases of migration CNs with the goal of tracing the modes of policymaking they undertake and/or are engaged in, in order to find out if and to what extent MLG emerges. Following Gerring's (2017, p. 98) diverse-method approach, my aim is to search for cases of migration CNs that "are intended to represent the full range of values characterising X1, Y or some particular X1/Y relationship."

More specifically, on the basis of the literature reviewed in Chapter 2 on CNs in general and in the above sections on migration CNs, two factors (X) emerge as key in accounting for the emergence of a CN-MLG nexus (Y), i.e. the particular EU opportunity structure (X1); and the problem pressure, namely the necessity for cities to deal with the extreme complexity of migration and mobility challenges (X2). These two factors represent the main dimensions underlying my case-selection strategy. The first factor (X1) can be operationalised in terms of the presence/absence of a supranational multilevel polity like the EU. The assumption behind this is that CNs will be more likely to engage in MLG policymaking in the EU multilevel context since specific opportunities are provided from above by the European Commission. The second factor instead, i.e. the problem pressure (X2), can be operationalised by considering the conditions leading to the mobilisation of CNs. As observed by Lacroix (2021), migration CNs can be directly promoted by cities themselves or by some external actor or 'patron' like an international organisation or an NGO.

Whereas networks established by cities can be expected to articulate local governments' concerns and needs, and therefore to respond to a specific problem pressure, externally mobilised CNs are more likely to follow the agenda of the organisation providing leadership, which might be oriented towards other different goals than addressing local issues perceived as critical by local policymakers.

In Fig. 3.3 I identify four different types of CNs and link them with different scenarios in terms of the migration CNs-MLG nexus that can be derived from the hypotheses present in the literature. For each case, I indicate a possible empirical referent, i.e. the CN that most closely approximates the characteristics of the hypothetical case identified in each square.

Case 1 is that of CNs directly promoted by cities in the context of the EU supranational system, like the Eurocities Working Group on Migration and Integration (WGM&I). On the basis of the literature, in this context we should expect a scenario characterised by the maximum level of MLG because of the combination of bottom-up direct mobilisation of cities with an opportunity structure favouring CNs inclusion in collaborative policymaking processes. Case 3 is somewhat conterminous for H1, in the sense that the opportunity structure is the same as case 1, yet it is very different case for H2 since engagement in MLG policymaking will

		Supranational level	
		Yes (EU)	No (US)
Mode of mobilisation	Directly promoted by cities	(1) Max. MLG scenario Working Group on Migration and Integration (WGM&I)	(2) No MLG for H1/High MLG scenario for H2 Cities for Action (C4A)
	Promoted by external actors	(3) High MLG scenario for X1/No MLG for X2 Intercultural Cities Programme (ICC)	(4) No MLG for X1/moderate MLG for X2 Welcoming America (WA)

Fig. 3.3 Case selection and expectations on the CN-MLG nexus

depend on the agenda promoted by the external 'sponsor.' The Intercultural Cities Programme established by the Council of Europe can be considered a case of an externally promoted CN that operates in the EU multilevel context.

Case 2 is a mirror image of case 1 and regards CNs directly promoted by cities to engage in complex MLG policy processes that, however, operate in a less favourable institutional opportunity structure, i.e. the US intended as traditional federalist state structure. A case in point is the Cities for Action (C4A) network, which is a local government-led initiative. In this scenario we should expect no MLG according to H1 and on the contrary high MLG for H2 because of bottom-up pressures from cities. Case 4 represents the least likely case for MLG in H1 because of the less favourable institutional structure. It should represent a least-likely case also for H2, since the CN is promoted by an external actor pursuing its own agenda. Yet the case selected, Welcoming America (WA), is a US-based CN mobilised by an NGO, that therefore presents a bottom-up genesis linked to pro-immigrant grassroots movements, as we will see more in-depth in Chapter 5. It can be reasonably assumed that this will represent a moderate MLG scenario for H2. Table 3.2 below provides a further specification of the hypotheses drawn from the literature in terms of causal arguments and expected causal observations.

However, the actor-centred interpretative approach that I have presented in Sect. 3.4 challenges the assumptions underlying these hypotheses. In this perspective, a critical role is assigned to actors' agendas, and more specifically to the agenda of CNs on the demand side and of gatekeepers, i.e. supranational institutions or international organisations and/or national governments on the supply side. It follows that, regarding factor X1, the presence of a supranational institution like the EU, which provides various financial and policy incentives for city mobilisation, might favour the emergence of greater vertical intergovernmental relations, as is actually pointed out in existing studies (Penninx, 2015), but does not seem per se conducive to MLG-like policy arrangements. On the other hand, regarding factor X2, whereas the literature tends to assume that CN leadership and policy agendas reflect cities' interest in obtaining access to high-level policymaking on the 'super-wicked' migration issue (see, e.g., Stürner & Bendel, 2019), taking an actor-centred perspective I conceptualise CNs as arenas where different actors can concur on shaping priorities and actions. The assumption that city-led initiatives will be more favourable for the establishment of MLG

Table 3.2 The CN-MLG link. Specification of the hypotheses drawn from the literature

Hypothesis	*Causal factors and mechanisms*	*Expected causal process observations*
H1. EU opportunity structure	EC programmes provide funding to cities and NGOs cooperative efforts • Cities start to collaborate in horizontal and vertical network to take advantage of the new resources	1. EU-based CNs involved in MLG policymaking venues and initiatives 2. No engagement of US CNs in MLG and less collaborative approach to policymaking
H2. Problem pressure	• New and/or increasingly worrisome immigration challenges hit cities Cities start to collaborate among them and with stakeholders to solve the issue • These networks put pressure on higher-ranked governmental authorities to establish modes of policy coordination	1. CNs directly established by cities, i.e. WGM&I and C4A, will put pressure for setting up MLG venues and initiatives 2. CNs established by NGOs like WA will show a moderate mobilisation for MLG policymaking; 3. No MLG engagement in case of ICC

policymaking interactions cannot be taken for granted, but depends on leaders' agenda.

Hence, the actor-centred interpretative framework for the migration CN-MLG nexus leads us to take an inductive theory-building approach to process tracing. Such a research path, by focusing on the in-depth reconstruction of the mechanisms leading to the—eventual—emergence of a CN-MLG nexus, allows going beyond the limits of existing explanations, in order to analyse more in-depth the role concretely played by CNs and other relevant governmental and non-governmental actors in migration policymaking. Table 3.3 presents the causal arguments and expected causal observations of the actor-centred and relational interpretative framework of the CN-MLG nexus, that will be assessed in Chapter 6.

3.5.2 *Data Sources and Empirical Research*

My empirical research developed through intensive case studies carried out between September 2018 and August 2020 on each of the four

Table 3.3 Operationalisation of the actor-centred and relational interpretative framework of the CN-MLG nexus

	Causal factors and mechanisms	*Expected causal observations*
Demand side	CNs articulating an agenda aimed at establishing collaborative relations on the vertical and horizontal dimension of multilevel policymaking processes	1. CNs leaders as brokers (rather than contenders) 2. Policy actions actively promoting multiple collaborations
Supply side	Gatekeepers interest in establishing MLG policymaking on migration-related issues EU 1. Supportive international organisations AND/OR 2. National governments interest and willingness to engage collaboratively US 3. National government interest and willingness to engage collaboratively	1. Discourses explicitly endorsing MLG policymaking 2. Actions, like platforms, consultation processes etc., to put into effect MLG policymaking 3. Participation to cooperative venues on migration policy established by other institutions

CNs introduced above. This required the collection of different types of data and the triangulation of various sources in a step-by-step process aimed at reconstructing migration CNs' modes of policymaking from their founding up to 2019.

The first step consisted in a systematic collection of CN official documents and webpages, which were downloaded in different time periods, i.e. in November–December 2018 for the first time and then in the spring and autumn of 2019 to check for new documents and updates. Overall, a corpus of 38 documents for the WGM&I, 41 for ICC, 31 for WA and 58 for C4A was constructed and qualitatively analysed in order to gather information on processes of involvement in MLG policymaking (see the Appendix). In a second step, I undertook a more in-depth search for documents on the websites of the institutions and organisations participating, together with the CNs analysed, in policymaking processes on migration. In total, 40 more documents were analysed. The third step involved a compilation of empirical narratives that were then systematically triangulated with the data collected during fieldwork research. This fourth step was carried out through qualitative interviews with key informants in the CNs (such as officers and/or political leaders) and other relevant institutions and organisations (see the list of interviews in the Appendix), and participant observation at some key events organised by the four networks in 2018–2019 and informal conversations with city representatives and other stakeholders participating in these events.

The interview partners were identified on the basis of the document analysis, yet the list was constantly discussed and amended during the interviews in order to add more relevant actors. Overall, the number of interviews per network varied reflecting the CNs' leadership structures, organisational articulations and ranges of initiatives. In total I collected four in-depth interviews in the cases of C4A and ICC, six in that of WA and ten for WGM&I. Formal face-to-face interviews were integrated with notes taken on more informal conversations and exchanges with policymakers and stakeholders mobilised in the CNs' activities, primarily city officials, mayors, NGO representatives, etc. Participation in CN events turned out to be extremely important in order to get more in-depth knowledge of the CNs' modes of working and initiatives. In general, I participated as an external expert, and in this role I engaged in workshops and discussions, acting as rapporteur or facilitator, depending on requests by the organisers. This active role enabled me to better understand the organisation of the CNs and interact on various occasions with staff officers and city leaders, e.g. before the events in the preparation of meetings and afterwards for the release of minutes and reports. In the empirical chapters, I present this rich research evidence through structured narratives. In particular, I follow a chronological order to reconstruct the sequence of events underlying the engagement by the four CNs in multilevel policymaking processes around migration and eventually their participation in instances of MLG.

Thick descriptions can easily run the risk of becoming simply descriptive and lacking in analytical focus. To avoid these pitfalls, the chronological narratives are structured around the key elements of the interpretative framework discussed in Sect. 3.4. With respect to the demand side of migration policymaking, i.e. CNs, attention has been paid to (1) the key leaders and processes of internal agenda setting and to (2) the main policy actions, initiatives and modes of policymaking actively promoted by each CN. As for the supply side of MLG, the analysis has attempted to flash out the interactions and relationships of CNs with other key stakeholders and policymakers in the multilevel migration policy field in order to detect the actors concretely promoting MLG instances of policymaking vis-à-vis specific challenges. More specifically, on the basis of the actor-centred and relational interpretative framework underlying the analysis, particular attention has been paid to the analysis of the discourses and actions put forward by actors that have a gatekeeping role, i.e. supranational and national governmental authorities (see Table 3.3 above).

Following this inductive approach to the process tracing method, for each of the four CNs I systematically investigate traces of within-case causal mechanisms and configurations of factors accounting for the emergence of MLG policymaking. Chapter 4 is dedicated to the two Europe-based CNs, i.e. the WGM&I and the ICC Programme, while Chapter 5 provides structured narratives on the two US-based networks, i.e. WA and C4A. At the end of each chapter, a cross-case comparative assessment of the CN-MLG nexus in each multilevel political context is provided. In Chapter 6 I further engage in transatlantic, cross-case comparison, in order to assess the validity of the interpretations presented in the literature and draw conclusions on the explanatory leverage of the actor-centred and relational interpretative framework to the CN-MLG nexus, and to highlight its contribution to ongoing debates on cities in the governance of global challenges.

Here below, I provide a brief introduction to the four CNs analysed in this study, and more specifically to their present structure, membership and main operating rules.

3.5.3 *The Selected Cases. An Introductory Note*

If certainly the four selected migration CNs do not exhaust the plurality of city initiatives operating in the EU and US contexts (Filomeno, 2017; Oomen & Baumgärtel, 2018), still, on the basis of a screening of Internet websites, policy reports and informal exchanges with experts, they result among the more active in the last decade and therefore represent significant cases for the exploration of multilevel policymaking dynamics on migration in the two continents.

Table 3.4 provides some general information on each of the selected CNs taking into account five main aspects: year of foundation, composition of membership, number of member cities, fees, decision-making organs and organisational structure. All these features will be examined more in-depth in the following chapters (Chapters 4 and 5). However, the synthetic summary offered by the table can give an idea of how the

Table 3.4 Main features of the four migration CNs analysed in the book

	WGM&I	*ICC*	*WA*	*C4A*
Year of founding	2004	2008	(2001) 2009	2014
Membership	City governments and metropolitan areas	City governments	Local governments (cities and counties), non-profit organisations	Mayors and county executives
Number of cities	97	145	79	200
Fee	Eurocities annual fee, ranging between €21,450 (full member) and €4,420 (associate partner)	€5,000	Annual fee ranging between $200 (General) and $2,500 (Premium)	No fee, private foundations supporting the network
Decision-making structure	1 Chair and 1 Vice-Chair from member cities; annual WG meetings (3 per year) gathering together cities and staff members	Annual Assembly of Member cities (together with the Secretariat)	Board of Directors (12 members from NGOs and including the founder and Executive Director) and a Network Leadership Committee (6 members, 3 of whom from local administrations)	Steering Committee (senior officials from 9 cities Atlanta, Boston, Los Angeles, New York City, Philadelphia, Providence, San Francisco, Chicago and Seattle)
Internal organisation	3 Eurocities staff units, 1 Policy Advisor and 2 Project managers	CoE Staff (1 director of programme, 2 assistants) 26 experts	16 staff members (Executive and Deputy Directors + 5 directors of programme)	3 officials of the Mayoral Office for Migrant Affairs (MOIA) of NYC (one of whom full time)

four CNs featured in 2019, when this research was carried out. Information has been drawn from various webpages of the official websites of each organisation, a list of which can be found in the Appendix to this book.

Where WGM&I, ICC and WA were founded in the first decade of the 2000s, C4A is a more recent initiative, dating back to 2014. Membership is reserved to local authorities with the only exception of WA, where other types of organisations are also featured, like NGOs, local development partnerships and civil rights associations. In total, WA has almost 200 members, 79 of which are municipal and/or county authorities. As for the other networks, C4A has the higher number of member cities, 200, and no fee is required to enter the organisation, even though commitment on the part of mayor and/or county executive officials appears extremely important, as we will see in Chapter 5. The ICC Programme and the WGM&I have 145 and 97 members, respectively, and both request a contribution from cities, as also does WA, whose registration fee varies according to the types of benefits members are entitled, from general to premium. On the contrary, the other two networks have more rigid fees; furthermore, in the case of WGM&I, cities actually register with the broader Eurocities network, and then decide in which forums and working groups want to engage.

With respect to the decision-making structure and internal organisation, in general the networks present a quite simple structure, which reflects the division between politics and administration characterising municipalities. Decision-making is assigned to assemblies of member cities in the cases of the WGM&I and ICC, that can rely also upon a dedicated secretariat, while C4A has a Steering Committee reflecting the core group of the founding cities. In this network, the implementation and coordination of the activities is ensured by the staff of Mayoral Office for Immigrant Affairs in New York City. A different structure is that of WA: strategic decisions are taken by a Board of Directors in collaboration with the Network Leadership Committee, while the functioning of the network relies upon 16 staff members in charge of overseeing the various programmes.

Hence, as is clear whereas the WGM&I, ICC and C4A appear pure cases of 'transnational municipal networks' (Kern & Bulkeley, 2009), intended as organisations formed by municipal governments, WA presents a more varied membership, as is also the case of other CNs in the migration policy field in Europe and elsewhere (Oomen & Baumgärtel, 2018).

However, as we shall see below, all of them, also the two US-based networks, appear to have engaged throughout the years in the building of multiple links with cities in different national/continental contexts. In other terms, migration CNs appear increasingly transnational and global actors, that articulate the complexity of migration and mobility challenges well beyond the boundaries of their states.

References

Adam, I., & Caponio, T. (2019). Research on the multi-level governance of migration and migrant integration. Reversed pyramids. In A. Weinar, S. Bonjour, & L. Zhyznomirska (Eds.), *The Routledge handbook of the politics of migration in Europe* (pp. 26–37). Routledge.

Alexander, M. (2007). *Cities and labour immigration: Comparing policy responses in Amsterdam, Paris, Rome and Tel Aviv*. Ashgate.

Alford, J., & Head, B. W. (2017). Wicked and less wicked problems: A typology and a contingency framework. *Policy and Society, 36*, 397–413. https://doi.org/10.1080/14494035.2017.1361634

Ambrosini, M. (2013). 'We are against a multi-ethnic society': Policies of exclusion at the urban level in Italy. *Ethnic and Racial Studies, 36*, 136–155. https://doi.org/10.1080/01419870.2011.644312

Ambrosini, M., & Boccagni, P. (2015). Urban multiculturalism beyond the 'backlash': New discourses and different practices in immigrant policies across european cities. *Journal of Intercultural Studies, 36*, 35–53. https://doi.org/10.1080/07256868.2014.990362

Bache, I. (2004). Multi-level governance and European Union regional policy. In I. Bache & M. Flinders (Eds.), *Multi-level governance* (pp. 165–179). Oxford University Press.

Banting, K. (2012). Canada. In C. Joppke & L. F. Seidle (Eds.), *Immigrant Integration in federal countries* (pp. 79–111). McGill-Queen's University Press.

Bauböck, R. (Ed.). (2006). *Migration and citizenship: Legal status*. Amsterdam University Press.

Beach, D., & Pedersen, R. B. (2019). *Process-tracing methods: Foundations and guidelines*. University of Michigan Press.

Boswell, C., & Geddes, A. (2011). *Migration and mobility in the European Union*. Palgrave Macmillan.

Bradford, N., & Andrew, C. (2011). *LIPs gathering momentum: Early successes, emerging challenges, and recommendations for the future*. Welcoming Communities Initiative.

Caponio, T. (2018). Immigrant integration beyond national policies? Italian cities' participation in European city networks. *Journal of Ethnic and Migration Studies, 44*, 2053–2069. https://doi.org/10.1080/1369183X.2017.1341711

Caponio, T., Baucells, O. J., & Güell, B. (2016). Civic integration policies from below: Accounting for processes of convergence and divergence in four European cities. *Ethnic and Racial Studies, 39*, 878–895. https://doi.org/10.1080/01419870.2015.1080379

Caponio, T., & Clément, A. (2021). Making sense of trajectories of participation in European city networks on migration. Insights from the cases of Turin (Italy) and Saint-Etienne (France). *Local Government Studies*. https://doi.org/10.1080/03003930.2021.1885378

Cianetti, L. (2018). Governing the multicultural city: Europe's 'great urban expectations' facing austerity and resurgent nativism. *Urban Studies, 57*, 2697–2714. https://doi.org/10.1177/0042098019884214

de Graauw, E. (2014). Municipal ID cards for undocumented immigrants: Local bureaucratic membership in a federal system. *Politics & Society, 42*, 309–330. https://doi.org/10.1177/0032329214543256

Dekker, R., Emilsson, H., Krieger, B., & Scholten, P. (2015). A Local Dimension of Integration Policies? A Comparative Study of Berlin, Malmö, and Rotterdam. *International Migration Review, 49*, 633–658. https://doi.org/10.1111/imre.12133

Della Porta, D. (Ed.). (2018). *Solidarity mobilizations in the 'refugee crisis': Contentious moves*. Palgrave Macmillan.

Edelman, M. (1985). *The symbolic uses of politics*. The University of Illinois Press.

Emilsson, H. (2015). A national turn of local integration policy: Multi-level governance dynamics in Denmark and Sweden. *Comparative Migration Studies, 3*, 1–16. https://doi.org/10.1186/s40878-015-0008-5

Filomeno, F. A. (2017). *Theories of Local Immigration Policy*. Palgrave Macmillan.

Flamant, A. (2017). Les cadres de l'action publique locale en charge des politiques d'intégration des étrangers. *Politique Europeenne, 57*, 84–115.

Fourot, A.-C., Aisling, H., & Flamant, A. (2021). French participation in transnational migration networks: Understanding city (dis)involvement and "passivism". *Local Government Studies*. https://doi.org/10.1080/03003930.2020.1857246

Freeman, G. P. (1995). Modes of immigration politics in liberal democratic states. *International Migration Review, 29*, 881–902. https://doi.org/10.1177/019791839502900401

Gebhardt, D. (2016). When the state takes over: Civic integration programmes and the role of cities in immigrant integration. *Journal of Ethnic and Migration Studies, 42*, 742–758. https://doi.org/10.1080/1369183X.2015.1111132

Gebhardt, D., & Güntner, S. (2021). We as leaders of the major European cities. The work of Eurocities to strengthen an urban perspective in EU migration and integration policy. *Local Government Studies*. https://doi.org/10.1080/03003930.2021.1938552

Gerring, J. (2017). *Case study research: Principles and practices* (2nd ed.). Cambridge University Press.

Guiraudon, V., & Lahav, G. (2000). A reappraisal of the state sovereignty debate: The case of migration control. *Comparative Political Studies, 33*, 163–195. https://doi.org/10.1177/0010414000033002001

Gulasekaram, P., & Ramakrishnan, S. K. (2015). *The new immigration federalism*. Cambridge University Press.

Hadj-Abdou, L. (2014). Immigrant integration and the economic competitiveness agenda: A comparison of Dublin and Vienna. *Journal of Ethnic and Migration Studies, 40*, 1875–1894. https://doi.org/10.1080/1369183X.2014.887462

Heimann, C., Müller, S., Schammann, H., & Stürner, J. (2019). Challenging the nation-state from within: The emergence of transmunicipal solidarity in the course of the EU refugee controversy. *Social Inclusion*, 7, 208–218. https://doi.org/10.17645/si.v7i2.1994

Hepburn, E., & Zapata-Barrero, R. (Eds.). (2014). *The politics of immigration in multi-level states*. Palgrave Macmillan.

Jessop, B. (2004). Multi-level governance and multi-level metagovernance: Changes in the European Union ad integral moments in the transformation and reorientation of contemporary statehood. In I. Bache & M. Flinders (Eds.), *Multi-level governance* (pp. 50–74). Oxford University Press.

Joppke, C. (2007). Beyond national models: Civic integration policies for immigrants in Western Europe. *West European Politics, 30*, 1–22. https://doi.org/10.1080/01402380601019613

Jørgensen, M. B. (2012). The diverging logics of integration policy making at national and city level. *International Migration Review, 46*, 244–278. https://doi.org/10.1111/j.1747-7379.2012.00886.x

Kaufmann, D. (2019). Comparing urban citizenship, sanctuary cities, local bureaucratic membership, and regularizations. *Public Administration Review, 79*, 443–446. https://doi.org/10.1111/puar.13029

Kemmerzell, J. (2019). Bridging the gap between the local and the global scale? Taming the wicked problem of climate change through trans-local governance. In N. Behnke, J. Broschek & J. Sonnicksen (Eds.), *Configurations, dynamics and mechanisms of multilevel governance* (pp. 155–172). Palgrave Macmillan.

Kern, K., & Bulkeley, H. (2009). Cities, Europeanization and multi-level governance: Governing climate change through transnational municipal networks. *JCMS: Journal of Common Market Studies, 47*, 309–332. https://doi.org/10.1111/j.1468-5965.2009.00806.x

Lacroix, T. (2021). Migration related city networks: A global overview. *Local Government Studies*. https://doi.org/10.1080/03003930.2021.1938553

Leo, C., & August, M. (2009). The multilevel governance of immigration and settlement: Making deep federalism work. *Canadian Journal of Political Science/revue Canadienne De Science Politique, 42*, 491–510. https://doi.org/10.1017/S0008423909090337

Levin, K., Cashore, B., Bernstein, S., & Auld, G. (2012). Overcoming the tragedy of super wicked problems: Constraining our future selves to ameliorate global climate change. *Policy Sciences, 45*, 123–152. https://doi.org/10.1007/s11077-012-9151-0

Light, I. (2006). *Deflecting Immigration: Networks, Markets, and Regulation in Los Angeles*. Russell Sage Foundation.

Maggetti, M., & Trein, P. (2019). Multilevel governance and problem-solving: Towards a dynamic theory of multilevel policy-making? *Public Administration, 97*, 355–369. https://doi.org/10.1111/padm.12573

Mahnig, H. (2004). The politics of minority-majority relations: How immigrant policies developed in Paris, Berlin, Zurich. In R. Penninx, K. Kraal, M. Matiniello, & S. Vertovec (Eds.), *Citizenship in European cities: Immigrants, local politics and integration policies* (pp. 17–37). Ashgate.

Massey, D. S., Arango, J., Hugo, G., et al. (1993). Theories of international migration: A review and appraisal. *Population and Development Review, 19*, 431–466. https://doi.org/10.2307/2938462

Mitnik, P., & Halpern-Finnerty, J. (2010). Immigration and local governments; Inclusionary policies in the era of state rescaling. In M. W. Varsanyi (Ed.), *Taking local control: Immigration policy activism in U.S. Cities and states* (pp. 51–72). Stranford University Press.

Moore, D. (2004). Migrants as mediators in a comparative perspective. In R. Penninx, K. Kraal, M. Martiniello, & S. Vertovec (Eds.), *Citizenship in European cities: Immigrants, local politics and integration policies* (pp. 17–37). Ashgate.

Newton, L. (2018). Immigration politics by proxy: State agency in an era of national reluctance. *Journal of Ethnic and Migration Studies, 44*, 2086–2105. https://doi.org/10.1080/1369183X.2017.1341714

Oomen, B. (2020). Decoupling and teaming up: The rise and proliferation of transnational municipal networks in the field of migration. *International*

Migration Review, 54, 913–939. https://doi.org/10.1177/0197918319881118

Oomen, B., & Baumgärtel, M. (2018). Frontier cities: The rise of local authorities as an opportunity for international human rights law. *European Journal of International Law, 29*, 607–630. https://doi.org/10.1093/ejil/chy021

Papadopoulos, Y. (2007). Problems of democratic accountability in network and multilevel governance. *European Law Journal, 13*, 469–486. https://doi.org/10.1111/j.1468-0386.2007.00379.x

Paquet, M. (2014). The federalization of immigration and integration in Canada. *Canadian Journal of Political Science/revue Canadienne De Science Politique, 47*, 519–548. https://doi.org/10.1017/S0008423914000766

Paquet, M. (2017). Wicked problem definition and gradual institutional change: Federalism and immigration in Canada and Australia. *Policy and Society, 36*, 446–463. https://doi.org/10.1080/14494035.2017.1361638

Penninx, R. (2015). European cities in search of knowledge for their integration policies. In P. Scholten, H. Entzinger, R. Penninx, & S. Verbeek (Eds.), *Integrating immigrants in Europe: Research-policy dialogues* (pp. 99–115). Springer International Publishing.

Penninx, R., Kraal, K., Martiniello, M., & Vertovec, S. (2004). *Citizenship in European cities: Immigrants, local politics and integration*. Ashgate.

Penninx, R., & Martiniello, M. (2004). Integration policies and processes: State of the art and lessons. In R. Penninx, K. Kraal, M. Martiniello, & S. Vertovec (Eds.), *Citizenship in European cities: Immigrants, local politics and integration policies* (pp. 139–163). Ashgate.

Pettrachin, A. (2019). When Asylum policies go local: The case of socially useful works for Asylum-seekers. *Italian Political Science, 14*, 1–20.

Piattoni, S. (2010). *The theory of multi-level governance: Conceptual, empirical, and normative challenges*. Oxford University Press.

Poppelaars, C., & Scholten, P. (2008). Two worlds apart: The divergence of national and local immigrant integration policies in the Netherlands. *Administration & Society, 40*, 335–357. https://doi.org/10.1177/0095399708317172

Ramakrishnan, K., & Wong, T. (2010). Partisanship, not Spanish: Explaining municipal ordinance affecting undocumented immigrants. In M. W. Varsanyi (Ed.), *Taking local control: Immigration policy activism in U.S. Cities and States* (pp. 74–96). Stranford University Press.

Rodriguez, D. X., McDaniel, P. N., & Ahebee, M.-D. (2018). Welcoming America: A case study of municipal immigrant integration, receptivity, and community practice. *Journal of Community Practice, 26*, 348–357. https://doi.org/10.1080/10705422.2018.1477081

Sassen, S. (1991). *The global city. New York, London, Tokio*. Princeton University Press.

Schertzer, R., McDougall, A., & Skogstad, G. (2016). *Collaboration and unilateral action: Recent intergovernmental relations in Canada*. Institute for Research on Public Policy.

Schiller, M. (2016). *European cities, municipal organizations and diversity: The new politics of difference*. Palgrave Macmillan.

Scholten, P. (2020). Mainstreaming versus alienation: Conceptualising the role of complexity in migration and diversity policymaking. *Journal of Ethnic and Migration Studies, 46*, 108–126. https://doi.org/10.1080/1369183X.2019.1625758

Scholten, P., Engbersen, G., van Ostaijen, M., & Snel, E. (2018). Multilevel governance from below: How Dutch cities respond to intra-EU mobility. *Journal of Ethnic and Migration Studies, 44*, 2011–2033. https://doi.org/10.1080/1369183X.2017.1341707

Scholten, P., & Penninx, R. (2016). The Multi-level governance of migration and integration. In B. Garcés-Mascareñas & R. Penninx (Eds.), *Integration processes and policies in Europe: Contexts, levels and actors* (pp. 91–108). Springer International Publishing.

Scholten, P. W. A. (2013). Agenda dynamics and the multi-level governance of intractable policy controversies: The case of migrant integration policies in the Netherlands. *Policy Sciences, 46*, 217–236. https://doi.org/10.1007/s11077-012-9170-x

Seidle, L. F. (2010). *Intergovernmental immigration agreements and public accountability*. Policy Options, retreived at https://policyoptions.irpp.org/wp-content/uploads/sites/2/assets/po/immigration-jobs-and-canadas-future/seidle.pdf

Spencer, S. (2018). Multi-level governance of an intractable policy problem: Migrants with irregular status in Europe. *Journal of Ethnic and Migration Studies, 44*, 2034–2052. https://doi.org/10.1080/1369183X.2017.1341708

Spiro, P. J. (2001). Federalism and immigration: Models and trends. *International Social Science Journal, 53*, 67–73. https://doi.org/10.1111/1468-2451.00294

Steil, J. P., & Vasi, I. B. (2014). The new immigration contestation: Social movements and local immigration policy making in the United States, 2000–2011. *American Journal of Sociology, 119*, 1104–1155. https://doi.org/10.1086/675301

Stoker, G. (2019). Can the governance paradigm survive the rise of populism? *Policy & Politics, 47*, 3–18. https://doi.org/10.1332/030557318X15333033030897

Stürner, J., & Bendel, P. (2019). The two-way 'glocalisation' of human rights or: How cities become international agents in migration governance. *Peace*

Human Rights Governance, 3, 215–240. https://doi.org/10.14658/pupj-phrg-2019-2-3

Thouez, C. (2020). Cities as emergent international actors in the field of migration: Evidence from the lead-up and adoption of the UN global compacts on migration and refugees. *Global Governance: A Review of Multilateralism and International Organizations, 26*, 650–672. https://doi.org/10.1163/19426720-02604007

Varsanyi, M. W. (2008). Rescaling the "Alien", rescaling personhood: Neoliberalism, immigration, and the state. *Annals of the Association of American Geographers, 98*, 877–896. https://doi.org/10.1080/00045600802223341

Varsanyi, M. W. (2010). Immigration policy activism in U.S. States and cities: interdisciplinary perspectives. In *Taking local control: Immigration policy activism in U.S. cities and states* (pp. 1–30). Stranford University Press.

Varsanyi, M. W., Lewis, P. G., Provine, D. M., & Decker, S. (2012). A multi-layered jurisdictional patchwork: Immigration federalism in the United States. *Law & Policy, 34*, 138–158. https://doi.org/10.1111/j.1467-9930.2011.00356.x

Wimmer, A., & Glick-Schiller, N. (2003). Methodological nationalism, the social sciences, and the study of migration: An essay in historical epistemology. *International Migration Review, 37*, 576–610. https://doi.org/10.1111/j.1747-7379.2003.tb00151.x

Zapata-Barrero, R., Caponio, T., & Scholten, P. (2017). Theorizing the 'local turn' in a multi-level governance framework of analysis: A case study in immigrant policies. *International Review of Administrative Sciences, 83*, 241–246. https://doi.org/10.1177/0020852316688426

CHAPTER 4

Migration City Networks in the EU Supranational Polity. Case-Studies

Abstract This chapter presents the research findings on the two Europe-based CNs, i.e. the WGM&I and the ICC Programme, using structured narratives. Following the causal process tracing method, I reconstruct the sequence of events underlying the two CNs' engagement in multilevel policymaking processes on migration and their eventual participation in instances of MLG. The narratives are structured around the key elements of the actor-centred and relational interpretative framework, and more specifically on the demand side (1) CN leaders and processes of internal agenda-setting and (2) the main policy actions, initiatives and modes of policymaking actively promoted by each CN. As for the supply side of migration policymaking, the analysis focuses on interactions and relationships with other key stakeholders and policymakers, and in particular on actors that have a gatekeeping role, i.e. supranational institutions and national government authorities. At the end of the chapter, I provide a cross-case comparative assessment of the CN-MLG nexus in the EU supranational political context.

4.1 Migration City Networks in the EU. An Overview of Institutional Factors and Problem Pressure

Historical studies (Ewen & Hebbert, 2007; Saunier, 2002; Saunier & Ewen, 2008) have looked at Europe as a key hub of the international

T. Caponio, *Making Sense of the Multilevel Governance of Migration*, https://doi.org/10.1007/978-3-030-82551-5_4

municipalist movement that underpinned the emergence of the first transnational city networks in the late nineteenth and early twentieth centuries. In the post-World War II context, European cities became even more entrepreneurial in promoting new networking initiatives (Ewen & Hebbert, 2007, p. 331), as is indicated by the literal explosion of twinning agreements between French and German cities and the foundation in 1951 of the Council of European Municipalities (CEM, then renamed CEMR, Council of European Municipalities and Regions) on the initiative of city councillors in French, West German, Italian and Swiss cities.

Since the mid-1980s, a key role in sustaining the flourishing of CNs started to be played by European supranational institutions. The Council of Europe's Charter of Local Self-Government is a clear case in point. Recognising the mandate of local authorities to regulate and manage their own affairs in the interests of the local population and within the confines of the law, this charter provided a legal framework allowing the strengthening of transnational collaboration (Ewen & Hebbert, 2007, p. 334). At the same time, the European Commission (EC) started to acknowledge the importance of the urban dimension of EU regional and cohesion policies, as is shown by the introduction of Urban Pilot Projects (1989–1993) first, and then of the Urban I Community Initiative (1994–1999) and Urban II (2000–2006). In these same years, other community initiatives were launched to sustain partnerships between territories across borders, like Interreg, sponsoring trans-frontier cooperation, Rechar, addressing coal mining areas, and Retex, for textile areas (Ewen & Hebbert, 2007, p. 336).

Throughout the 1990s, interurban networking was constantly expanding, reflecting the dynamics of local government Europeanisation (e.g. Schultze, 2003; Dossi, 2017; Huggins, 2018a, 2018b; Marshall, 2005) favoured by the specific EU institutional structure. In fact, as Heinelt and Niederhafner (2005, p. 77) note, because of its quite thin bureaucratic apparatus considering the size and importance of its tasks, the European Commission has always relied on cities and their organisations to gather much needed information and expertise on implementation in various policy fields. In 2019 Tortola and Couperos (2020, pp. 6–7) identified 96 networks operating fully or partially in the EU territory, comprising 30 CNs, 30 regional networks and 36 with mixed membership, i.e. including both cities and regions. The great majority of the networks were established in the 1990s and the first decade of the 2000s, i.e. 33 and 32 new networks respectively, confirming the key role played by EU policies in sustaining the expansion of networking initiatives.

Regarding the migration policy field, Penninx (2015, p. 107) notices that the first CN initiatives in the EU began to take hold after 2004 in response to new funding opportunities provided by the EC on the issue of immigrant integration through the Integration of Third Country Nationals (INTI) programme (2004–2006), which had the goal of financing specific local integration measures. Even though this local-based approach was revisited by the following—and financially more substantial—European Integration Fund (2007–2013), which assigned to member states the responsibility for taking into account the perspective of local implementing authorities in the process of drawing up their national integration programmes (see also Caponio & Borkert, 2010, p. 12), the EC continued to directly finance initiatives by local authority networks through a share of the EIF budget (7% of the total) reserved for Community Actions.

Penninx (2015) identifies four main EU-based CNs on immigrant integration issues (pp. 107–110), i.e. Cities for Local Integration Policies, founded in 2006 by the Congress of Local and Regional Authorities of the Council of Europe, the City of Stuttgart and the European Foundation for the Improvement of Living and Working Conditions (Eurofound); Integrating Cities, a project funded by the EIF and carried out by Eurocities, as we will see in more depth below, which started in 2007 and involved the mobilisation of a sub-group of cities within the broader network; Intercultural Cities, which started as a joint action by the Council of Europe and the European Commission in 2008; and the European Coalition Against Racism (ECCAR), which was established in 2004 on the initiative of UNESCO to share experiences and promote learning on local policies to fight racism, discrimination and xenophobia. Although the CLIP network, which included in the partnership a consortium of research institutions and focused on research-policy dialogue, was discontinued in 2011 with the ending of the funding provided by Eurofound,[1] the other networks represent established actors in migration policymaking in the EU (Caponio, 2019; Taran et al., 2016).

[1] The research results of the CLIP project are available at the following website: https://www.eurofound.europa.eu/clip-european-network-of-cities-for-local-integration-policies-for-migrants (last accessed 20th November 2020).

Along with these highly institutionalised migration CNs, in the context of the increasing arrival of asylum seekers and refugees in the last decade, new activist networks have emerged. According to Lacroix (2021), these grassroots initiatives differ in terms of their levels of militancy and anti-state policy stances, yet a common feature is their engagement in producing and disseminating narratives on migration that counter the security-oriented rhetoric commonly underlying national policies (p. 8). These CNs appear particularly prominent in the Mediterranean area, where tensions around the reception of asylum seekers have been particularly heightened, as has been shown by the surge of populist parties and the criminalisation of migrant rescue and support. While these networks are primarily embedded in their national contexts, the analysis of the dynamics of their political mobilisation reveals the key role played by certain mayors and NGOs like Open Arms and Seebrücke in bridging movement organisations and upscaling activism to the cross-Mediterranean level (Lacroix et al., 2020, p. 6).

Thus, not all migration CNs in Europe appear to be linked to the multilevel policymaking dynamics triggered by the EU institutional polity. The sense of pressure created by the asylum and refugee issue in the mid-2010s seems to have heralded a contentious era in the mobilisation of European cities marked by the emergence of new alliances between mayors and social movements. A case in point is the mayor of Barcelona, Ada Colau, whose leadership appears crucial in most of the recent non-institutional militant CN initiatives, like the Ciutat Refugi Plan in Spain (Irgil, 2016) and the international Fearless Cities movement (Russell, 2019; for the link between the two movements, see: Agustín & Jørgensen, 2019).

Against this background, in this chapter I present an in-depth analysis of two highly established initiatives in the European context: the Working Group on Migration and Integration (WGM&I) and the Intercultural City Programme (ICC). As emblematic cases of the first generation of city mobilisation on migration in Europe, as Penninx (2015) suggests, we should expect a high level of engagement in MLG policymaking, therefore enabling observation of the dynamics underpinning the emergence of the migration CN-MLG nexus in Europe. However, these two cases also present a key difference in their modes of mobilisation (see Sect. 3.5). Whereas WGM&I is a case of transnational mobilisation directly promoted by municipalities, ICC in contrast is more of an externally promoted initiative since, as mentioned above, it was set up by the

Council of Europe and with the support of the European Commission. Hence, both have a clear transnational membership yet differ in their modes of creation insofar as the first represents an instance of grassroots mobilisation and the second of a co-opted network (Lacroix, 2021, p. 8).

Below, by using structured narratives I present research evidence collected through empirical in-depth studies carried out on the two CNs. At the end of each account, I present a brief summary of the research findings in terms of: (1) the CN leaders' agendas; (2) modes of policymaking; and 3) interactions with other key stakeholders and policymakers.

4.2 The Eurocities Working Group on Migration and Integration

4.2.1 *An Introduction to Eurocities*

Official documents date the origins of Eurocities back to a conference held in 1986 in Rotterdam on 'The city. The engine behind economic recovery' (Bloomfield, 2011), in which eleven big European cities gathered together to discuss the urban and regional dimension of economic transformation. According to Payre (2010, p. 264), however, a key role in the gradual institutionalisation of the movement was played by the city of Barcelona, which in 1988 launched a second conference on 'The role of cities in the European construction.' This was held in the context of the EU-funded programme Recite, which involved five more 'second' cities, i.e. in the European policy jargon "cities which do not have the status of capitals but are nonetheless keen to have a presence on the international stage by setting themselves apart from the capital city and from the dependent relationship that they may have with it" (Payre, 2010, p. 264). These cities were Birmingham, Frankfurt, Lyon, Milan and Rotterdam.

The early history of Eurocities (see: Ewen & Hebbert, 2007; Payre, 2010; Kübler & Piliutyte, 2007) reflects the 'local turn' in EU policy during the Jacque Delors EC presidency, as was epitomised by the reform of the European Regional Development Fund in 1989. In this context, Eurocities emerged as a transnational lobbying association to represent the interests of cities with populations over 250,000 inhabitants and influencing EU policies on urban matters (Ewen & Hebbert, 2007; Heinelt & Kübler, 2005; Payre, 2010). At the same time, Eurocities benefitted considerably from EU resources for its consolidation. In 1991, the EC co-funded three Eurocities sub-projects involving 21 cities with the European Regional Development Fund. Furthermore, some of these resources contributed to the setting up of the Brussels office and the organisation's secretariat (Bloomfield, 2011, p. 10).

Rapid expansion in the 1990s brought an increasing institutionalisation of the internal structure, also in terms of horizontal city-to-city collaboration. At the annual conference in Birmingham in September 1991, the member cities agreed that the Executive Committee would be composed of the six founding partner cities combined with the chairs of the then six working groups, i.e. culture, economic development, environment, knowledge, mobility and social affairs (Bloomfield, 2011, p. 12). The organisational structure was further developed during the mandate of Eurocities Secretary General Catherine Parmentier (2000–2008), who played a key role in professionalising the network through an enlargement of its staff (30 officers), the involvement of over 130 cities and the setting up of 6 forums and 40 working groups on more specific issues (Bloomfield, 2011, p. 13).

Against this background, my study has focused on the Working Group on Migration and Integration from its genesis up to 2019. In the following, I combine existing research studies on the genesis of the network with fresh data and evidence on the more recent years, i.e. from 2012 onwards (for details of the methods and data sources see Sect. 3.5).

4.2.2 The Genesis of the WGM&I Lobbying as Second-Tier Migration Cities

In 2001 in the turbulent context of 9/11 and debates on 'fortress Europe,' the municipalities of Rotterdam and Barcelona started to mobilise a group of 15 cities to set up a migration observatory and carry out a first mapping of their integration policies (WGM&I_doc1, p. 63; WGM&I_int1). In the early 2000s Eurocities official documents (for an extensive analysis, see: Gebhardt & Güntner, 2021) lamented the neglect of the local dimension in the making of national migration policies and laws and revealed the ambition to have a say in the definition of the 'European Framework on Integration,' which was formally introduced in 2002 in the context of the 1999 Tampere Programme (Carrera, 2008).

> Regarding the policies of national governments we recommend [...] that in the design of policy concerning immigration and asylum, reception and

> integration, national governments take into account the most essential element: the impact of policy at the local level… [p. 6]. Regarding the policies of the European Union […] [w]e advise the Commission to develop a consultation framework with the large cities and their associations in Europe in order to be adequately informed of all the issues concerned and the impact of European policies at the local level. (WGM&I_doc2)

Hence, rather than MLG, the political goal of the cities taking the lead on the migration policy issue was to establish a system of collaborative intergovernmental relations with national and EU institutions. Cities' knowledge of the situation on the ground was presented as a key asset "to adequately respond to the challenges of immigration and integration, to benefit from the important opportunities offered by immigration and to maintain and promote social cohesion" (WGM&I_doc2, p. 6).

In Turku in 2005 the Working Group on Migration and Integration was formally established as one of the Eurocities Forum for Social Affairs working groups by a group of 15 cities including Berlin, Leeds, Malmö, Southampton, Stockholm, Helsinki, Mannheim, Rotterdam, Tampere, Turku, Utrecht and Vienna (Flamant, 2017, p. 90). As Gebhardt and Güntner (2021) report and as was confirmed by my interviewees, the people mobilised in the first period were primarily city officers from 'like-minded cities' that "knew each other well from previous meetings in other contexts such as the Social Affairs Forum, had expertise and experience in EU policy and were active in other networks and European-level bodies. There was a solid working basis between city delegates and the Eurocities policy officers, who produced position papers and other documents in a teamwork spirit" (p. 7).

Among the activities carried out in this early period, Gebhardt and Güntner (2021) mention collaboration with the Migration Policy Group (MPG), a think tank based in Brussels, to contribute examples of good city practices to the first edition of the *Handbook* on *Integration for Policymakers and Practitioners* (Niessen & Schibel, 2004), which was published in 2004, and to the European Website on Integration (WGM&I_web1). Both projects were funded by the Directorate General for Justice, Freedom and Security of the European Commission in the context of the INTI programme. The *Handbook* defined immigrant integration as a 'shared responsibility' and linked policy-effective implementation to MLG policymaking:

> (…) to avoid becoming too removed from programme delivery, ministries in charge should systematically provide the implementing agencies with feedback channels and access to policy design. Local and regional governments, social partners, NGOs and migrants associations are all part of the 'integration nexus' along with the state and the individual migrants it admits. (Niessen & Schibel, 2004, pp. 21–22)

The close relationships among the city officials mobilised in the WGM&I, the MPG and the EC in this period favoured the emergence of an agenda focused on immigrant integration, which was defined as a 'two way process' implying adaptation on the part of both migrants and the receiving societies (Gebhardt & Güntner, 2021). This framing marginalised other possible agendas and interpretations of migration-related challenges for cities, like, for instance, discrimination, racism and urban segregation, which were particularly debated in UK cities, and irregular status, which was highly topical for southern European cities (see, Flamant, 2017, p. 91). According to Gebhardt and Güntner (2021), the WGM&I adopted the integration framing and language "pragmatically and in some instance opportunistically" (p. 10) with the goal of being present in relevant EU forums and consultations.

This strategy turned out to be rewarding for Eurocities in both symbolic and material terms. At the symbolic level, the 'Common Basic Principles for Integration' agreed by the Justice and Home Affairs Council in November 2004 and then the Communication on a Common Agenda for Integration approved by the European Commission in 2005 explicitly acknowledge that "integration takes place at the local level as part of daily life and […] [e]ngaging local communities in working together is thus crucial" (COMM(2005)289 final, p. 3). At the more practical level, in 2006 an institutionalised partnership between Eurocities and the EC was established in Rotterdam: the so-called Integrating Cities process.

4.2.3 *The Integrating Cities Process as a Case of—intergovernmental—EC-City Partnership*

Political leadership also played a key role in this process. By convening the first Integrating Cities conference, the mayor of Rotterdam, Ivo Opstelten, lent political legitimacy to the more technical work carried out within the WGM&I with the aim of establishing local authorities as partners implementing the EC integration strategy. Thus, through intense lobbying activities, the WGM&I succeeded in establishing a mode of policymaking based on cooperative intergovernmental interactions.

The Milan Declaration, which was signed during the second Integrating Cities Conference in 2007, formally confirmed the commitment of the two parties, i.e. local authorities as represented by Eurocities and the EC, to "a constant dialogue and co-operation for the success of immigrant integration, pursuing policies based on the principles of partnership, empowerment and good governance" (WGM&I_doc3, p. 3). It also detailed the instruments of the partnership, i.e. the Integrating Cities conferences and a working programme coordinated by Eurocities consisting of bi-annual projects funded by the EC (WGM&I_web2 and WGM&I_web3).

Looking in more depth at what has been carried out under the umbrella of the Integrating Cities process, a strong emphasis on goals such as policy learning and benchmarking can be found. The Inti-Cities project (2007–2009; see WGM&I_web4), funded by the European Integration Fund, is a case in point.

> Our aim is to provide a platform for municipal integration experts to meet with counterparts in other cities and find inspiration in approaches to local integration policy taken elsewhere. Our ambition was to organise this exchange in an intensive and focused way. To this end, the project chose to implement a peer review process based on a common benchmark and standardised methodology. (WGM&I_doc4, p. 6)

Taking the same approach, the Dive (2008–2010; see WGM&I_web5) project provided the background for the elaboration of the Eurocities Charter on Integrating Cities, which lists the commitments to which cities should subscribe to provide equal opportunities and to promote migrant integration in their roles as 'policy-makers,' 'service providers,' 'employers' and 'buyers of goods and services' (WGM&I_web6). Evaluation Reports were compiled in 2013 and 2015 based on surveys carried out in the signatory cities (22 in 2013 and 30 in 2015). The reports presented the cities' self-assessments and provided examples of good practices, de facto validating cities' different approaches to dealing with the obligations in the Charter. The following Mixities (2010–2012), ImpleMentoring (2012–2014) and Cities Grow (2017–2019) projects centred on policy exchange and mutual learning through a 'city-to-city mentoring' methodology (WGM&I_web7). In concrete terms, cities with experience in the specific issues addressed by each project (e.g. in the case of ImpleMentoring, managing diversity in public administration and service provision, enhancing participation in diverse neighbourhoods and promoting the political participation of migrants through local consultative bodies) assumed the role of 'mentors,' while other cities willing to address a policy gap with respect to the issues were identified as 'implementing' partners.

As is clear, the projects promoted in the context of the Integrating Cities process emphasised the centrality of the multiple responsibilities of local authorities in integration policies, implying an understanding of the horizontal dimension as centred on city-to-city peer learning and policy exchange. In this context, relations with non-public actors like NGOs and stakeholders were essentially conceived as—eventually—linked to municipal integration strategies and policies. However, no specific venues for dialogue between policymakers from local authorities and non-public organisations were organised under the aegis of Integrating Cities.

A key leadership role in the EU-sponsored Integrating Cities process was assumed by public officials from the cities mobilised in the projects and by Eurocities staff officers. According to Gebhardt and Güntner (2021, p. 5), the Integrating Cities partnership "brought staff from the secretariat acting as coordinators to the fore and led to a more managerial culture in the migration work." This was also confirmed by my interviewees: in 2008 Eurocities hired a policy advisor responsible for the area of migration and employment and other project managers were recruited later (WGM&I_int1; WGM&I_int2).

Eurocities Staff Officers also took the lead in the organisation of the Integrating Cities conferences, which had the goal of engaging different categories of policymakers interested in cities' approaches to integration, ranging from international organisations like the International Organisation for Migration and the United Nations High Commissioner for Refugees to national governments, international research institutes and think tanks, NGOs and immigrant rights organisations. However, these conferences were primarily conceived as highly symbolic events and no formal policymaking dialogue followed.

The technical character of the Integrating Cities process might have had the effect of somewhat alienating the political leadership of mayors. In fact, Gebhardt and Güntner (2021) note a disengagement of political leadership in this period and attribute it to a hostile climate regarding migration taking hold in some cities, with Rotterdam in first place. With the closure of the ImpleMentoring project in 2014 and the rapid unfolding of the so-called European refugee crisis, the Integrating Cities process seemed to stall, since no new projects were initiated until 2017.[2]

4.2.4 *Beyond Integration. Political Mobilisation on the Eve of the Refugee Crisis*

Gebhardt and Güntner (2021) consider the crisis a watershed in the development of Eurocities' relations with the European Commission, from the consensus underpinning the partnership to a more political—and seemingly contentious—approach with the Solidarity Cities initiative. However, as a result of my interviews and document analysis, a different interpretation can also be put forward which actually points to the emergence, already at the beginning of the 2010s, of contentious political issues within the CN. Traces of this emerging political agenda can be clearly found in the minutes of the meeting of the WGM&I on 1–2 October 2012 in Brussels (WGM&I_doc5) and in the programme of the fifth Integrating Cities Conference held in Tampere in 2013 (WGM&I_web8).

In fact, in the Brussels meeting the technical aspects of Integrating Cities continued to remain central on the agenda but a more political discussion also started to take place on how the partnership with the EC would be reconfigured following the approval of the new Agenda for the Integration of non-EU Migrants in 2011 (COM(2011)455 Final). Similarly to the first Agenda (European Commission 2005; see above), the new document emphasised the centrality of local action (p. 4). However, a need to improve 'multilevel cooperation' was now also stressed.

> Even if integration measures are mainly for local authorities, close cooperation between the different levels of governance is important to coordinate the provision, financing and evaluation of services. Effective integration can only be realised in partnership between the whole range of stakeholders such as the European institutions, Member States and national, regional and local actors. The EU can provide a framework for monitoring,

[2] See the chart of the Integrating Cities Processes published on the official website (WGM&I_web2).

> benchmarking and for the exchange of good practice among the various governance levels, as well as creating incentives promoting good local and regional models. (COM(2011)455 Final, p. 8)

In compliance with this new multilevel cooperation strategy, the minutes of the Brussels meeting report on a meeting with representatives of DG Home and the Committee of the Regions (CoR) in which the former announced the intention of the EC to formalise a 'strategic partnership' with CoR "to be a bottom-up process and avoid duplication with existing initiatives" (WGM&I_doc5, p. 2). However, it was also stated that "The shape or format of this dialogue is still to be decided." In turn, the CoR representative stressed CoR's political support for the strategic partnership:

> The opinion of the CoR on the new agenda for integration called for cities and regions to come together to discuss the issue [...] Basic preoccupation of the partnership is not to duplicate existing networks but add to what is happening on the ground [...] CoR counts on the cooperation and know-how of EUROCITIES and members to contribute to the partnership as it takes shape. (WGM&I_doc5, p. 2)

The WGM&I members' comments on these updates appear quite critical or at least not particularly enthusiastic. A need for clarification of the added value of the new partnership to the existing structures was stressed. At the same time, the participants in the meeting identified three critical issues on which the new partnership could eventually contribute: (1) bridging the local/national divide; (2) getting the voice of cities and regions heard on particularly sensitive issues like asylum; and (3) exploring the possibility of a more stable partnership with DG Home in order to "ensure more long-term planning outside the project cycle" (WGM&I_doc5, p. 2).

Thus, in discussions on MLG the asylum issue started to be put on the table. In another point on the agenda (WGM&I_doc5, p. 3), cities were invited to take advantage of the opportunities offered by the Share Network on refugee resettlement, a project promoted by the International Catholic Migration Commission and co-funded by the EU with the aim of establishing partnerships for the inclusion of refugees in local communities across Europe.[3]

However, asylum was not the only topic discussed at the Brussels meeting. Two more 'politically delicate' issues were also raised by different coalitions of cities. The first was that of intra-EU mobility and the integration of EU citizens. As reported in the minutes, in September of that year Germany and the Netherlands hosted a conference on the topic organised by the city of Rotterdam (WGM&I_doc5, p. 4). The conference was attended by "representatives from central, regional and local authorities from 21 EU Member States, Norway and Switzerland, the European Commission, the Council of Europe, Eurofound, Eurocities, academics, employers and various civil society organisations and migrant associations" (ibid.). The summary of the conference reported a general agreement on the benefits and potential of freedom of movement, yet also stressed the negative socio-economic impacts at the local level in both receiving and sending countries "such as rupture of families and brain drain and questions with regard to the capacity of local authorities to welcome newcomers and to maintain social cohesion" (ibid.). A second conference on the topic was announced to take place in Austria in 2013 in order to strengthen inter-governmental dialogue on the topic of—economic—participation by 'migrating EU citizens.' The representative of the city of Rotterdam asked for the issue to be regularly put on the agenda of the WGM&I and to take an active role in the organisation of the next conference. The second issue discussed at the Brussels meeting was irregular migration. Two initiatives were announced (WGM&I_doc5, p. 5): the participation by the city of Barcelona as representative of Eurocities in an event organised by PICUM (Platform for International Cooperation on Undocumented Migrants) in Brussels (12 December 2012) on undocumented migrants' access to health care; and a research initiative coordinated by Compass at Oxford University to investigate the motivations of cities to grant basic services.

Hence, discussions in 2012 within the WGM&I confirmed the internal divisions identified by Flamant (2017) with respect to the framing of migration and integration. Whereas continental cities put the issue of local—negative—impacts of intra-EU mobility to the fore (see: Scholten

[3] See: http://www.resettlement.eu/page/welcome-share-network. Last Accessed: 3rd May 2020.

et al., 2018), southern European cities seemed more concerned with irregular migration and the reception of asylum seekers.

The sixth Integrating Cities conference held in Tampere in September 2013 entitled 'European cities shaping the future of integration' reflected these different emerging agendas (see: WGM&I_web8). A workshop on 'Finding the key to multilevel governance' was organised by the CoR and the Hessen Region (Germany) reflecting the EC's intention to somewhat dilute the partnership with Eurocities in a broader multilevel cooperation system. Furthermore, beyond integration, workshops were also organised on the topics of refugee resettlement, intra-EU migration and undocumented migrants.

In the following years, the topics of irregular migration and asylum catalysed more and more attention within the WGM&I, also spurring mobilisation on the part of city political leaders with the unfolding of the refugee crisis. In October 2014 in partnership with Eurocities and with the financial support of the Open Society Initiative for Europe, the city of Barcelona and Compass (University of Oxford) organised a two-day roundtable seminar on 'City responses to irregular migrants' to discuss the challenges European cities faced in responding to the needs of undocumented migrants and share experiences and good practices. Representatives from 11 cities in eight European countries took part in the discussion: Barcelona, Brighton, Brno, Frankfurt, Genoa, Ghent, Helsinki, The London Borough of Islington, Milan, Terrassa and Utrecht. At the end of the meeting, these cities agreed to form a WGM&I sub-group to continue dialogue and exchanges of policy learning and best practices, and work "towards the mainstreaming of irregular migrants within relevant areas of European Union policy and funding" (WGM&I_web9).

If until 2014 the discussion on irregular migration had involved primarily city officials, the heightening of the crisis in 2015 brought political actors to the fore. The continual arrivals of asylum seekers led to increasing pressure on EU cities, spurring activism on the issue within the WGM&I, especially vis-à-vis the incapacity of the member states to manage the situation and come to an agreement on a solidarity plan. On the impulse of cities hardly hit by the crisis like Milan and Athens, together with traditionally active members like Barcelona, Amsterdam, Berlin and Ghent, on 13 May the WGM&I published the Eurocities Statement on Asylum in Cities (WGM&I_doc6). The document had a clear political tone and criticised the EU for not addressing the "whole range of migration and integration issues especially with respect to the issue of asylum," advocated for acknowledgement of the role of cities "as frontline service providers" and called for direct involvement by national and EU institutions in the implementation of a Common European Asylum System (p. 3). Another critical issue stressed in the document was that of funding.

> A better balance of European and national funding is needed between border protection and security and structural support for reception and integration at the local level. This is even more important at a time when many cities have had budgets and resources cut due to austerity policies at the European and national levels. In addition, adequate financial resources need to be available in the long term for structural integration policies and not only for the pilot and mutual learning phase. (WGM&I_doc6, p. 4)

Following this statement, Eurocities multiplied its activities to raise awareness and put pressure on the EU and governments regarding the issue of asylum in cities. However, these initiatives seemed to reveal two different underlying agendas and approaches to the issue. Whereas actions promoted by the WGM&I staff officers and Eurocities officials were framed in typical EU-integration language and in continuity with the 'learning by example' (Gebhardt & Güntner, 2021) agenda promoted by the Integrating Cities process, those launched by mayors and city political representatives took a more confrontational approach, denouncing a 'lack of solidarity' in the EU.

Examples of the first agenda are a series of articles entitled "Cities welcome refugees" published on the Eurocities website (WGM&I_web10) reporting welcoming initiatives by member cities like Vienna, Gdansk and Munich (WGM&I_web11a, b and c). In an article published on the Euractiv website, Eurocities Secretary General Annalisa Boni clearly articulated the integration policy frame (WGM&I_web12).

> But it is not all about the challenges; we must also identify and make the most of the opportunities that migration presents. Giving asylum seekers the right to seek gainful employment and be treated without discrimination, including while their claims are being processed, would help them to integrate better into society. Ensuring that their qualifications are properly recognised and making the most of their entrepreneurial potential would allow them to make a lasting contribution to our societies and the local economies, as well as relieving some of the burden on the authorities. A

failure to properly integrate refugees, migrants and asylum seekers into our societies is not only a failure to respect their fundamental human rights, but a missed opportunity to realise the full benefits of immigration. Member states need to work with cities to ensure that effective and long-term solutions can be developed that ensure the long-term integration of asylum seekers and recognised refugees.

This approach underlay the Cities Grow project, again funded by the EC under the Integrating Cities process aegis in 2017 with the goal of "enhancing mutual learning between cities and improving the implementation of migration policies through concrete actions to facilitate the integration of migrants and refugees" (WGM&I_web13).

As for the second agenda, it was articulated through various political initiatives aimed at claiming a seat for cities in the discussions surrounding EU migration policy and specific financial resources to face the situation. Cases in point are represented by speeches by the vice-mayor on social cohesion of the city of Milan, Marco Granelli, to the LIBE (Civil Liberties, Justice and Home Affairs) Committee of the European Parliament in June 2015 (WGM&I_web14) and by the deputy mayor of Helsinki, Ritva Viljanen, at the "Investing in an open and secure Europe" conference organised by DG Home on 29 September 2015 (WGM&I_web15). In both cases, the political leaders advocated for direct access by cities to the EU Asylum, Migration and Integration Fund (AMIF) and in particular to emergency funding reserved in AMIF regulations for member states, international organisations and NGOs.

Building on these footsteps, in April 2016 the then Mayor of Athens George Kaminis launched a new initiative, Solidarity Cities, which my interview partners described as a 'plea' or 'call for action' to provocatively advocate for a bottom-up asylum-seeker redistribution mechanism managed by cities (WGM&I_int1; WGM&I_int2; WGM&I_int6; WGM&I_int7).

At the beginning, Solidarity Cities was an initiative that aimed to convey a strong message: the capital cities of the EU were getting together to put pressure on member states and the EU to take up their responsibility on asylum. Solidarity was the key message, solidarity not only between cities but also member states, and between member states, cities and the EU. Furthermore, we wanted to put the issue of asylum on the fore. When you work with the Commission, the Commission gives the tone, and all the attention was on working with cities on immigrant integration [...] We

> had this strong message for capital cities in the first place, but then a lot of cities responded and not only capitals... and so also Eurocities stepped in and took it from there. (WGM&I_int7)[4]

Thus, in 2016, along with the resumption of intergovernmental cooperation with the EC as shown by the approval of the Cities Grow project, political representatives of the WGM&I member cities were engaged in lobbying the EC and national governments to fully acknowledge the role of cities vis-à-vis contentious asylum issues. The potential contradictions of this agenda with Eurocities' long-standing collaboration with the EC on integration were managed by the CN staff officers through a strategy of 'internalisation' of Solidarity Cities. The new initiative was officially presented during the Eurocities Social Affairs Forum held in Athens in October 2016 and a programme of activities centred on knowledge exchange, capacity building and advocacy was started.

> The Mayor of Athens shed light on the work of cities in the midst of the emergency ... yet from the beginning there was a need to go beyond mere criticism of national non-policies. Eurocities was able to shape a programme of actions attracting the attention not only of mayors but also of policymakers at different levels of government. (WGM&I_int2)

More specifically, for knowledge exchange the WGM&I launched two surveys among its members to collect information and data on the education of newly arrived refugees and asylum seekers and on labour market inclusion. As regards capacity building, thanks to a grant from the Open Society Foundation, in 2017 the WGM&I organised mentoring visits on education for refugee children in cities. As for advocacy, an information campaign was launched together with The Guardian to showcase 'Refuge Cities' (see: WGM&I_web16).

4.2.5 *Engagement in MLG. The Urban Agenda for the EU*

At the beginning of 2016, engagement in MLG policymaking was not an obvious development for the WGM&I. On the vertical dimension, the partnership with the EU had come to a halt in 2014 and was about to

[4] See also the interview with Mayor Georgios Kaminis published on World Mayor: http://www.worldmayor.com/contest_2016/interview-athens-mayor.html.

be resumed with a new project focusing on asylum in 2017. At the same time, mayors seemed more interested in lobbying for acknowledgement of the central role of cities in policymaking processes than in collaborating on specific projects. On the horizontal dimension, dialogue and cooperation with NGOs and civil society appeared almost absent on the topic of integration, since these types of interactions were left to the initiative of municipalities in the context of the local implementation of EU-funded projects. As for asylum, Eurocities started a partnership with ICMC and other NGOs in the Share project (2012–2016, see above). However, from the documents I have analysed and my interviews this never emerged as a particularly strategic line of action but rather as "an opportunity for our members to benefit from the experience of other cities and NGOs to improve their resettlement practices or find out how to become a resettlement city" (WGM&I_web17).

On the other hand, the plan pursued by the Barroso II EC and DG Home Commissioner Malmström (2010–2014) to establish a strategic partnership on integration with a coordinating role of CoR not only did not consider asylum but remained vague with respect to modes of coordination with cities and NGOs. Regarding the latter, since 2009 the European Integration Forum, re-named European Migration Forum in 2015, had provided a platform for NGOs "to express their views on migrant integration issues and to discuss with the European institutions challenges and priorities" (WGM&I_web18). How to integrate EMF in the broader partnership was, however, unclear.

Thus, overall in the mid-2010s the context did not seem very favourable for the emergence of MLG policymaking.

> Commissioner Frattini [DG Home, Barroso I EC] was very open towards cities and relations with Eurocities were positive … Then things became more difficult, and you can see that from the participants in the Integrating Cities Conferences. They [DG Home] always sent the Head of Unit, to have the Commissioner was impossible. The European Commission chaired by Junker kept this way of doing things, matters of migration were dealt with by national governments only … In the midst of the crisis, though, we saw a change of attitude. States were not collaborating at all and the European Commission risked remaining isolated … Cities started to be regarded again by the DG Home as allies, like with Commissioner Frattini when the Integrating Cities project was launched. (WGM&I_int1)

In fact, according to other interviewees (WGM&I_int4 and WGM&I_int5; see also Gebhardt & Güntner, 2021), in spring 2016 the mayor of Amsterdam together with the mayors of other cities mobilised in the Solidarity Cities initiative, like Barcelona, Athens, Ghent, Helsinki, Berlin, Leipzig, Malmö, Paris and Rome, met Dimitris Avramopoulos, then Commissioner for Migration, Home Affairs and Citizenship, to denounce the failure of EU refugee redistribution and ask for direct support for cities.

It was exactly in this complicated context that the Dutch presidency of the EU Council launched the Urban Agenda for the EU as a bi-annual programme to achieve 'better regulation, better funding and better knowledge' on urban matters (WGM&I_web19). The so-called Pact of Amsterdam was signed in May 2016 by all the ministers responsible for urban matters in the 27 EU member countries.

> The so-called Pact of Amsterdam, other than the name might suggest, had very few relations with the city ... The preparation meetings took place in Amsterdam, but the whole process was steered by our colleagues of the Ministry of the Interior, who have responsibility over urban planning-related issues [...] There were already the groups on housing, air quality and poverty working as pilot, and there was a fourth theme they [people in the Ministry] were looking at, migration and inclusion... The then mayor, Eberhard van der Laan, had this idea that Amsterdam should be a responsible capital city, and take on responsibility on international issues... and so we, as the city of Amsterdam, we stepped in and offered to chair the Partnership.... Parallel to the mayor's political contacts, we approached DG Home officers and proposed them to co-chair the Partnership with us. (WGM&I_int8)

Thus, the Urban Agenda for the EU provided a window of opportunity to set up a Partnership for the Integration of Immigrants and Refugees, which for the first time was characterised as a proper instance of MLG. Bottom-up pressure from Solidarity Cities mayors—more than from the WGM&I as such—indeed contributed to this result.

More specifically, besides the city of Amsterdam and DG Home as coordinators, the Partnership included representatives of such different actors as local authorities, i.e. Eurocities, the mayors of Athens, Barcelona, Berlin and Helsinki, the Council of European Municipalities and Regions (CEMR), CoR and the Urbact Programme; EU Member States, i.e. Denmark, Greece, Italy and Portugal; other EC DGs like DG Regio and

Employment and Social Affairs, the Joint Research Centre, other European institutions like the Council of Europe Development Bank (CEB) and the European Investment Bank (EIB) and think tanks like the European Council for Refugees and Exiles (ECRE) and the Migration Policy Group (MPG). The Partnership's action plan, the result of a year-long decision-making process, also engaged NGOs and migrant associations through specific work conferences (WGM&I_web19).

Eurocities took responsibility for the implementation of Action 4, 'Improving access for cities to EU integration funding' (WGM&I_doc9, p. 14 and pp. 22–24). According to interviews and informal conversations, together with CEMR and DG Home staff officers, representatives of the WGM&I engaged in the drafting of "Recommendations for improving cities' use of and access to EU funds for the integration of migrants and refugees in the new programming period" (WGM&I_doc10). These recommendations advanced two main requests: an increase in EU funding for local integration policies; and the establishment of a 'structured multi-level governance framework' based on the 'principle of conditionality,' whereby in order to have access to funding national governments first had to establish partnership agreements with local authorities on implementation.

The recommendations of the Partnership were officially presented by the then mayor of Amsterdam to several European Commissioners and agreed on by the Civil Liberties, Justice and Home Affairs Committee of the European Parliament in its proposal for the reform of the Asylum and Migrant Integration Fund regulations (WGM&I_doc13). However, my interviewees reported a much less supportive stance on the part of the European Council of Home Affairs Ministers, especially regarding the principle of conditionality, and only mild engagement by the EC in supporting the reform of EU funding in this direction. As I observed during the final conference of the Cities Grow project (Milan, 7–8 November 2018), some members of Solidarity Cities were clearly putting pressure on the DG Home to support the introduction of the conditionality principle in EU funding, somewhat challenging the more accommodative stance prevailing among Eurocities executive directors and staff officers.

4.2.6 Policy Agendas, Modes of Policymaking and Relations

A process-tracing analysis of the WGM&I's engagement in policymaking processes from its founding in 2004 until 2019 enables identification of four main periods characterised by different modes of mobilisation in policymaking: (1) lobbying and political advocacy (2004–2007); (2) intergovernmental partnership with the EC (2007–2014); (3) lobbying and political advocacy again (2012–2016); and 4) renewed intergovernmental partnership (2016–2019). Table 4.1 presents this sequence of events as a process of mobilisation on the demand and supply sides of migration policymaking along the lines of the actor-centred interpretative framework presented in Chapter 3.

The first period coincides with the genesis of the WGM&I and was dominated by the Eurocities agenda to claim a seat at 'high level' migration policymaking tables in order to establish collaborative intergovernmental relations with national and EU institutions. This move upwards was rewarding at least with respect to the EU: the Integrating Cities process, which started in 2007, opened the second period, that of intergovernmental partnership with the EC. This period was marked by close collaboration between DG Home and city officials and the shaping of a coordinated agenda on immigrant integration. This collaborative turn also led to an increasing professionalisation of the WGM&I with the consolidation of an internal staff of project managers supporting the working group in the implementation of EU projects. These projects often required collaboration at the local level with NGOs, which started to be somewhat indirectly involved in WGM&I initiatives.

However, around 2012, in parallel with the consolidation of intergovernmental partnership on the Integrating Cities process, especially on the initiative and with the support of the WGM&I staff officers, at a political level the EC promoted a redefinition of immigrant integration policymaking around a multilevel 'strategic partnership' coordinated by the Committee of the Regions. In this context, cities, and more specifically civil servants and political leaders, started to take a critical stance towards the EC and mobilise a more politically contentious agenda around 'delicate' issues such as intra-EU mobility, undocumented migration and asylum. These topics were closely intertwined for some cities like Milan, which as early as 2013 had started to receive increasing numbers of asylum seekers from the south of Italy (see the above-mentioned speech by Marco Granelli, Deputy Mayor on Social Cohesion, to the LIBE Committee

Table 4.1 WGM&I: Causal process observations and modes of policymaking

	Causal process observations	*Modes of policymaking*
1. 2004–2007	**Demand side** Advocacy agenda and city leadership • 2004 policy statement **Supply side** EC acknowledges cities' role in the CBP (2004); engagement in collaborative projects funded by the INTI programme • Integrating Cities Process	Lobbying and political advocacy Intergovernmental partnership
2. 2007–2014	**Demand side** Internal professionalisation to manage EU projects **Supply side** Projects funded in the context of the Integrating Cities project	Intergovernmental partnership
3. 2013–2016	**Supply** *Barroso II Commission calls for improved cooperative multilevel policymaking and engagement of the Committee of the Regions* **Demand** Mobilisation on particularly contentious issues (asylum, undocumented migrants, internal EU mobility), with the issue of asylum seeker reception becoming more and more topical on the eve of the **2015 refugee crisis** **Supply side** *No access to policymaking. Junker Commissionprivileging relations with member states* **Demand side** Eurocities Statement on Asylum in Cities and Solidarity Cities	Political advocacy and Lobbying

(continued)

in June 2015). The spectacular numbers of arrivals through the Eastern European route in 2015 finally brought the issue to the top of the agenda, also leading to the mobilisation of mayors of cities that had previously been almost absent from the WGM&I like Athens.

Table 4.1 (continued)

	Causal process observations	*Modes of policymaking*
4. 2016–2019	**Supply side** Dutch government initiative to set up an Urban Agenda for the EU City of Amsterdam and the EC collaborate to establish the Partnership for the Inclusion of Migrants and Refugees as an **MLG-like instance of policymaking** **Demand side** WGM&I lobbying, together with other organisations representing local authorities, mayors and DG Home officials, on access to EU resources **Supply side** Increased collaboration in venues also open to non-profit organisations	Renewed intergovernmental partnership with the DG Home

Thus, starting in 2013, a new phase of political mobilisation in the WGM&I seemed to unfold, at times also with a contentious tone, as indicated by the Eurocities Statement on Asylum in Cities and the Solidarity Cities initiative. As in the early 2000s, the aim was to again advocate for a seat at high-level policymaking tables, considering also that the Junker Commission, which entered into office in November 2014, did not show any interest in engaging cities in decision-making processes on migration. In this context, city representatives became particularly vocal in lobbying for direct access to EU funding, which existing EIF regulations before and AMIF (2014–2020) afterwards assigned to national governments. In principle, these governments should have engaged all 'relevant stakeholders,' local authorities included, in the definition of national implementation programmes. However, city representatives lamented that this did not take place in many countries. The conditionality principle aimed precisely to make consultation unavoidable, since access to funding was made conditional on city participation in national decision-making. Eurocities' engagement in the Partnership on the Inclusion of Migrants and Refugees of the Urban Agenda for the EU took place against this increasingly politicised background. Whereas on paper the Partnership was characterised as a quintessential MLG process, in practice for the WGM&I it represented another venue to advance mayors' political agendas.

However, in the context of setting up the Partnership and then its concrete working, a new phase of collaboration between the WGM&I, and more specifically staff officers and city officials, and DG Home officials started again. On the one hand, DG Home officials actively collaborated in drafting the new regulation for the post-2020 Asylum and Migration Fund, which was approved by the EC in 2018 (COM(2018) 471 final).[5] This proposal incorporated a recommendation advanced by the Partnership to reduce the share of funding administered by member states from 88 to 60%, thus reserving 40% of the financial resources for Community Actions, in which cities traditionally represent a key group. On the other hand, the WGM&I actively collaborated in the implementation of the Urban Academy on Integration, a policy action coordinated by DG Home in the context of the Partnership with the goal of creating a "strategic learning environment [for] practitioners and policy-makers working on integration at the local, regional and national levels, with a focus on cities" (WGM&I_web20 and WGM&I_doc9). Overall, this action appears to be very close to the expertise matured by the working group through the Integrating Cities projects in supporting processes of policy learning and exchange of good practices.

Thus, despite the tensions created in the midst of the asylum and refugee crisis by Solidarity Cities' contentious political agenda, through participation in the Partnership the WGM&I project officers and city officials were able to strengthen relations with the EC, and more specifically with DG Home, by uploading the WGM&I political agenda on direct city access to funding. In its turn, through its renewed bilateral partnership with WGM&I staff officers, DG Home engaged in downloading to local authorities an agenda aimed at strengthening cooperation with NGOs and civil society organisations in the implementation of AMIF projects. In fact, WGM&I staff officers together with DG Home officials actively contributed to the organisation of the 5th European Migration Forum (EMF, 3–4 April 2019) by coordinating the workshop

[5] Available at: https://ec.europa.eu/commission/sites/beta-political/files/budget-may2018-asylum-migration-fund-regulation_en.pdf.

'From global to local governance of migration: the role of local authorities in managing migration' (WGM&I_web21 and WGM&I_doc14). Furthermore, during the Forum, Eurocities was elected for a term of two years to represent 'EU-level organisations' in the Forum Bureau (WGM&I_doc14, p. 4). Last but not least, the need for a stronger link between local governments and non-public actors was at the centre of the VALUES project (Volunteering Activities to Leverage Urban and European Social integration of migrants, 2019–2021), which was funded by AMIF in the context of the Integrating Cities Process (WGM&I_web22).

It has to be underlined, however, that the mobilisation of the WGM&I mayors and political leaders in the mid-2010s not only targeted the EC but also had the aim of exerting pressure for a profound redefinition of relations with national governments. In this respect, as mentioned above, the results appear far less satisfactory. Not only did national governments oppose the conditionality principle but also the EC was judged by my interviewees to be 'mild' on this issue. Hence, overall intergovernmental collaboration appears to have been limited to the partnership with the EC.

4.3 The Council of Europe Intercultural Cities Programme

4.3.1 An Introduction to the Council of Europe's Engagement with Subnational Governments

The ICC Programme can be characterised as an initiative started by an international organisation, i.e. the Council of Europe (CoE), with the goal of supporting engagement by subnational governments and transnational networking on the specific topic of interculturalism. It reflects a long-standing tradition of CoE engagement with local authorities in Europe (see: Ewen and Hebbert, 2007; Tavares, 2016). In fact, as early as 1952, four years after its foundation, the CoE Parliamentary Assembly decided to set up a Special Committee on Municipal and Regional Affairs. In 1955 the Special Committee proposed convening an annual 'European Conference of Local Authorities' to the Parliamentary Assembly. This then took place in Strasbourg on 12 January 1957. On a decision by the Committee of Ministers, in 1961 the Conference became biannual and in 1975 it was opened to participation by regional authorities.

In 1985 on the occasion of the 20th European Conference of Local and Regional Authorities, the European Charter of Local Self-Government was opened for signature by the member states. As mentioned above, the Charter recognised local authorities' mandate to regulate and manage their own affairs in the interests of the local population and within the confines of the law. Furthermore, it affirmed the entitlement of local authorities to adhere to "an association for the protection and promotion of their common interests and to belong to an international association of local authorities" (Art. 10.2). According to Ewen and Hebbert (2007), the Charter represented a key reference for the international mobilisation of municipalities. Applied in combination with the Outline Convention on Transfrontier Cooperation between Territorial Communities or Authorities, which was introduced in 1980, again by the CoE, it favoured the flourishing of over 100 inter-municipal networks "forming a continuous tissue across the boundary lines of member states, a unique phenomenon in international law" (Ewen & Hebbert, 2007, p. 334).

Thus, as is clear, the engagement of CoE with subnational authorities was crucial in the development of transnational CNs in Europe (Tavares, 2016, p. 109). In this context, the ICC Programme stands at the crossroads of the activities of three different Directorates General: the Democracy DG, where the Congress of Local and Regional Authorities is located and which has developed various programmes on cultural diversity and democratic citizenship; the Human Rights DG, which has competence over migrant protection and minority rights issues; and the Rule of Law DG, which oversees freedom of expression and pluralism in the media.

4.3.2 *The Genesis of ICC. Building a Learning Community*

The ICC Programme was officially launched in 2008 as a joint initiative by the CoE and the EC for the European Year of Intercultural Dialogue (ICC_doc1). The foundations of the programme can be found in three sources of inspiration (ICC_doc2, p. 18): work on conflict prevention and reconciliation carried out by the CoE since 1957, which culminated in the White Paper on Intercultural Dialogue, adopted by the foreign ministers of the 47 member states in 2008; the preparatory documents for the European Year of Intercultural Dialogue; and research work carried out by the British think tank Comedia on the management of diversity in urban contexts (Bloomfield & Bianchini, 2004; Wood & Landry, 2008). More specifically, with respect to the CoE, the ICC Programme was initially developed by the Diversity and Intercultural Dialogue Policy Division. A dedicated staff or Secretariat was established, which was initially formed of three CoE officials, which over the course of time became four, one of whom with supervision tasks.

Together with the EC, a call for proposals was launched for the selection of cities to participate in a two-year (2008–2010; see ICC_doc1, p. 45) pilot programme with the goal of reviewing their governance, policies, discourse and practices from an intercultural perspective. More specifically, the programme had three main objectives:

- To stimulate an inclusive debate, review and policy reformulation in pilot cites on the basis of an intercultural approach to migration, integration and social cohesion;
- To encourage pilot cities to develop comprehensive intercultural strategies for the management of urban diversity;
- To elaborate model intercultural strategies and strategy development and evaluation methods as an example and inspiration for other cities in Europe (ICC_doc2, p. 18).

To this end, ICC was conceived as an action research and policy development programme (ICC_doc2, p. 18) in which a group of international and national experts were engaged in working with the eleven selected cities[6] (ICC_doc1). A key role in the research group was played by Phil Wood, senior researcher at Comedia, which in 2004 had led 'The Intercultural City: Making the Most of Diversity' research programme funded by the Joseph Rowntree Foundation, and was engaged as principal advisor to the CoE/EU Intercultural Cities programme (ICC_web1).

Thus, in this first phase the main instruments used by the ICC Secretariat to guide cities in the process of understanding and engaging with the concept of interculturalism were essentially drawn from previous work by Comedia on the intercultural city model, which was defined by Wood in the following terms:

[6] Berlin Neukölln (Germany), Izhevsk (Russian Federation), Lublin (Poland), Lyon (France), Melitopol (Ukraine), Neuchâtel (Switzerland), Oslo (Norway), Patras (Greece), Reggio Emilia (Italy), Subotica (Serbia) and Tilburg (The Netherlands).

> Most citizens regard diversity as a resource, not as a problem, and accept that all cultures change as they encounter each other in the public space. The city officials publicly advocate respect for diversity and a pluralistic city identity. The city actively combats prejudice and discrimination and ensures equal opportunities for all by adapting its governance structures, institutions and services to the needs of a diverse population, without compromising the principles of human rights, democracy and the rule of law. In partnership with businesses, civil society and public service professionals, the intercultural city develops a range of policies and actions to encourage greater mixing and interaction between diverse groups. The high level of trust and social cohesion helps to prevent conflicts and violence, increase policy effectiveness and make the city attractive for people and investors alike. (ICC_doc2, p. 17)

A policy assessment grid was developed along these lines, leading to the compilation of narrative reports and city profiles (ICC_doc2). However, in the course of the first pilot project, a need for a more systematic methodological approach emerged, leading to the elaboration of the so-called Intercultural Cities Index (ICC_web2; see also ICC_doc3 and ICC_doc4). As was explained in the document *The Intercultural City Step-by-step* (ICC_doc4), which was published in 2013 to provide an overview of the ICC philosophy, policy model and key achievements, the Index had primarily a practical goal:

> The INDEX is not intended to be a scientific tool. It would be impossible to reduce the essence of interculturality to a few measurements, or to establish clear-cut relationships of cause and effect between policies and actions and outcomes in something so subjective. The intercultural city approach is not a science but a general set of principles and a way of thinking. Thus, the Intercultural City INDEX aims to highlight a few common facts and phenomena – or what we might describe as crucial "acupuncture" points–which give an indication of the level of interculturality of a city, and which enable the beginning of a discussion whereby one city can be compared with another. However, it is not the intention of the project to use the INDEX for the simple "ranking" of cities. Rather, it should be used to encourage greater self-reflection, learning and improvement. (ICC_doc4, p. 109)

To monitor policies and prepare a viable intercultural city strategy, this same document provides a list of the relevant local actors that should be involved. Along with the Mayor, City Councillors with competence on diversity-related issues and city officials in relevant departments for the implementation of the strategy, other civil society actors are mentioned, like representatives of cultural communities and/or minority groups, of local media organisations, educational and cultural operators, of religious communities and organisations of non-believers, of businesses, trade unions, housing associations and any other relevant partners, of organisations carrying out integration/intercultural projects on the ground, of research and statistical institutes, individual artists and entrepreneurs (ICC_doc4, p. 113).

In 2011, nine more cities joined the initial group[7] "to benefit from peer and expert support for their intercultural policy-making" (ICC_doc4, p. 23). Furthermore, national networks of intercultural cities started to be established, like the Italian network 'Cities of Dialogue' (*Città del dialogo*, ICC_web3) and the Norwegian 'City Network on Diversity and Equality Policies' (ICC_web4) in 2010, the Spanish *Reci—Ciudades Interculturales* in 2011 (ICC_web5), the Portuguese Network of Intercultural Cities (RPCI) in 2012 (ICC_web6) and the Ukrainian Intercultural Cities Network in 2015 (ICC_web7). The constant increase in the number of member cities led to greater structuring of the network, which, as is explained on the website (ICC_web8), has three tiers of membership:

> Cities can be full members of the network with privileged access to all international activities and dedicated expert support. Alternatively, they can focus on exchanges within a national Intercultural cities network, where such a network exists, or opt only for diagnostic of their policies through the Intercultural cities index. (ICC_web8)

This flexible networking organisation, which allows cities to choose their level of engagement 'à la carte,' appears to be consistent with the more general purpose of the ICC Programme to build 'a learning community' by helping cities to re-design their policies and to re-shape their governance structures in order "to manage diversity positively and realise the diversity advantage" (ICC_web9; see also ICC_doc4).

[7] Botkyrka (Sweden), Copenhagen (Denmark), Geneva (Switzerland), Dublin (Ireland), Lisbon (Portugal), Limassol (Cyprus), London Lewisham (UK), Pécs (Hungary) and San Sebastian (Spain).

Thus, the network's general goals and early history reveal the centrality of the vertical dimension in the ICC Programme, seemingly taking a top-down direction from the CoE Secretariat and, during the pilot phase, the EC, where the programme was conceived and managed, downward to the cities engaged in implementing the intercultural strategy. In more concrete terms, the ICC Programme assumed the form of a partnership between supranational institutions and local authorities. As noted above, stakeholders, and more specifically businesses and civil society organisations, were considered important partners in order to develop policies and actions aimed at encouraging mixing and interaction between diverse groups, "increase policy effectiveness and make the city attractive for people and investors alike" (ICC_doc4, p. 26). However, cities, understood as local authorities, have always represented the main targets and key partners of the actions promoted by the CoE through the ICC Programme. With respect to the Index, for instance, the *The Intercultural City Step-by-step* clearly describes the key role of cities in the review process.

> Following the accession process, member cities set up an intercultural support group and start the process of reviewing different urban policies from an intercultural perspective, re-shaping them and integrating them into a comprehensive policy strategy… The cities are encouraged to involve citizens broadly in the strategy development process, identifying indicators for success, monitoring progress and implementation. A methodological guide for this work is available […] the Council of Europe can provide experts and facilitators for the policy discussions within the city. (ICC_doc4, p. 9)

The involvement of stakeholders and citizens is therefore encouraged during the review process, yet city leadership is the key pre-condition. More generally, the engagement of non-public actors takes place at the local level through the specific projects put in place by member cities, as is shown by the initiatives presented under the heading 'Thematic Initiatives' on the ICC Programme website. The Deli Project (Diversity in Economy and Local Integration) funded by the European Integration Fund and implemented in 2014–2015 with the support of the Migration Policy Group, for instance, was based on a partnership network of ten pilot cities that worked towards 'systemic change' in economic integration by "fostering more efficient local policies in support of migrant-owned SMEs and migrant entrepreneurship" (ICC_web10). Another action started in 2014 again with the support of EU funding is the Cities for Integration project (C4i), which engaged eleven ICC member cities in developing an anti-rumour strategy, building on innovative social communication practices already developed by the city of Barcelona in partnership with civil society organisations (ICC_web11; ICC_doc6). However, municipal leadership was regarded as crucial:

> While not all anti-rumour strategies are led by local governments, we would argue that an anti-rumour strategy must at least secure real political commitment, support and even leadership. Moreover, the decision to promote an anti-rumour strategy must be consistent with existing diversity policies and cannot run counter to the discourses and policies being implemented by the municipality (ICC_doc6, p. 15)

4.3.3 *Going Global. The 2014 Montréal Forum*

In building a transnational 'learning community' of cities, the CoE Secretariat has always sought to go beyond the European Union, consistently with the broader membership of the CoE as an institution which counts 47 signatory states. In the early group of member cities, Melitopol in Ukraine and Izhevsk in Russia figure prominently. Furthermore, Mexico City started to be affiliated with ICC in 2010 and took its first full diagnostic study in 2014 (ICC_doc5), while the city of Montreal participated in the 2012 ICC meeting in Barcelona and the 2013 meeting in Dublin and in May 2014 organised the 'Montreal Forum on Intercultural Cities' (White, 2018, p. 4). As is stressed in the edited book resulting from this experience,

> The Intercultural Cities Programme (ICC) of the Council of Europe has played a central role in bringing together not only officials from different parts of the globe but also various types of actors involved in the field of intercultural research (policymakers, planners, policy analysts, researchers, practitioners, elected officials, community organizers). [...] the Forum in Montreal is part of the story of how ICC – whose primary mission was limited to the member states of the European Union – became involved in intercultural policy on a global scale. (White, 2018, p. 4)

In this same book, Irena Guidikova, head of division at the Directorate of Democratic Governance and in charge of overseeing the ICC Programme, reflected on the shift from intercultural dialogue to interculturalism. The latter was defined as an 'urban policy paradigm' pursuing power symmetry and the creation of a "'we culture' complementing the culture of human rights and antidiscrimination to build a pluralistic, dynamic, constantly renegotiated collective identity which helps remove mental barriers and prejudice and foster trust and cohesion" (Guidikova, 2018, p. 57). For Guidikova, the transatlantic perspective of the Forum encouraged "out-of-the-box thinking and the acquisition of new perspectives, which is difficult when actors remain within overly familiar conceptual spaces (either European or North American)" (Guidikova, 2018, p. 60).

These quotations are indicative of the ambition of the ICC Programme to build a global dialogue on the intercultural paradigm. In this process, a key role was played by experts and more specifically by the group mobilised around the Laboratory for Research on Intercultural Relations (Labbri) of the University of Montreal. Bob White, director of Labbri, is included in the list of experts supporting the activities of the ICC Programme, together with 12 other experts including academics and independent researchers like Phil Wood of Comedia, who—as seen above—contributed to the specification of the intercultural city model and to the first initiatives promoted by the network (ICC_web12).

> Experts have always been vital for the development of the ICC programme as well as for the national networks. My role was not so much to facilitate processes of mutual learning, this is also part of the programme, but more is involved... Experts are engaged in contributing to the realisation of a quite abstract model in real cities facing different situations. Knowledge from policy practice is as important as more abstract competence on interculturalism. At the same time, experts have also contributed to make dialogue between cities in different continents not only possible, but lively and constructive. The Montreal Forum is a case a point. (ICC_int1)

The expansion of the ICC Programme beyond Europe continued in the following years, as is shown by the Annual Reports of Activities regularly published on the website since 2016.[8] In 2016, under the South Programme II, a joint action by the CoE and the EU, a national ICC network was set up in Morocco and based in Tangier (ICC_doc10, p. 5),

[8] The annual reports are available in the section 'Documents' of the ICC website: https://www.coe.int/en/web/interculturalcities/documents. Last accessed on 3 December 2020.

Table 4.2 ICC member cities (2016–2019)

	Total no. of m. cities	*New m. cities*	*New members from outside Europe*
2016	104	16	Bursa-Osmangazi (Turkey), Haifa (Israel), Amman (Jordan)
2017	120	16	Ballarat (Australia), Klaksvik (Faroe Islands), Hamamatsu (Japan), Agadir, Meknes, Rabat, Marrakech, Chefchaouen, Tetouan, Kenitra, Martil, Larache and Tanger (Morocco)
2018	134	14	Melton and Maribyrnong (Australia), Rochester Minnesota (United States), Kepez (Turkey)
2019	136	2	Kobe (Japan) and Ansan (South Korea) expressed interest

Sources ICC_doc10; ICC_doc12; ICC_doc22; ICC_doc27

followed in 2019 by the Australiasian network of ICC Cities, including cities in Australia, South Korean, Japan and New Zealand (ICC_web13). Table 4.2 reports data on the number of member cities in the last four years, showing a constant increase in membership from Europe, understood in the enlarged sense mentioned above which includes Russia and all the Balkan and Caucasian area.

The expansion of ICC seems to have come to an end in 2019, when only two new members joined the network, even though more cities outside Europe expressed their interest in the programme as is shown in the table. This slow-down appears consistent with the goals set by the document *Intercultural Cities Programme—Medium-term strategy 2016–2019* (ICC_doc8), which suggested a need for a 'controlled expansion' of the network's membership in order to maintain the level and quality of support provided to cities and ensure participation opportunities for all the member cities (p. 3). To this end, the document proposed a more proactive strategy aimed at encouraging membership in still under-represented countries and more specifically old European immigration countries, like Germany, Austria, Belgium, France and the UK, and Eastern European ones, like Hungary, the Czech Republic and

Turkey. At the same time, expansion in the southern European neighbourhood and in other regions/continents was also to be continued, even though Europe remained 'a priority' (ICC_doc8, p. 3).

4.3.4 *And Back to Europe Again. Building Instances of Multilevel Governance Policymaking*

The expansion of the ICC network was marked by two main developments: increasing political recognition by the CoE's political organs of the value of interculturalism as a more general model of immigrant integration in Europe; and growing internal structuring of the network organisation and modus operandi.

With respect to the first development, in the context of the unfolding European refugee crisis, in January 2015 the Committee of Ministers approved the 'Recommendation CM/Rec 2001 on Intercultural Integration,' explicitly recommending that the governments of member states should take "the urban model of intercultural integration into account when revising and further developing national migrant integration policies or policies for intercultural dialogue and diversity management" (ICC_doc7). Furthermore, in May 2016 the Commissioner for Human Rights issued a policy paper entitled 'Time for Europe to get migrant integration right' (ICC_doc9), which criticised states' unilateral attempts to cut back on migrant reception standards and pledged for coordinated integration policies, emphasising the positive outcomes of the intercultural approach in the education and health sectors.

Regarding internal structuring, as our interviewees explained, the growing number of member cities, their extremely diverse situations and the multiplication of the activities of the programme put on the table a need to rethink internal modes of decision-making and organisation of the work (ICC_int1 and ICC_int3). Whereas in the first phase the CoE Secretariat had always had a key role in setting the network agenda, which was then presented to the cities in the main annual events, the *Medium-term strategy 2016–2019* introduced a more participatory procedure, since it envisaged that the ICC annual programme of activities had to be designed jointly by the Secretariat and member cities, with experts providing support in the process. More specifically, the programme had to be presented and validated at the annual coordinators' meeting (ICC_doc8, p. 7), where the officials in charge of coordinating

ICC initiatives in member municipalities and/or national ICC networks were represented.

Against this background, the *Medium-term strategy 2016–2019* proposed an explicit MLG agenda which however, as we shall see below, took a more intergovernmental mode in its concrete implementation, reflecting the mediation between the ICC Secretariat original ideas and the more political agenda articulated by member cities in the Coordinators' Meeting. In fact, on 23 May 2016, members of the ICC Secretariat, policymakers and experts from academia and NGOs met at a brainstorming meeting at the EUI in Florence to explore "the further strategic development of the Intercultural cities programme by addressing the challenge of how to export the intercultural policy model at the regional and national levels" (ICC_web14 and ICC_web15). A key idea discussed during the meeting was that of launching a new initiative under the aegis of the CoE and the ICC Programme called 'The Squared Circle: Inclusive Integration Policy Laboratory.' The goal was to involve city, regional and national officials, experts and NGO representatives in developing "policy ideas based on the intercultural approach but tailormade for regional and national levels" (ICC_web15).

> [...] There are clear limits to the mandate and scope of action of local authorities, which make it important to introduce this policy approach at the national level as well [...] For the Intercultural integration approach to effectively influence policies across Europe, it is necessary to enlarge not only the number of cities which embrace it but also to reach out to other important actors, in particular regional and national authorities, academia and NGOs. (ICC_doc8, p. 5)

Reflecting these ideas, the *Medium-term strategy 2016–2019* document emphasised a need to set up specific structures and platforms to transfer policy know-how from the local to the national level and favour multi-stakeholder policy exchanges. The Inclusive Integration Policy Lab was to be structured as a series of events with officials, academics and NGOs "to help raise a community of ICC advocates and thinkers who can help propagate the concept but also enrich it" (ICC_doc8, p. 6).

The proposal was discussed and accepted at the annual meeting of ICC coordinators held in Reykjavik September 2016, as was reported in the minutes (ICC_doc11). However, the representatives of the cities present at the meeting remarked on the scarce engagement of Mayors and

Deputy Mayors in ICC and the risks deriving from changes in local political majorities in terms of commitment to the programme. To strengthen the political visibility of ICC, it was agreed in the meeting to organise a 'milestone event' for the 10th anniversary of ICC in November 2017 and to launch on that occasion the first Policy Lab. Contrary to the original design discussed in Florence, the Concept Paper prepared in April 2017 as a background for the first Policy Lab emphasised the importance of fostering coordination between public actors at different territorial scales, while there was no mention of collaboration with non-public actors.

> The Policy Lab aims to ensure policy consistency and complementarity and enable transfer of innovation and good practice from local to regional and national levels. It could also encourage national and/or (whenever appropriate) regional authorities to adopt an intercultural approach to migrant and refugee integration policies as a means of building more inclusive societies. (ICC_doc13, p. 1)

Thus, in its concrete implementation the Policy Lab became more of an intergovernmental venue than a proper MLG instance of policymaking. In fact, while the milestone event held in Lisbon in November 2017 brought together a wide range of participants, 271 in total, including civil servants and political leaders (mayors and/or deputy mayors) of member cities and of state authorities, academics, intercultural experts and NGOs (ICC_doc15), the Policy Lab that took place at the end of the event only gathered representatives of public institutions. From the documents available on the internet, the list of participants included six representatives of ICC cities (London Lewisham, Olso, Reggio Emilia, Tenerife, Paris, Stavanger), four of national governments (Spain, Germany, Portugal and Ireland), one of the Canton of Neuchatel and representatives of the CoE and experts from the Migration Policy Group (ICC_doc16). This is consistent with the Lisbon Declaration, presented by ICC at the end of the milestone event.

> One of our priorities for the next 5 years will be to work systematically with national authorities, with support by the Council of Europe, to design and implement coherent inclusive integration policies. [...] We are confident that a relationship of trust and cooperation with national authorities, as well as dynamic partnerships with local, national and international organisations that support this agenda, will help make our societies and communities stronger. (ICC_doc17, p. 2)

Three more Policy Labs followed, in Strasbourg in June 2018 (ICC_doc19) and in Helsinki (ICC_doc23) and Limassol, Cyprus (ICC_doc25) in May and November 2019, respectively. In these meetings, discussions focused on the drafting of the so-called Policy Framework for Intercultural Integration for the National Level to represent "an inspirational model to foster common understanding, a coherent approach, and shared responsibilities among all levels of governance in relation to migrant integration" (ICC_doc25, p. 1). This confirms that the Policy Lab worked essentially from the perspective of intergovernmental relations with the goal of achieving policy coherence through cooperation between levels of government.

In this context, the horizontal dimension of collaboration with non-public actors, which underlay the initial design of the Policy Lab as pointed out above, was put aside. However, this dimension seems to have had some relevance in the Portuguese national Policy Lab held in Lisbon in October 2018, where the main national NGOs were invited to the table and included in the partnerships established for the implementation of the actions agreed on in the meeting (ICC_doc21, 4). In contrast, the national Policy Lab organised by the Italian ICC network and held in Rome in May 2017 substantially followed the intergovernmental pattern of the international Labs (see ICC_doc14).

Rather than through the Policy Labs, the ICC Secretariat seems to have developed relations with non-public actors through the Building Inclusive Societies Action Plan approved by the CoE in March 2016 (ICC_doc10, p. 7). In fact, two pilot projects were launched under the aegis of the ICC Programme with the goal of engaging the private sector in local diversity policies. More specifically, Diversity Rating for Businesses had the goal of assessing the economic potential of workforce diversity in private companies and encouraging them to diversify their workforce, while the Diversity Connector for Start-ups consisted of visits by the interested ICC member cities to explore good practice examples of how to design diverse business incubators (ICC_doc10, pp. 7–8). However, NGOs do not seem to have been the target of these specific actions.

> Many ICC cities have already in place an intercultural approach entailing cooperation with NGOs. NGOs are key partners, hence there is no need to further develop instruments to involve NGOs. These are already very much active, this is the work of the cities and they have to do it in an intercultural perspective. The NGOs have always to be there. Yet this is not always the

> case of the private sector. In some cities businesses are involved, in others less. The cities need our support to see how to approach the private sector. Businesses at a local level are key actors because they employ immigrants, yet it can be more difficult to engage them in local policy. We choose this as a focus area in order to generate knowledge on how to build good partnerships and tools to attract private firms and bring them closer to the intercultural integration mind-set. (ICC_int3)

In fact, as mentioned above, NGOs had been somewhat indirectly involved in ICC activities since the very outset as partners of member cities in the implementation of best practices and in compiling policy reviews for the ICC Index reports. Furthermore, NGOs also contributed to the organisation of so-called Thematic Events, that is, intercultural initiatives promoted by the ICC Programme and organised by member cities. Cases in point are: the seminar 'Social innovation for refugee inclusion' held in Brussels on 12–13 September 2016 and aimed at promoting local partnerships in support of refugees between social innovators, NGOs, local authorities, businesses and service professionals (ICC_doc10, pp. 2–3); the initiative 'Human Rights in the Intercultural City' organised on 14–15 June 2017 in cooperation with the city of Oslo to build stronger alliances between cities and advocates of human rights (ICC_doc12, pp. 3–4); and the thematic event 'Fighting discrimination and hate speech: is interculturalism the solution?' held in Turin on 18–19 June 2019 (ICC_doc27, pp. 2–3), gathering together member cities, the ICC team, academic experts and NGOs with specific expertise on discrimination and conflict mediation.

4.3.5 Policy Agendas, Modes of Policymaking and Relations

A process-tracing analysis of the ICC Programme from its founding in 2008 until 2019 reveals two main phases underpinned by two distinct modes of policymaking: (1) an intergovernmental—supranational-local—partnership phase (2008–2015); and (2) a MLG-like phase (2016–2019). Table 4.3 provides an overview of the sequence of events underlying the mobilisation on the demand and supply sides of migration policymaking following the actor-centred and relational interpretative framework presented in Chapter 3.

In the first phase, the agenda was essentially set by the ICC-CoE Secretariat in collaboration with experts and more specifically Comedia in the

Table 4.3 ICC: Causal process observations and modes of policymaking

	Causal process observations	*Modes of policymaking*
1. 2008–2016	**Demand side** Mobilisation of a group of 11 cities on the part of CoE around the theorisation of the intercultural model of immigrant integration • Collaborative and inclusive agenda **Supply side** CoE and EC provide funding and support for projects aimed at concretely implementing the model • ICC Index • Anti-rumour strategy • DELI project (business sector)	Intergovernmental partnership (local-supranational levels)
2.2015–2019	**Demand side** 1. ICC Secretariat and experts engage in a revision of ICC in the MLG direction • Florence meeting • *Medium-term strategy 2016–2019* 2. City Coordinators start to articulate a political advocacy agenda **Supply side** CoE Secretariat provides a venue for MLG policymaking, the Policy Labs • Intergovernmental fora more than MLG • An exception in the case of Portugal	MLG skewed towards intergovernmental relations

early years and then other academics and an increasing number of experts from independent institutes. This appears to be consistent with the aim of the ICC Programme in this period: to define an original approach to migrant integration based on CoE legislation and taking into account specific expertise on urban policy. The process of global expansion was also essentially driven by the Secretariat, often by engaging experts from the cities joining the programme (like the Labbri group in the case of Montreal). Contacts with cities in Morocco and the Middle East (Jordan and Israel) were instead facilitated by the support offered by another CoE-EU joint programme, i.e. South II.

Thus, in this period, a seemingly top-down direction prevailed in agenda-setting, from the Strasbourg Secretariat to member cities.

However, cities always took an active role in reviewing their policies and validating the ICC Index, engaging in collaborative relations together and with the ICC-CoE team. Overall, a mode of policymaking based on intergovernmental—supranational-local—cooperation was established. Relations with NGOs and the non-profit sector more generally, while considered important in the theoretical definition of interculturalism, were always of an indirect type, in the sense that these organisations were engaged in ICC initiatives only through the networks established with local authorities for the implementation of specific projects.

Between 2015 and 2016, in parallel with the process of global expansion described above and in the politically tense context of the European asylum crisis, the agenda of the ICC Programme started to take a new direction. On the initiative of the Secretariat and in collaboration with experts, the importance of engaging cities in broader MLG-like governance relations with public and non-public actors at different territorial scales was affirmed with the aim of favouring the adoption of the intercultural approach to integration beyond the city level.

However, as pointed out above, the concrete implementation of this MLG agenda had to take cities' standpoints in consideration. In fact, the reports of the coordinators' meetings published on the internet reveal the emergence of a city agenda prioritising relations with national governments rather than MLG. This is clearly articulated in the report of the 2017 Lisbon meeting:

> The ICC Programme is certainly among the core actions of the Council of Europe in the fields of diversity management and migrant integration. Still, there is a need to make this work (and its outcomes) much more political and visible. Besides, cities also feel that a strong political support is key for greater impact and thus the support of political leaders – from both the local and national levels – seems crucial. (ICC_doc18, p. 3)

Based on these considerations, the city coordinators asked the ICC team for support in improving relations with city political leaders through initiatives like intensive political information sessions, small working groups on concrete issues to keep politicians informed of ICC activities and the appointment of local leaders as 'ICC Ambassadors' to be involved in delivering public statements on behalf of the network, preparing articles for national media on specific themes and commenting on issues of interest to public opinion, etc. In other words, the coordinators asked the ICC secretariat to help cities to "increase their impact and make their voice better heard, both at the national and international levels" (p. ICC_doc18, p. 4). It follows that the Policy Labs were also appreciated insofar as they could contribute to establish informal work with governments "to build confidence and involve them in the ICC work" (ICC_doc).

Hence, rather than as instances of MLG, as in the ICC Secretariat's original plan, from the perspective of the cities the Policy Labs were conceived as intergovernmental fora aimed at enabling direct engagement and eventually the emergence of partnerships with national authorities. In the conclusions of the 2018 Meeting of Coordinators in Rijeka (ICC_doc20) and of the 2019 meeting in Odessa (ICC_doc24), explicit mentions were made to the necessity of expanding the coalition to leaders of NGOs and other local stakeholders, including private companies and the academia. However, according to the conclusions of the meeting in Odessa, these are regarded more as strategic partners in implementation processes (ICC_doc24 p. 16) than as stakeholders to be invited to take part in the Policy Labs.

4.4 Comparative Insights

According to Penninx (2015), the WGM&I and the ICC Programme could be characterised as two exemplary cases of the emergence of new city-EU coalitions in the MLG of migration in Europe (p. 106). The two CNs were founded more and less in the same years (the WGM&I in 2005 and the ICC Programme in 2008), and in fact some collaboration was also solicited by the EC in the context of the European Year for Intercultural Dialogue (ICC_doc1). Nevertheless, my in-depth reconstruction of the sequences of events underlying the engagement by the two CNs in multilevel policymaking around migration reveals more differences between them than similarities, somewhat echoing the words of one of my interviewees:

> In fact, we were supposed to collaborate together but this did never really take off… It was difficult to share the agenda, each network had its priorities, identity, initiatives etc. In the end, we are very different indeed. (ICC_Int1)

Whereas the WGM&I represents a case of political mobilisation started from below by mayors with the goal of claiming a seat at high-level policy-making tables, ICC is instead an instance of activation from above, i.e. by a supranational institution, the CoE, pursuing the realisation of the intercultural policy paradigm. This dynamic of top-down activation is clearly reflected in the key role assumed by experts, engaged since the beginning in defining the inspirational model for a new policy of integration. In the case of the WGM&I, on the contrary, the expertise that acquired relevance over the course of time was that of internal project managers supporting member cities in the development and implementation of the project proposals to be presented for funding to the EC.

Notwithstanding these structural differences, my in-depth study shows a remarkable similarity in terms of scarce engagement by both CNs in MLG policymaking. In fact, the prevailing mode of policymaking emerging from the evidence collected is intergovernmental cooperation between a supranational institution, i.e. the EC in the case of the WGM&I and the CoE in that of ICC, and local level authorities. On the side of cities, this kind of collaboration seems to have engaged primarily civil servants or technical staff, whereas politicians, especially in the WGM&I but to some extent also in ICC, appear to have been more involved in political advocacy and lobbying. MLG, on the other hand, emerges as an initiative from above, i.e. by the Dutch Presidency of the EU through the Urban Agenda in the case of the WGM&I and by the Strasbourg Secretariat in that of ICC. Above all, it is a mode of policymaking that, in its concrete occurrences, does not seem to engage civil society and private actors on an equal footing as governmental authorities.

This is particularly clear in the case of the Partnership for the Integration of Immigrants and Refugees, where NGOs and civil society organisations were included through specific conferences but did not participate on a regular basis in the decisions and implementation of the final action plan. However, the ICC Programme also seems to have experienced limits in this respect: even if partnership with non-profit and economic actors was in principle crucial for the building of an intercultural model of immigrant integration, the Policy Labs took an intergovernmental format, with the only exception of the Portuguese one. Relations with NGOs remained a prerogative of cities, while with respect to economic actors ad hoc projects were undertaken that, however, did not imply engagement in the Policy Labs.

To conclude, from the trajectories of the two European CNs analysed, MLG emerges as a mode of policymaking skewed, in its practical implementation, towards intergovernmental relations and taking place in the "shadow of hierarchy" (Börzel, 2010), and even more precisely in the case of the WGM&I of the will of national governments. Nevertheless, CNs seem to have represented an interesting opportunity for mayors and/or deputy mayors to raise their voices vis-à-vis national governments and supranational institutions by building on and taking stock of specific projects managed by civil servants and administrative staff, often in partnership with local non-profit and civil society organisations. However, the latter do not appear to have been directly involved in the decisions regarding CN initiatives, de facto representing secondary partners in MLG policymaking in the EU context.

References

Agustín, Ó. G., & Jørgensen, M. B. (2019). Solidarity cities and cosmopolitanism from below: Barcelona as a refugee city. *Social Inclusion, 7*, 198–207. https://doi.org/10.17645/si.v7i2.2063

Bloomfield, J. (2011). *Developing Europe's urban model: 25 years of Eurocities*. Eurocities.

Bloomfield, J., & Bianchini, F. (2004). *Planning for the intercultural city*. Comedia.

Börzel, T. (2010). European governance: Negotiation and competition in the shadow of hierarchy. *JCMS: Journal of Common Market Studies, 48*, 191–219. https://doi.org/10.1111/j.1468-5965.2009.02049.x

Caponio, T. (2019). *City networks and the multilevel governance of migration: Policy discourses and actions*. EUI RSCAS, 2019/08, Migration Policy Centre. Retrieved from Cadmus, European University Institute Research Repository, at http://hdl.handle.net/1814/60666

Caponio, T., & Borkert, M. (2010). *The local dimension of migration policymaking*. Amsterdam University Press.

Carrera, S. (2008). *Benchmarking integration in the EU: Analyzing the debate on integration indicators and moving it forward*. Bertelsmann Foundation, Gütersloh

Dossi, S. (2017). *Cities and the European Union: Mechanisms and modes of Europeanisation*. Rowman & Littlefield Publishers / ECPR Press.

Ewen, S., & Hebbert, M. (2007). European cities in a networked world during the long 20th century. *Environment and Planning c: Government and Policy, 25*, 327–340. https://doi.org/10.1068/c0640

Flamant, A. (2017). Les cadres de l'action publique locale en charge des politiques d'intégration des étrangers. *Politique Europeenne, 57*, 84–115.

Gebhardt, D., & Güntner, S. (2021). 'We as leaders of major European cities'—how Eurocities works to influence EU migration and integration policies. *Local Government Studies*. https://doi.org/10.1080/03003930.2021.1938552

Guidikova, I. (2018). Intercultural integration: From an ideology of the oppressed to the mainstream. In B. W. White (Ed.), *Intercultural cities: Policies and practice for a new era* (pp. 55–64). Palgrave Macmillan.

Heinelt, H., & Kübler, D. (Eds.) (2005). Metropolitan governance, democracy and the dynamics of place. In Heinelt, H. & Kübler, D. (Eds.) *Metropolitan governance in the 21st Century: Capacity, democracy and the dynamics of place* (pp. 8–28). Routledge.

Huggins, C. (2018a). Subnational transnational networking and the continuing process of local-level Europeanization. *European Urban and Regional Studies, 25*, 206–227. https://doi.org/10.1177/0969776417691564

Huggins, C. (2018b). Subnational government and transnational networking: The rationalist logic of local level Europeanization. *JCMS: Journal of Common Market Studies, 56*, 1263–1282. https://doi.org/10.1111/jcms.12740

Irgil, E. (2016). Multi-level governance as an alternative: The municipality of Barcelona and the Ciutat Refugi Plan. *Glocalism: Journal of Culture, Politics and Innovation*, 1–21. https://doi.org/10.12893/gjcpi.2016.3.1

Kübler, D., & Piliutyte, J. (2007). Intergovernmental relations and international urban strategies: Constraints and opportunities in multilevel polities. *Environment and Planning c: Government and Policy, 25*, 357–373. https://doi.org/10.1068/c0637

Lacroix, T. (2021). Migration related city networks: A global overview. *Local Government Studies*. https://doi.org/10.1080/03003930.2021.1938553

Lacroix, T., Hombert, L., & Furri, F. (2020). *Migration and municipal militancy in the Mediterranean*. EuroMed Research Network on Migration.

Marshall, A. (2005). Europeanization at the urban level: Local actors, institutions and the dynamics of multi-level interaction. *Journal of European Public Policy, 12*, 668–686. https://doi.org/10.1080/13501760500160292

Niessen, J., & Schibel, Y. (2004). *Handbook on integration for policy-makers and practitioners*. DG Justice, Freedom and Security, European Commission, Brussels.

Payre, R. (2010). The importance of being connected. City networks and urban government: Lyon and Eurocities (1990–2005). *International Journal of Urban and Regional Research, 34*, 260–280. https://doi.org/10.1111/j.1468-2427.2010.00937.x

Penninx, R. (2015). European cities in search of knowledge for their integration policies. In P. Scholten, H. Entzinger, R. Penninx, & S. Verbeek (Eds.),

Integrating immigrants in Europe: Research-policy dialogues (pp. 99–115). Springer International Publishing.

Russell, B. (2019). Beyond the local trap: New municipalism and the rise of the fearless cities. *Antipode, 51*, 989–1010. https://doi.org/10.1111/anti.12520

Saunier, P.-Y. (2002). Taking up the bet on connections: A municipal contribution. *Contemporary European History, 11*, 507–527. https://doi.org/10.1017/S0960777302004010

Saunier, P.-Y., & Ewen, S. (Eds.). (2008). *Another global city: Historical explorations into the transnational municipal moment*. Palgrave Macmillan.

Scholten, P., Engbersen, G., van Ostaijen, M., & Snel, E. (2018). Multilevel governance from below: How Dutch cities respond to intra-EU mobility. *Journal of Ethnic and Migration Studies, 44*, 2011–2033. https://doi.org/10.1080/1369183X.2017.1341707

Schultze, C. J. (2003). Cities and EU governance: Policy-takers or policy-makers? *Regional & Federal Studies, 13*, 121–147. https://doi.org/10.1080/714004785

Taran, P. A., Neves de Lima, G., & Kadysheva, O. (2016). *Cities welcoming refugees and migrants: Enhancing effective urban governance in an age of migration*. UNESCO.

Tavares, R. (2016). *Paradiplomacy—Cities and states as global players*. Oxford University Press.

Tortola, P. D., & Couperus, S. (2020). *Differentiation from below: Sub-national authority networks as a form of differentiated cooperation*. EUIDEA: EU Integration and Differentiation for Effectiveness and Accountability.

White, B. W. (2018). From policy to practice and back again: The montreal forum on intercultural cities. In B. W. White (Ed.), *Intercultural cities: Policies and practice for a new era* (pp. 1–18). Palgrave Macmillan.

Wood, P., & Landry, C. (2008). *The intercultural city: Planning for diversity advantage*. Earthscan.

CHAPTER 5

Migration City Networks in the US Federal System. Case-Studies

Abstract This chapter presents the research findings on the two US-based CNs, i.e. WA and C4A, using structured narratives. Following the causal process tracing method, I reconstruct the sequence of events underlying the engagement by the two CNs in multilevel policymaking processes on migration and their eventual participation in instances of MLG. The narratives are structured around the key elements of the actor-centred and relational interpretative framework, and more specifically on the demand side (1) CN leaders and processes of internal agenda setting and (2) the main policy actions, initiatives and modes of policymaking actively promoted by each CN. As for the supply side of migration policymaking, the analysis focuses on interactions and relationships with other key stakeholders and policymakers, and in particular on interactions with federal authorities, which have a gatekeeping role on migration issues in the US. At the end of the chapter, I provide a cross-case comparative assessment of the CN-MLG nexus in the US federal political system.

5.1 Migration City Networks in the US. An Overview of Institutional Factors and Problem Pressure

As was already mentioned in Sect. 3.3, intergovernmental relations around migration in the US have always been characterised as highly contentious since a key stake is represented by law enforcement

T. Caponio, *Making Sense of the Multilevel Governance of Migration*, https://doi.org/10.1007/978-3-030-82551-5_5

(Gulasekaram & Ramakrishnan, 2015; Ridgley, 2008). More specifically, the 287 (g) programme introduced in 1996 as part of the Illegal Immigration Reform and Immigrant Responsibility Act (IIRIRA) requires state and local police to collaborate with the federal government to enforce federal immigration laws (Williamson, 2018, p. 7). Further direct requirements to participate in the removal and detention of undocumented migrants were imposed by the so-called Secure Communities programme launched by George W. Bush in 2008, which was rescinded by President Obama and then reinstated by Trump (Varsanyi et al., 2017).

The gradual expansion of the Sanctuary Cities movement can be regarded as a reaction of local authorities to this highly contentious and politicised institutional structure. However, its origins in San Francisco as a faith-based movement date back to the 1980s (Kuge, 2020, p. 46), well before IIRIRA, and therefore are linked to civil society activism in support of victims of civil wars in Central America. Sanctuary Cities have never formed a proper network organisation, instead being characterised as a patchwork of policies and practices that differ from city to city and serve the purpose of accommodating undocumented migrants and refugees in urban communities, therefore challenging national immigration laws and policies (see, e.g. Bauder, 2017, p. 174).

Issues linked to law enforcement have spurred not only pro-immigrant movements as in the case of Sanctuary Cities but also restrictive mobilisation based on arguments like ensuring the security of the local community and the need to limit access to social services. This is the case of conservative organisations promoting local restrictive ordinances (Colbern & Ramakrishnan, 2018, p. 363). More specifically, Gulasekaram and Ramakrishnan (2015) draw attention to the key role played by Numbers USA and the Federation for American Immigration Reform in drafting and spreading anti-immigrant local ordinances between 2006 and 2007 across the US states. A case in point is that of so-called landlord ordinances, which mandate that landlords should check the immigration status of their tenants and terminate the leases of residents without federal legal status.

With respect to settlement, according to existing laws and Supreme Court rulings, municipalities in the United States are expected to provide basic services concerning education, health and language access (Williamson, 2018, p. 6). Some of these services, like English-language programmes and emergency care for those who cannot pay, should be provided by public schools and local health providers accepting public funding regardless of the migrant's legal status. However, because of the lack of dedicated federal programmes, a laissez-fair approach has prevailed in which migrants and the local communities they live in are expected to take the initiative (Bloemraad & de Graauw, 2013), leading to the emergence of very differentiated situations across the country in terms of initiatives by both non-profit organisations and local governments (de Graauw, 2019; Williamson, 2018).

Scholars have noticed a growing activism of US municipalities in the local governance of integration since the mid-2000s (de Graauw, 2019; Huang & Liu, 2018), leading to an expansion of the number of city immigrant offices and, since 2010, of so-called welcoming ordinances, which explicitly affirm openness to migrants and refugees (McDaniel, 2014; McDaniel et al., 2019). Huang and Liu (2018) identify the genesis of these policies in the post-2007 Great Recession years, when policy agendas centred on regional competitiveness and economic development started to emphasise the contribution of migrants' skills and ideas to the growth of receiving communities (Peri, 2010).

Among the various local organisations and networks that are engaged in the welcoming movement (Filomeno, 2017; McDaniel et al., 2019), two key components can be identified: organisations based on political leadership, usually mayors and other elected politicians; and grassroots associations. Networks of city political leaders mobilised around migration include some generalist organisations such as the National League of Cities,[1] the US Conference of Mayors,[2] the National Conference of State Legislatures[3] and CNs dealing exclusively with migration issues. Cases in point are Cities for Citizenship, which was launched in 2014 by the mayors of New York, Los Angeles and Chicago with the aim of increasing naturalisation rates among eligible permanent residents and encouraging cities across the country to invest in citizenship programmes,[4] and Cities for Action, which is one of the case studies treated in more depth below. As for grassroots organisations, existing research emphasises the

[1] https://www.nlc.org/about/. Last accessed: 3 December 2020.

[2] https://www.usmayors.org/. Last accessed: 3 December 2020.

[3] https://www.ncsl.org/aboutus.aspx. Last accessed: 3 December 2020.

[4] http://www.citiesforcitizenship.com/c4c-celebrate-5-years-of-impact. Last accessed: 3 December 2020.

key role assumed since 2010 by Welcoming America (WA) in mobilising an increasing number of cities and counties around the inclusion of migrants in local communities, from main gateway cities to small and medium-sized towns (de Graauw, 2019; Rodriguez et al., 2018). Unlike initiatives by city political leaders, WA is a civil society-based organisation bringing together municipalities and NGOs, as I will illustrate below.

Hence, the introduction of local integration policies and the emergence of CN organisations appear as strictly intertwined processes, with the latter providing a "growing support infrastructure to sustain and expand municipal efforts for immigrant integration" (de Graauw, 2019, p. 170). As is clear, if law enforcement continues to represent an issue of contention in the American federal system, welcoming and integration increasingly emerge as topics in the relations between federal and local authorities around migration in the US.

5.2 Welcoming America

5.2.1 *The Genesis of Welcoming America. A Movement of Communities*

The origins of WA date back to 2001, when the Tennessee Immigrant and Refugee Rights Coalition (TIRRC) was founded in Nashville by the founder of WA, David Lubell. Described in an official video as "a coalition of immigrants, refugees and allies,"[5] TIRRC engaged in various initiatives to support integration in Nashville. Unlike traditional immigration gateway cities like New York, Nashville was a 'new destination' that between 1990 and 2005 had undergone fast rates of immigrant population growth, generating increasing anxieties and hostility among the resident population (WA_doc1). Facing this situation, in 2006 TIRRC launched the Welcoming Tennessee Initiative (WTI). According to David Lubell, this was

> [...] a new experiment that differed from traditional programming focusing on integrating immigrants into American life. We dedicated a substantial amount of our time and resources to engaging Tennessee's 'immigrant receiving communities,' the long-term residents of towns or cities that had

[5] 'Nashville Welcomes,' https://www.youtube.com/watch?v=Mt49BNoAOAs&feature=youtube, last accessed on November 25, 2019.

> recently experienced an influx of immigrants and/or refugees. (WA_doc1, p. iv)

The WTI experience is reported in official documents and by our interviewees as particularly important for the development of WA. Starting with the mobilisation of civil society and immigrant organisations in grassroots initiatives like community dialogues and presentations by local immigrants, WTI was “able to start changing the policies and programmes of the Nashville government to help it become the most welcoming city in the southeast, which it is today” (see footnote 5). Particular attention was also devoted to building a discourse on ‘the concrete benefits’ of being welcoming, emphasising the positive contributions that immigrants were bringing to Tennessee (WA_doc1, iv; WA_int2).

The Nashville experiment attracted the interest of other local coalitions promoting immigrant integration across the US, spanning from Nebraska to Massachusetts (WA_int1). From 2008, campaigns across the country started to be organised under the WA banner, leading to the emergence of a ‘movement of communities’ (WA_int2 and WA_int3) that was constituted as a formal organisation in Atlanta in 2009, with David Lubell as executive director.

> For us it was important not to be a Washington DC-based organisation, but rather being present at a grassroots level, where communities are. Atlanta was a rising city... There was indeed leadership there, since the mayor was interested in our approach and supported us in putting together a partnership beyond the municipality, including NGOs, employers, immigrant and refugee communities etc. All these actors collaborated to draft an agenda. This agenda strengthened the mayor’s actions, since his efforts were supported by a group of stakeholders demanding to set up a commission for immigrant affairs ... Metro Atlanta was the first major metropolitan area to adopt a regional welcoming plan and today represents a model for other regions. (WA_int2)

According to our interviewees, in its early years the main focus of WA activity was on “changing mentalities and promoting the ‘moral value’ of welcoming” (WA_int2). The document *The Receiving Communities Toolkit: A guide for engaging mainstream America in immigrant integration* can be considered the main achievement of this initial period. The toolkit was the result of a two-day event organised together with the Center for American Progress and the J. M. Kaplan Fund which brought together academics and practitioners "to discuss how best to engage mainstream Americans to promote inclusion and ease conflict" (WA_doc2, p. 2). Three strategies are suggested as "having tremendous potential for improving community climate: contact, communication and leadership" (WA_doc2, p. 3). The actions illustrated under each heading address local policy practitioners in a broad sense, including NGOs, immigrants' rights coalitions, community organisations, business leaders and the like.

5.2.2 *Engaging with City Governments to Build Local Partnerships*

The *Receiving Communities Toolkit* is indicative of a process of internal structuration of the WA policy agenda, from essentially being centred on promoting the 'moral value of welcoming,' as was the case with WTI, to the definition of a more precise welcoming strategy and operational tools (WA_int3). A key initiative in this respect is the National Welcoming Week, which was celebrated for the first time in September 2012 and since then has been regularly organised every year (WA_web1). The goal is that of bringing together long-term and new immigrant residents to take part in local community projects organised by WA and its affiliate organisations across the country. The Welcoming Weeks testify to the central role of civil society organisations and grassroots voluntary groups in the WA identity as a 'movement of communities.'

However, at the turn of the 2010s, WA civil society leaders also started to acknowledge more and more the importance of engaging counties and city governments, which could provide crucial contributions to the realisation of welcoming environments though the promotion of specific public policies.

> At the beginning the network was formed primarily by NGOs. There were also some pro-active municipalities but these were rather the exception. However, with the passing of time we realised that in order to move from affirming the moral value of welcoming to the promotion of a more pro-active approach the engagement of local governments was crucial. Hence, from a NGO-based membership, in a second step WA developed in the direction of engaging more and more local authorities. (WA_int2)

This local government turn in the WA agenda can be understood in the context of the increasing mobilisation of local authorities around the welcoming messages and ideals described above in Sect. 5.1. As is emphasised in the document *Welcoming Cities: Framing the Conversation* (WA_doc3) published in 2012 and written in collaboration with the German Marshall Fund, at the turn of the 2010s many states and cities had actively engaged in pro-immigrant policies like opening immigrant affairs offices or introducing Welcoming Resolutions. It was acknowledged that Welcoming Resolutions, defined as "formal proclamations by elected officials that articulate openness to migrants [...] are also important steps towards creating more actionable and comprehensive welcoming plans" (WA_doc3, p. 5).

Building on these footsteps, with the support of the German Marshall Fund and other partners like the American Society/Council of the Americas,[6] the Maytree Cities of Migration and the cities of Chicago and New York, in June 2013 WA launched the Welcoming Cities and Counties Initiative (WA_web2). Its goal was to promote the sharing of innovative policies and practices and develop new tools to support "economic development and create vibrant global communities that are great places to live, work and do business" (WA_web2). Seventeen cities and counties joined the new initiative: Allegheny County, Pennsylvania; Austin, Texas; Baltimore, Maryland; Boise, Idaho; Chicago, Illinois; Columbus, Ohio; Dayton, Ohio; High Point, North Carolina; Lincoln, Nebraska; Macomb County, Michigan; Montgomery County, Maryland; New York, New York; Oakley, California; Philadelphia, Pennsylvania; San Francisco, California; St. Louis, Missouri (city and county).

In this same period and in parallel with the Welcoming Cities and Counties initiative, WA continued to consolidate its centrality in the context of the welcoming movement by establishing a Welcoming Economy Global Network (WA_web3). This gathered together leaders from several economic development partnerships and initiatives across the Mid-West, like Global Detroit,[7] which in 2012 had started to develop welcoming discourses and initiatives emphasising the positive contribution of diversity, immigrant talents and entrepreneurship to the growth of the regional economy. The network was formalised in 2013, when the first Convening was held in Detroit (6 June 2013; see WA_web3). In 2014

[6] See: https://www.as-coa.org/about/about-ascoa. Last access: 23 August 2019.

[7] See: http://www.globaldetroit.com/#horizontalTab2. Last accessed: 25 November 2019.

the Welcoming Economy Global Network became a WA project in partnership with Global Detroit (WA_web4, WA_doc4), bringing under the WA flag 20 local development coalitions in the Rust Belt area (WA_web4 and WA_web5) including Global Pittsburgh, Welcome Dayton and Saint Louis Mosaic and the cities of Akron, Chicago, Cincinnati, Columbus and Pittsburgh (WA_doc4, 4). Thanks to contributions by private foundations, early initiatives were directed at developing and consolidating communication activities, creating a state and local policy playbook on strategies for building inclusive local economies and supporting five city-to-city visits (WA_doc4, 4; WA_doc12).

In 2013 President Obama publicly recognised the key role assumed by WA in mobilising local communities on immigrant welcoming by assigning the prestigious Champions of Change award to ten WA leaders (WA_web6 and WA_int2). Furthermore, in 2012, WA was directly approached by the US Office of Refugee Resettlement (ORR), the federal agency in charge of providing assistance to facilitate the inclusion of refugees in the United States,[8] because the refugee service providers they were overseeing began to report growing fears among US-born residents about refugees and realised they needed help in stepping up engagement and bridging with local communities (WA_int4). Following these contacts, WA launched the Fostering Community Engagement and Welcoming Communities Programme, which was funded by ORR until 2017 and aimed to provide technical assistance to the nation's refugee resettlement network, and more specifically specialised training and practical toolkits to strengthen relations with local communities, foster participation and promote a positive climate regarding refugees (WA_web7).

Thus, as is clear, in the early 2010s WA had considerably grown in terms of initiatives and programmes, leading to an increasing structuration of the internal organisation and professionalisation of the network. According to our interviewees, whereas at the beginning the organisation was animated primarily by volunteers, in 2011 it counted four full-time staff members, a number that gradually increased over the years to reach 16 in 2018.

[8] See: https://www.acf.hhs.gov/orr. Last accessed: 25 November 2019.

5.2.3 The Welcoming Communities Campaign. An MLG Exercise

The increasing engagement of WA with counties and local governments seems to have represented a key asset favouring contacts with the federal government in the context of President Obama's *Federal Strategic Action Plan on Immigrant and Refugee Integration* (WA_doc5) of April 2015. On 21 November 2014, the President issued a Presidential Memorandum for the Heads of Executive Departments and Agencies entitled *Creating Welcoming Communities and Fully Integrating Immigrants and Refugees* with the aim "to develop a Federal immigrant integration strategy that is innovative and competitive with those of other industrialised nations" (WA_web8). To this end, the President established a White House Task Force on New Americans, which was defined in the memorandum in the following terms:

> An interagency effort to identify and support State and local efforts at integration that are working and to consider how to expand and replicate successful models. The Task Force, which will engage with community, business and faith leaders, as well as State and local elected officials, will help determine additional steps the Federal Government can take to ensure its programs and policies are serving diverse communities that include new Americans. (WA_web8)

The Task Force, which was co-chaired by the Director of the Domestic Policy Council and Secretary of Homeland Security, included: the Secretary of State; the Attorney General; the Secretary of Agriculture; the Secretary of Commerce; the Secretary of Labour; the Secretary of Health and Human Services; the Secretary of Housing and Urban Development; the Secretary of Transportation; the Secretary of Education; the Chief Executive Officer of the Corporation for National and Community Service; the Director of the Office of Management and Budget; the Administrator of the Small Business Administration; the Senior Advisor and Assistant to the President for Intergovernmental Affairs and Public Engagement; the Director of the National Economic Council; the Assistant to the President for Homeland Security and Counterterrorism; and the Director of the Office of Science and Technology Policy (WA_web8).

Thus the Task Force sought to engage and coordinate all relevant federal agencies that were somehow involved in promoting immigrant integration policies and at the same time in the spirit of developing a comprehensive plan it undertook extensive consultations with numerous stakeholders in both the public and non-public sectors and at all government levels. The plan, which was presented by the Task Force in April 2015 and entitled *Strengthening Communities by Welcoming all Residents* (WA_doc5, pp. 2–5), outlined the goals of the new federal strategy: to build welcoming communities; to strengthen existing pathways to naturalisation and promote civic engagement; to support skill development, entrepreneurship and protect New American workers; to expand opportunities for linguistic integration and education; and to strengthen the federal immigrant and refugee integration infrastructure. For each goal, the document detailed a series of recommended actions to be implemented with the participation of public institutions at different levels and all relevant civil society stakeholders:

> Critical to the success of our implementation efforts are maintaining a continued coordinated effort across the federal government and an open dialogue with stakeholders. None of this can, nor should, be done by the federal government alone. The pillars of civic, economic and linguistic integration cannot be supported without the collaboration of state and local governments, the non-profit and private sectors, schools, philanthropic organisations, community-based organisations, immigrant- and refugee-serving organisations, religious institutions and private citizens. (WA_doc6, ii)

It is in the context of the MLG policymaking strategy deployed by the Task Force that WA became more and more engaged in vertical and horizontal collaborative relations that developed in the policy process of the *Federal Strategic Action Plan*, from initial consultations to the implementation of the integration measures agreed upon, as was reported by one of our interviewees:

> During the Obama administration we started to have conversations on how the federal government could support the work which was taking place at the community level. They were interested in understanding our work and the way they could direct more support to communities. There started to be individual meetings with different federal agencies. We were able to feed into that process and we co-launched with them the campaign Building Welcoming Communities. (WA_int2)

The main outcome of this process was the Building Welcoming Communities Campaign, which was announced during the annual WA Welcoming

Week in September 2015 (WA_web9). The campaign had the goal of engaging cities and counties in creating positive environments for migrants and the resident population more generally. Forty WA member communities agreed to participate in the programme from the very start (for the full list, see WA_web9) and a call was issued to engage new ones (WA_doc6). Communities could participate in the campaign by committing to one of three tiers of involvement: making a formal statement declaring the intention to develop policies, programmes or initiatives aimed at building welcoming communities; establishing a multisector partnership to create a vision, a strategy and a comprehensive plan; or serving as national models by demonstrating exceptional progress on key action areas like immigrant and refugee participation in civic life (WA_doc6, pp. 6–8).

In more concrete terms, the Task Force agreed to support three types of measures (WA_doc5 and WA_doc6). The first was the launch of a Building Welcoming Communities Campaign webinar series to offer cities and counties the opportunity to get access to information from federal agency experts on federal programmes, policies and initiatives and learn about best practices from other cities and counties. Furthermore, always in the spirit of facilitating access to resources and enhancing coordination between federal agencies and local communities, in October 2015 the Task Force hosted the White House Building Welcoming Communities Convening in Washington, DC, which brought together more than 175 participants from cities and counties and from relevant federal agencies (WA_doc6, p. 7).

The second action consisted in the provision of extra staff for community work through the Corporation for National and Community Service and in partnership with the YMCA, Catholic Charities and national refugee resettlement organisations (WA_doc5, p. 2; WA_int2 and WA_int4). In more concrete terms, a civil service (AmeriCorps Vistas[9]) programme was launched to "help communities to increase capacity, expand multi-sector networks and develop and implement local integration plans" (WA_doc5, p. 2). As for the third measure, the Task Force sponsored the publication of new tools "to provide guidance to those communities interested in creating more welcoming inclusive environments" (WA_doc6, 7). This is the case of the *Community Planning Process*

[9] See: https://americorps.gov/serve/fit-finder/americorps-vista. Last Accessed: 25 November 2019.

Guide (WA_doc7), which was based on the experience of Boise, Idaho and presented as a model of a positive community climate and policies for welcoming immigrants and refugees. Furthermore, together with WA the Task Force created a *Roadmap to Success*, providing a menu of options for committed localities to transform the Building Welcoming Communities Campaign principles into action (WA_doc6 and WA_doc8):

> Using this Roadmap, communities can choose from a menu of specific ideas for action that are built around the principles of strategic planning and infrastructure development, equitable access and trust-building, awareness of pathways to citizenship and civic engagement, skill development, entrepreneurship, worker protection, linguistic education and integration. The Roadmap offers concrete ideas so that localities can tailor welcoming efforts to meet unique community needs. (WA_doc6, p. 7)

Furthermore, the Task Force also confirmed the continuation of the partnership of the Office for Refugee Resettlement with WA (see above) "to provide refugee resettlement organisations with the tools and support needed to enhance and sustain their community-engagement and public-awareness work in local communities, deepen their practices and local collaborations, and develop broader support for refugees" (WA_doc6, p. 11). In more concrete terms, the Welcoming America Welcoming Refugees project created a series of toolkits and webinars on matters such as refugee reception, messaging and communication on refugee issues, volunteering with refugees and refugee entrepreneurs (see, e.g. WA_doc9 and WA_doc13; WA_web7).

With the November 2016 presidential election and the victory of Donald Trump, the Task Force was discontinued, de facto ending the Building Welcoming Communities Campaign. No more contacts between WA and the White House appear to have taken place since then. In addition, the partnership with the Office for Refugee Resettlement came to an end in 2018 (WA_web7). Relations with the national level seem to have been limited to contacts with members of the Congress and Senate:

> We have to row against the ideological momentum … continue our work in local communities, consolidate our approach and show that it works. We annually bring a delegation of our members from several parts of the US to meet members of Congress, and we present our work to both conservative Congress Representatives and Senators [...] Furthermore, we have informal

relations with individual Senators because of the contacts of our members with the representatives of their districts. (WA_int2)

In 2019, WA organised a visit to Capitol Hill by delegations from Atlanta, Austin, Salt Lake City and Saint Cloud to receive training on advocacy and meet Congress members and staff to engage allies across the political spectrum on the impact of welcoming work at the local level (WA_doc14, p. 7).

5.2.4 Back to Community Work. Network Governance and Transnational Links

Since 2016, following the discontinuation of the Building Welcoming Communities Campaign, WA activities seem to have concentrated on the horizontal dimension of policymaking processes, understood both as city-to-city and public–private actor networks. Regarding city-to-city relations, two initiatives primarily targeted city governments and local administrations: the Welcoming Standards and Certified Communities programme; and the Welcoming International (WI) network.

The first initiative can be considered a step forward in the process initiated with the *Roadmap to Success*. The Welcoming Standards, developed together with 'leading experts,' i.e. practitioners, academics and business and civic leaders (WA_web10 and WA_doc10), provide a set of 'rigorous benchmarks and requirements' that welcoming communities have to meet in order to be certified as such. The certification process has to be initiated by a city or a county government, yet "Partners, such as non-profits, can contribute at any stage, including completing the application, contributing to the self-assessment, and being consultants during the site visit" (WA_web10). Furthermore, the assessment criteria regard collaboration and partnership as a key strategy in order to build welcoming and cohesive communities (WA_doc10, p. 11). The full certification fee amounted to 6,000 US dollars in 2019 but municipal governments could also apply for the dedicated WA scholarship programme (WA_web11). In December 2019, seven communities had successfully completed the certification process, while thirteen more had started the procedure (WA_web10).

As for Welcoming International (WA_web12), this programme started to take shape in 2013, when representatives of WA were invited by German cities, through The German Marshall Fund, to exchange ideas and practices around the advancement of local migrant and refugee inclusion (WA_web13). Thanks to financial support from various foundations like the Heinrich Böll Stiftung North America, and in collaboration with Cultural Vistas, a non-profit organisation specialised in organising international exchange programmes,[10] three rounds of visits between US and German cities were organised between 2016 and 2018 involving 30 municipalities in total with the goal of favouring peer-to-peer mutual learning on city integration policies (WA_doc11, p. 27; WA_web14). Furthermore, since 2016 Welcoming International has been supporting welcoming initiatives involving cities in Australia, New Zealand and the UK (WA_web10). In Australia the welcoming movement started to develop in 2015 with contacts between WA and the states of Queensland and Victoria, which led to the establishment of an NGO, Welcoming Australia, which is supported by the Scanlon Foundation and currently unites 39 city and regional authorities.[11] As for New Zealand, the first contacts were established by New Zealand Immigration, a national government agency, with the purpose of piloting a city network initiative on migration. In the case of the UK, relations developed with the Inclusive Cities programme of Oxford University's Centre on Migration, Policy and Society (COMPAS), which is supported by the Paul Hamlyn Foundation and engages five municipal governments across the country (WA_web10).

Regarding networks of public authorities and private/civil society stakeholders, WA has always continued the flagship initiatives mentioned above, i.e. Welcoming Economies and the Welcoming Weeks. More specifically, Welcoming Economies is presented on the website as a competitive opportunity for the members of the network to get access to professional support from WA and Global Detroit in advancing immigrant economic inclusion and contributing to local economic development in the form of virtual training sessions, coaching and tailored support (WA_web15). As for the Welcoming Weeks, over the years they have mobilised an increasing number of stakeholders beyond municipalities. In 2016, for instance, a partnership was launched with the YMCA which contributed to organising, together with 20 other organisations, 50 events in local YMCA headquarters around the country (WA_doc11,

[10] https://culturalvistas.org/about-us/. Last accessed: 25 November 2019.

[11] See: https://welcomingcities.org.au/what/. Last accessed: 25 November 2019.

pp. 18–19). In 2019 over 3,000 events were organised in partnership with the YMCA, the eBay Foundation and the American Alliance of Museums (WA_doc14, p. 6).

Along with these two long-standing programmes, new initiatives have also been established in recent years with the aim of fostering partnerships with non-profit organisations, like the Gateways for Growth programme and the National Inclusion Campaign. Gateways for Growth, which was launched in 2015 together with New American Economy,[12] is a competitive challenge that "offers resources to communities that demonstrate a public–private commitment to creating a welcoming environment for all residents" (WA_web16). The resources offered are of two types: customised research by NAE on the demographic and economic contributions of immigrants to their communities; and technical assistance from WA and NAE on drafting, executing and communicating 'a multi-sector immigrant integration strategy.' As for the National Inclusion Campaign, it started in 2019 with support from the Walmart Foundation. WA provided small grants and technical assistance to three communities in Missouri, Idaho, and Kentucky to pilot 'Do-It-Together' strategies designed to bring people from different backgrounds together (WA_doc14, p. 6). The activities at the pilot sites have been informed by a broader national inclusion campaign led by WA and the American Immigration Council that includes as its key component a media campaign led by the Ad Council, an advertising agency with "a long history of designing communications campaigns to address public issues and stimulate action" (WA_doc14, p. 6; WA_web17).

5.2.5 *Policy Agendas, Modes of Policymaking and Relations*

The process-tracing analysis of WA's engagement in policymaking processes on migration from its genesis in 2001 in Tennessee until 2019 enabled me to identify three main periods characterised by different modes of mobilisation: (1) prevailing network governance (2009–2014); (2) MLG policymaking (2014–2016); (3) network governance again (2016–2019). Table 5.1 presents the sequence of events as a process of mobilisation on the demand and supply sides of migration policymaking,

[12] NAE is a bipartisan research and advocacy organisation: https://www.newamericaneconomy.org/about/. Last accessed: 25 November 2020.

Table 5.1 WA: Causal process observations and modes of policymaking

	Causal process observations	*Modes of policymaking*
1.2009–2014	**Demand side** Collaborative agenda • Welcoming Cities and Counties • Welcoming Economies **Supply side** Request for collaboration on refugees in local communities (2012) • Partnership with ORR	Network governance Intergovernmental partnerships limited to the topic of refugees
2. 2014–2016	**Supply side** Task Force for New Americans • Involvement of cities and WA in the consultation process **Demand side** • Building Welcoming Communities programme	MLG policymaking
3. 2017–2019	**Supply side** Trump administration anti-immigration stance • Cancellation of previous programmes • End of collaboration between WA and ORR **Demand side** Programmes emphasising community work and international links • Certified communities • National Inclusion Campaign • Gateways for Growth • Welcoming International	Network Governance

consistently with the actor-centred and relational interpretative framework presented in Chapter 3.

In general, from my empirical account it emerges that over the years WA has been engaged primarily in a networking mode of policymaking, consistently with the civic engagement background of its founder David Lubell and other leaders of the organisation. In other words, WA stands out for its horizontal collaborative policy agenda, reflecting its origins as a civil society led organisation and 'movement of communities.' Favouring partnerships between different stakeholders in local communities has always been a key aim of WA projects and programmes, which as my interviewees admitted at the beginning did not pay particular attention to the role that local authorities could play in local networks. The mobilisation of municipalities and counties acquired greater relevance after collaboration with the German Marshall Fund started in 2012, leading to the Welcoming Cities and Counties programme. However, WA activists have always conceived city governments as key actors in broader local partnerships. This was clearly highlighted by the Welcoming Economies network, which includes economic development coalitions led by both public and non-profit actors, and by the emphasis that the Welcoming Standards and Certified Communities programme—a flagship WA action since 2016—puts on the engagement of non-profit and migrant groups in local welcoming policies. Hence, local policy is understood not as an endeavour of enlightened municipalities or counties but rather as a result of efforts by various actors impinging on the local community.

In this context, intergovernmental cooperation and MLG have always had secondary relevance. These modes of policymaking, as shown in Table 5.1, were undertaken primarily on solicitation from above, i.e. by the federal administration. This was the case during the Obama presidency (2009–2016). Intergovernmental cooperation clearly underpins the Welcoming Refugees Programme, which is defined on the official website as a 'cooperative agreement' with the federal Office for the Resettlement of Refugees (WA_web7), from which WA received funding between 2013 and 2017. WA committed to carry out initiatives aimed at building capacity to receive and integrate refugees in local communities through the engagement of local authorities and prominent stakeholders, including the private business sector. At least until March 2021, the website still featured the main outputs (webinars, toolkits etc.) of this collaboration and served as a repository for the resources produced using the federal grant (WA_web7).

As for MLG, this mode of policymaking is reflected in the experience of the Building Welcoming Communities Campaign. My empirical account has shown how this developed on an initiative by the White House Task Force for New Americans, which provided the overall framework for undertaking collaborative action between WA, relevant federal agencies and national NGOs. In the course of the consultation processes, WA was able to articulate an agenda on immigrant integration that, reminiscent of the initial steps of the movement in Tennessee at the beginning of the 2000s, looked beyond gateway cities and stressed the importance of welcoming in new destinations, and especially in small and medium-sized towns. According to my interviewees, this agenda represented a 'source of inspiration' for the White House, as the name of the federal campaign also seems to suggest. However, MLG not only underpinned the decision-making and policy-design phase but also characterised the implementation. In fact, the initiatives promoted by the Task Force at the same time engaged WA, representing the local authorities mobilised in the network, the Corporation of National Community Service on behalf of the federal government, the YMCA, Catholic Charities and national refugee resettlement organisations in the non-profit sector.

Vertical relations dissolved with the change of administration and the discontinuation of the policy programmes in which WA was involved. The anti-immigrant stance of the Trump presidency was strongly criticised by WA, as is shown in the position it took on the Executive Order of 27 January 2017, which by suspending the resettlement of Syrian refugees and introducing a travel ban to the US on non-citizens from seven Muslim-majority countries imposed a pause in the overall refugee resettlement programme[13]:

> We vehemently oppose any proposal or statements calling for a ban on refugees, as well as discrimination based on religion or nationality. As a nation founded in part by refugees and immigrants, these kinds of discriminatory policies dishonour our history, beliefs and values.
>
> This Executive Order will not make us safer. It simply feeds the rhetoric of fear and distrust in the United States, and marginalises new Americans who want to contribute to their new communities and country. (WA_web18)

However, apart from this statement and another regarding the ending of DACA (WA_web19), the press releases issued by WA during the years of the Trump administration avoided employing an openly contentious political tone (see: WA_web20). To face the political climate of increasing hostility to migrants and refugees, WA civil society leaders seem to have stressed even more strongly the importance of focusing on local communities and working at the grassroots level. This message is clearly conveyed

[13] The executive order was partially revised in March that same year. For an analysis of the two President Trump Executive Orders, see https://www.migrationpolicy.org/sites/default/files/publications/Trump-EO-RevisedTravelBan-FINAL.pdf.

in the *2019 Report of Activities* (WA_doc14), which celebrated 10 years since the founding of the network in 2009 by showcasing the programmes and events put in place in recent years to continue building "a movement around belonging" (p. 6), like the National Inclusion Campaign, Gateways for Growth and the Welcoming Week. Furthermore, community work seems to have also been directed at resisting and countering federal policies, as was indicated by some of the working sessions organised in the context of the 2019 Welcoming Interactive and Welcoming Economies Annual Convening[14] on topics like 'Building Resilience in Welcoming Communities' and 'Understanding and Responding to Federal Immigration Policies and Priorities.' The latter in particular engaged professional experts on federal immigration policy, primarily lawyers, to answer specific questions on law enforcement, detention and the treatment of undocumented migrants.

Another strategy underlying WA mobilisation that became particularly relevant in the aftermath of the Trump administration was messaging and communication on the positive impact of welcoming on local communities. The *Belonging Begins with US* media campaign, which started in 2019 with the Ad Council, is a clear case in point. Furthermore, again during the 2019 annual convening, panel sessions were devoted to communication-related issues, like 'Communicating Inclusion in Contentious Times' and 'Changing the Frame: Engaging Hateful Rhetoric in a Charged Political Environment.' In this process of communicating the impact of grassroots community work, data and research emerge as key resources. The workshop 'How to Use Data to Support and Advocate for Integration in Your Community,' in fact, discussed possible data sources and independent institutes that can provide useful research to make a case for Welcoming Communities.

Thus, WA's initiatives during the Trump years seem to stress the key relevance of the community dimension as a context for resistance to national restrictive laws, although without going so far as to explicitly endorse sanctuary policies. Again in the 2019 convening, WA seemed to instead put more emphasis on building a transnational movement of communities through the Welcoming International initiative, which since 2017 had been the main endeavour of its founder. A policymaking mode

[14] An overview of the programme of the Convening can be found at https://welcomingconference2019.sched.com/. The notes below are based primarily on my participation at the event, which took place in Pittsburgh on 25–26 May 2019.

based on peer-to-peer networking has therefore started to complement grassroots networking, even though community work to put in practice welcoming values and standards remains the fundamental *modus operandi* underlying the Welcoming Communities philosophy.

5.3 Cities for Action

5.3.1 *The Genesis of Cities for Action. Mayoral Leadership in Intergovernmental Relations*

Cities for Action (C4A), initially called Cities United for Immigration Action, was launched on 8 December 2014 by a group of twenty-five mayors who convened in New York City to discuss how cities could support and help implement President Obama's executive action on immigration announced in November (C4A_int1 and C4A_int2; C4A_web1, C4A_web2 and C4A_web3). More specifically, the convened mayors considered two measures particularly relevant for cities: the Extended Deferred Action for Childhood Arrivals (DACA) Programme; and the extension of Deferred Action for Parents of Americans and Lawful Permanent Residents (DAPA).[15] DACA was introduced as early as 2012 to provide temporary relief for so-called dreamers, i.e. immigrants that came to the United States as children. The Extended Action had the goal of enlarging the pool of eligible migrants. DAPA, on the other hand, was a new programme that granted a temporary reprieve from deportation to parents of US citizens and permanently resident children.

To pursue these goals, a steering committee was set up composed of the representatives of the nine most active cities: New York City, Los Angeles, Atlanta, Boston, Chicago, Philadelphia, Providence, San Francisco and Seattle (C4A_int1). From the organisational point of view, C4A was established as a programme of the Mayoral Office for Immigrant Affairs (MOIA) of New York City and was funded primarily by private foundations. It could rely on MOIA's Chief of Staff and Senior Policy Advisor, both of whom were engaged in developing and overseeing the programme strategic plan, and a dedicated C4A Programme Manager acting as the operational point of contact for the coalition.

[15] For an overview of President Obama's executive actions, see https://www.dhs.gov/archive/immigration-action. Last accessed: 14 January 2020.

Therefore, at least at the beginning C4A can be characterised as reflecting the emerging leadership of the main American cities on migration and their willingness to articulate their views and interests in national policymaking on the issue:

> The President's action on immigration will strengthen our cities. It will keep families together, grow our economies and foster additional community trust in law enforcement. We are ready – and together we're rolling up our sleeves to turn this policy into a better reality for millions of hardworking people in the communities we serve. (C4A_web1)

This statement clearly highlights the three motivations driving the mobilisation of the mayors: favouring social cohesion, boosting the local economy and fostering law enforcement through community trust. These motivations seem to have underpinned the C4A mayoral agenda in 2015 and 2016, which was essentially centred on two main topics: President Obama's executive actions and citizenship policy more generally; and federal and state policies on undocumented migrants and refugees.

Regarding the first topic, in January 2015 New York City mayor Bill de Blasio and Los Angeles mayor Eric Garcetti launched a coalition between C4A, which already counted 30 member cities, the National League of Cities and the US Conference of Mayors to file a friend-of-the-court brief in response to an order by a Texas federal judge that blocked President Obama's executive actions (*Texas vs. United States*; see C4Adoc_1 and C4Adoc_2). This was just the first of four amicus briefs handled by C4A during the litigation process, which reached the Supreme Court at the end of 2015. In each stage of the lawsuit the number of municipalities joining the action increased to include, along with the largest cities, also suburbs and rural areas. In April 2015, there were 73 cities signing the brief (C4A_doc3), at the petition stage to the Supreme Court there were over 80 signatories (C4A_doc12) and in the last brief in March 2016 to urge the Supreme Court to move forward with implementation there were 118 (C4A_doc14). The C4A arguments in support of Obama's policy regularly stressed the need to take cities' interests and points of view on migration seriously into consideration, since the coalition had broadened over time and in 2016 claimed to represent "an estimated 55million people" (C4A_doc14, p. 1).

> The cities and counties [...] argue that the district court judge who temporarily blocked implementation of the programs failed to consider the significant harms to America's local governments caused by this delay [...] the public interest across the country is served clearly and overwhelmingly by implementing immigration reform by executive action. [...] The brief also argues that the District Court judge's decision to block executive action with a preliminary injunction is bad for the economy, hurts families, threatens law enforcement priorities, and will stall desperately needed changes to the federal government's immigration policies. (C4A_doc3, pp. 1–2)
>
> Cities and counties joining the brief are seeking to advance their longstanding economic, public safety and community-based interests that are being jeopardised by the delayed implementation of the President's executive action on immigration. [...] The nationwide injunction should not have been entered in this case without any consideration of local interests and the harms to localities caused by the injunction. (C4A_doc14, p. 7)

Along with direct engagement in the long legal battle for the implementation of Obama's executive actions, C4A has also supported 'days of action,' i.e. city mobilisation events to sensitise people on DACA and DAPA like workshops, conferences and forums with migrants, information sessions with NGOs, migration movie screenings etc. These actions days took place in April 2015 during the Immigrant Heritage Week (C4A_doc5), in May 2015 (C4A_doc6) and in November 2015 to commemorate a year since the launch of President Obama's policy (C4A_doc11). Furthermore, support for the policies of the Obama administration was also expressed on the occasion of the release of the task force's final report and recommendations on New Americans, "which were shaped by contributions from cities including New York, Los Angeles, Boston and Seattle." (C4A_doc4, p. 1). Last but not least, on 17 September 2015 to celebrate Citizenship Day, C4A engaged in organising naturalisation ceremonies and other events in partnership with the White House, the National Partnership for New Americans, Cities for Citizenship, Welcoming America and other national organisations (C4A_doc7).

In the face of a decision by the Supreme Court on 23 June 2016 to uphold the injunction against Obama's executive actions, C4A confirmed its commitment "to continu[e] the fight for common-sense immigration reforms" (C4A_doc16, p. 1). In July 2016, C4A issued an open letter to the next US President entitled *Mayors and Municipal Leaders Call for Immigration Reform* (C4A_doc17) that emphasised the broad social basis of the network, representing "over 55 million people from more than half the states in the nation" "from large to small" cities and its bipartisan composition, bringing together "red states and blue states:"

> This is why we call on national leaders to take action on urgently needed immigration reform. Our country has the opportunity now to build a stronger and more inclusive society through reform that: creates a broad, humane and timely path to citizenship; supports local economic growth while protecting the rights and labor standards of all workers; upholds immigrants' due process rights and the rights of those seeking refuge; offers robust local implementation and immigrant integration support. (C4A_doc17, p. 2)

The second topic underlying C4A mobilisation in 2015–2016 was the protection of undocumented residents and refugees. This second line of action was clearly outlined in a series of C4A official statements and other documents. In October 2015, for instance, C4A issued a letter to the US Senate leaders urging opposition to legislation withholding federal funds from Sanctuary Cities (C4A_doc9). The letter also provided detailed data and information to illustrate how the proposed cuts would affect crucial social programmes for cities and negatively impact local residents in general. Furthermore, in January and May 2016, C4A expressed concern about reports of federal administration—Immigration and Customs Enforcement (ICE)—raids targeting families of adults and children from Central America in member cities, stating that "We believe that the United States must continue to be a welcoming nation that protects individuals who are fleeing persecution and violence" (C4A_doc13 and C4A_doc15). These openness and welcoming positions were echoed in several statements expressing support for President Obama's commitment to increase the overall number of refugees to be resettled in the US. A case in point is a letter issued by C4A on the occasion of Pope Francis's visit to the country on 23 September 2015:

> As the mayors of cities across the country, we see first-hand the myriad ways in which immigrants and refugees make our communities stronger economically, socially and culturally. We will welcome the Syrian families to make homes and new lives in our cities. Indeed, we are writing to say that we stand ready to work with your administration to do much more and to urge you to increase still further the number of Syrian refugees the

> United States will accept for resettlement. Our cities have been transformed by the skills and the spirit of those who come to us from around the world. The drive and enterprise of immigrants and refugees have helped build our economies, enliven our arts and culture and enrich our neighbourhoods. (C4A_doc8, p. 1)

C4A also continued to uphold these positions in the face of the terror attacks in Paris in November 2015, which were followed by restrictive statements on the part of several state governors declaring their unwillingness to accept Syrian refugees in their territory (C4A_10).

Contacts with the White House became particularly intense after the election of Donald Trump in November 2016, as testified in an open letter to President Obama published on 29 December 2016 (C4A_19). The letter reports on contacts between C4A mayors and county leaders and the White House to discuss the complete removal of the National Security Entry-Exit Registration System (NSEERS) programme, a special registration system for migrants from 25 Muslim-majority countries introduced in the aftermath of the 9/11 attacks and already suspended in many respects in 2011,[16] which was then finally removed on 23 December 2016. In the letter, C4A thanked the President for abolishing a norm perceived as discriminatory and creating "great fear and turmoil within our communities, particularly among Muslim immigrants, while not providing any increase in security" (C4A_19). Furthermore, C4A encouraged the President to continue to support immigrant communities in the last weeks of his presidency by: (1) accepting early renewal applications for DACA holders and implementing additional privacy protections to reassure recipients "that they will not be punished as a result of coming out of the shadows;" (2) extending Temporary Protection Status (TPS) "to protect immigrants from countries that recently experienced extraordinary conditions that have made return unsafe, including Haiti and Ecuador" (C4A_19).

In parallel with mayoral political statements and initiatives, C4A has also promoted the sharing of best practices and innovative programmes on issues considered of key relevance for cities, like undocumented migrants, access to services, translation services etc., "starting from the assumption that successful policies already in place in some cities can eventually

[16] https://www.dhs.gov/dhs-removes-designated-countries-nseers-registration-may-2011, last accessed 4 December 2020.

help to solve problems in other cities" (C4A_Int1). In May 2015 in New York City, C4A convened the first conference on Municipal Identification Card (ID) programmes, gathering together 28 local government officials from 22 cities and counties to share successful models and providing practical support for cities interested in this type of policy (C4A_doc18, p. 3). According to our interviewees, C4A annual meetings are attended primarily by migration commissioners and senior officers and have the very practical goal of showcasing best practices in order to help officers who are working on an issue to implement a specific policy. To this end, the New York first conference led to the publication of a toolkit on local ID policies (C4A_doc18) providing insights on specific experiences and practical information on laws and other constraints at the state and federal levels.

5.3.2 Contentious Mobilisation and Policy Learning in the Trump Era

If during the years of the Obama presidency C4A had been able to establish relations with the White House on various issues as shown above, with the entry into office of the Trump administration in January 2017 contacts ceased, reflecting the strong anti-immigrant stance of the new presidency. In this period, the C4A agenda appeared to be driven by the controversial immigration policies promoted by the White House and the Congress, as is shown by its numerous statements criticising or condemning specific acts and measures aimed at dismantling Obama programmes and/or introducing new restrictions on immigration regulation.

In fact, the new restrictive turn became clear as early as 25 January 2017. President Trump's executive order *Enhancing Public Safety in the Interior of the United States* re-defined enforcement priorities by putting all unauthorised migrants at risk of deportation, including families, long-term residents and dreamers.[17] Furthermore, the executive order required the Departments of Justice and Homeland Security (DHS) to consider stripping federal funding from sanctuary cities. C4A's reaction arrived the

[17] For an overview of the Executive Order *Enhancing Public Safety in the Interior of the United States,* see https://www.americanimmigrationcouncil.org/sites/default/files/research/summary_of_executive_order_enhancing_public_safety_in_the_interior_of_the_united_states.pdf. Last accessed: 20 December 2020.

same day and vocally restated the mission of the network to advocate for inclusive policies.

> Today's executive orders do not change who we are or how we govern our cities, and we will fight against attempts to undermine our values and the security of our cities. Representing cities and counties across the country, we are united in our commitment to remain inclusive cities, providing for the public safety of all. As mayors and county executives nationwide have made clear today, we will continue to provide for all in our communities – regardless of where they come from – and work to continue building trust between city residents and law enforcement. (C4A_doc21)

Trump's executive order was challenged in the Federal Court by the county of Santa Clara and the city and county of San Francisco on the grounds of violating the division of powers between jurisdictions and the Constitution more generally. The Court's decision ruling in favour of local authorities was welcomed by C4A as sending the "clear message that the Trump administration goes beyond its authority with threats to withhold vital funding to municipalities" (C4A_doc27). However, the introduction of measures sanctioning sanctuary cities continued to be discussed in Congress. On 28 June 2017, C4A took a position on the *No Sanctuary for Criminals Act* (Bill 3003), in discussion in the House of Representatives, which threatened to withhold national funding for various social programmes from cities not cooperating with national immigration enforcement. In a letter to Congress, C4A asserted that "these bills undercut localities' public safety efforts, hinder local law enforcement's ability to keep communities safe, and threaten to separate families" (C4A_doc30). The approval of the bill the next day was condemned by C4A for "unjustly targeting immigrant communities and the cities that welcome them" (C4A_doc31).

A second controversial Trump administration decision prompting C4A mobilisation was Executive Order no. 13769 of 27 January 2017 entitled *Protecting the Nation from Foreign Terrorist Entry into the United States*, also known as the 'travel ban.' This executive order lowered the number of refugees to be admitted into the US in 2017 to 50,000, indefinitely suspended the admission of Syrian refugees and more generally suspended entries from Iran, Iraq, Libya, Somalia, Sudan, Syria and Yemen. In February, C4A announced that 34 cities and counties 'representing 23 million people' had filed a local government amicus brief in support of the plaintiffs in the *Darweesh v. Trump* case (C4A_doc22 and C4A_doc23). The arguments put forward by the group of cities, which however did not represent all the C4A members, emphasised the harm caused by the ban "to millions of residents by interfering with local economies, immigrant integration and public safety efforts" (C4A_doc22 and C4A_doc23, p. 1). The President introduced a second travel band on 7 March 2017 (Executive Order no. 138780). This was again condemned by C4A (C4A_doc24), which issued a report on the responses put forward by the main international airports to face the consequences of the ban on families and travellers from targeted countries (C4A_doc25). The report emphasised the contribution of local officials in facilitating communication among family members and with volunteer attorneys, customs officials and Congressional representatives:

> The response was successful because of advocacy from a range of stakeholders, coordination of lawyers and elected officials by mayors' offices, and strategic communication through traditional and social media channels. Based on the January events, cities are recommended to deepen relationships with local advocates, elected officials and attorneys for future coordinated efforts, and to develop and utilise a social media plan during rapid response situations. Mayors' offices are also recommended to create an office of immigrant affairs or designate dedicated immigration staff members. (C4A_doc26, p. 10)

Even though federal judges intervened by blocking the entry into effect of parts of the second ban (C4A_doc25) and some C4A members joined several amicus briefs against the ban, in June 2018 the Supreme Court decided to uphold the executive orders. C4A expressed disappointment while re-stating its commitment "to [build] inclusive communities and [protect] the rights of our Muslim and immigrant neighbours" (C4A_doc42).

Chronologically, a third controversial issue in the Trump period regarded the extension of temporary protection status (TPS) to specific groups of migrants threatened with deportation. In May 2017, C4A issued a letter to the then Secretary of Homeland Security John Kelly and Secretary of State Rex Tillerson urging them to extend TPS for the Haitian community (C4A_doc28). Other letters followed this regarding Hondurans and Nicaraguans in November (C4A_doc34), Salvadorans and Syrians in January 2018 (C4A_doc37 and C4A_doc38) and Yemenis and Somalis in June and July respectively (C4A_doc43 and C4A_doc44). Whereas for South Americans the letters emphasised the contribution these migrants made to the economy and their enduring ties with local communities, including the presence of children born in the US at risk of being separated from their families, humanitarian arguments prevailed in the case of refugees from the Middle East. Negative decisions by the President were condemned as 'inhumane' in the case of Nicaraguans and Hondurans (C4A_doc35 and C4A_doc40), 'abhorrent' in that of Haitians (C4A_doc36) and 'cruel and counter-productive' in the case of Salvadorans (C4A_doc37). Equally condemned in October 2019 was the decision to further curtail the annual ceiling of refugee admissions from 30,000 entries in 2019 to 18,000 in 2020,[18] the lowest annual refugee cap ever. C4A stated its disappointment was motivated by a mix of humanitarian and economic arguments (C4A_doc45 and C4A_doc 51):

> Mayors and county executives support the U.S. Refugee Admissions Program because it saves lives and enriches communities. Refugees and their families contribute to public life and cultural institutions and fill jobs in a variety of key U.S. industries, including manufacturing, lumber, hospitality and food production. (C4A_doc51)

A fourth matter of contention with the Trump administration was the rescission in June 2017 of President Obama's deferred action policy for dreamers and their parents, i.e. the expanded DACA and DAPA programmes (C4A_doc29), even though the original DACA remained in place. On 15 August, DACA's fifth anniversary, C4A issued a letter calling on the President to continue the programme until a legislative solution was enacted for all undocumented immigrant young people (C4A_doc32). However, on 5 September President Trump announced his intention to terminate DACA. This was immediately condemned by C4A, which called on Congress to take immediate action and make a "bipartisan effort" to approve a legislative solution (C4A_doc33 and C4A_doc39). On 5 June 2018, a letter signed by 110 C4A mayors was sent to Congress to urge the approval of the so-called *American*

[18] For an overview of refugee admissions in the US, see https://www.migrationpolicy.org/programs/data-hub/charts/us-annual-refugee-resettlement-ceilings-and-number-refugees-admitted-united#:~:text=For%20FY%202019%2C%20the%20number,the%20lowest%20level%20on%20record. Last accessed: 20 December 2020.

Dream and Promise Act, which would provide dreamers with a path to citizenship (C4A_doc41). In fact, although court decisions had allowed DACA recipients to apply for their status to be renewed, the signatory mayors lamented that uncertainty over the future of the programme was preventing DACA holders from applying. The passage of the act in the House of Representatives on 19 June 2019 was commended by C4A for bringing "dignity and safety to millions" (C4A_doc49). According to our interviewees, ensuring access to DACA by providing eligible migrants with support and information was a key priority for the cities engaged in C4A during the Trump years (C4A_int1 and C4A_int2), as was also testified by the publication in 2020 of a toolkit entitled *Cities for Daca—Resource Guide for Daca Recipients and Impacted Communities*[19] (C4A_doc52).

In 2018, two more contentious issues emerged on the C4A agenda: the so-called public charge rule and the family separation crisis. The 'public charge' rule is the principle according to which, under Section 212(a)(4) of the Immigration and Nationality Act (INA), an alien seeking admission to the United States or seeking to become a permanent resident (obtain a Green Card) is inadmissible if "at the time of application for admission or adjustment of status, [he/she] is likely at any time to become a public charge." In September 2018, President Trump put forward a proposal to define public charge in more restrictive terms. An alien was to be considered a 'public charge' if he/she had received one or more public benefits for more than twelve months in total over a period of 36 months.[20] C4A denounced this measure as 'a back-door immigration ban' (C4A_doc48). Introduced on 12 August 2019, the 'public charge' rule change was condemned by C4A as a 'draconian and wrongheaded rule' (C4A_doc49) penalising both migrant families and local economies:

> By forcing immigrants and their families to make a choice between obtaining permanent residency and utilising public programs that support health, nutrition and economic security, this proposal would deal immigrant communities a harsh blow, particularly the elderly and people

[19] At the time I carried out interviews on C4A the DACA guide was under preparation.

[20] For details, see https://www.uscis.gov/news/public-charge-fact-sheet#:~:text=Introduction,become%20a%20lawful%20permanent%20resident. Last accessed: 20 December 2020.

> with disabilities. It would stand to increase poverty and inequality among already vulnerable populations and damage our local economies. (C4A_doc50)

As for the 2018 family separation crisis, together with the Lumos Foundation C4A compiled a report outlining best practices in dealing with separated children in New York City, in the city and county of Los Angeles and San Antonio (C4A_doc46 and C4A_doc47). While emphasising the key role played by mayors in raising public awareness, the report, entitled *On the Frontline of the Family Separation Crisis—City Response and Best Practices for Assisting Families*, also stressed the importance of local networks of legal service providers and local partnerships in sharing information and coordinating outreach and service delivery (C4A_doc47, p. 4).

Thus, along with advocacy in favour of migrants' rights and against restrictive national policies, local officials continued to collaborate on best practices and policy innovation exchange, as is shown in the reports on local actions concerning the family separation issue and the consequences of the travel ban. Furthermore, issues such as DACA, temporary protection status, the public charge rule change and services for separated families were at the centre of the two C4A convenings held in 2019 in Atlanta (May, see: C4A_web5) and Seattle (September, see: C4A_web6).

Furthermore, in 2018 C4A engaged in collecting signatories for the 2018 Marrakech mayoral declaration 'Cities Working Together for Migrants and Refugees,' which was adopted at the 5th Mayoral Forum for Human Mobility, Migration and Development on 8 December 2018 (C4A_web4). Our interviewees stressed the coordinating role played by the New York City MOIA in this process (C4A_int1 and C4A_int3). Thanks to this, migration officers and commissioners from C4A member cities were able to contribute to the drafting of the declaration, contributing their perspective on how to support the rights and dignity of migrants and refugees around the world.

5.3.3 Policy Agendas, Modes of Policymaking and Relations

The analysis above shows that over the years C4A has enacted a double-edged agenda. On the one hand, mayors have articulated political advocacy on critical policy issues, responding reactively and pro-actively to the implementation of federal policy at the local level; on the other hand, local officials, and more specifically immigration commissioners and senior officers, have engaged in policy learning and exchange of best practices to support effective local policy solutions. The two agendas, which have being developing in parallel, reflect a persistent mode of policymaking characterised by a matching of contentious political advocacy on the part of mayors with peer-to-peer networking on the part of city officers, as is illustrated in Table 5.2.

Regarding the mayoral agenda, it has primarily involved mobilisation on the vertical dimension and has been marked by a high level of contentiousness. More specifically, rather than seeking collaboration, city mayors have engaged in affirming their city leadership vis-à-vis other government authorities and institutions in the US federal system. By building a broad coalition of local political leaders, C4A has sought to lend legitimacy to a vision of migration policymaking as essentially and inherently city-centred. This vision was clearly stated in various documents and interviews:

Table 5.2 C4A: Causal process observations on modes of policymaking

	Causal process observations	*Modes of policymaking*
1. 2014–2016	**Demand side** Mayoral leadership agenda • Amicus briefs • Public statements supporting/criticising federal and/or state policies • City models and best practices (developed by city officers) **Supply side** Cooperation on specific issues • Citizenship Day initiatives • Removal of the NSEERS programme	Political advocacy and lobbying (Limited) intergovernmental cooperation
2. 2017–2019	**Supply side** Trump administration anti-immigrant stance **Demand side** Mayoral progressive leadership • Amicus briefs against federal orders • Public statements and letters criticising federal/state policies • City models and best practices	Contentious political advocacy

> Over the past two years, more than 100 cities and counties have advocated for inclusive immigration policies and programs. Our cities and counties – representing over 55 million people across the country – are leveraging our resources and power to push for the changes our communities deserve. As we transition to a new presidential administration, Cities for Action mayors and county executives renew their commitment to driving the national debate, embracing new immigrants and engaging with stakeholders to win on immigration policies. (C4A_doc20)
>
> Because large numbers of immigrants reside in cities, C4A is well positioned to understand and advocate for the needs of diverse immigrant populations in urban environments. C4A members in smaller cities and counties help represent the perspectives of smaller and even rural communities. [...] It's important for mayors and county executives across the United States to take a stand on important issues like global migration because city officials are best placed to understand the challenges and solutions associated with migration in urban environments. (C4A_web3)

During the Obama administration, C4A's city-centred vision of migration policy resulted primarily in actions providing support for President Obama's inclusion strategy, as for instance in the friend-of-the-court briefs issued in favour of the President's executive orders and the 'action days' organised to sensitise people on DACA and DAPA. Certain forms of intergovernmental collaboration with the White House were also established, as in the case of the celebration of Citizenship Day and the removal of the National Security Entry-Exit Registration System (NSEERS) programme. However, C4A also took a critical stance on ICE raids and on attempts by states to sanction sanctuary cities, arguing that these policies risked jeopardising local communities by threatening social cohesion and migrants' contributions to the local economy and therefore did not sufficiently take into account local authorities' perspectives on the issues.

Contentious mobilisation clearly prevailed in the years of the Trump administration. C4A took part in legal battles around the more controversial anti-immigrant policies promoted by the new administration and issued various letters and statements showing how these policies went against the interests and needs of local communities. However, in taking a more confrontational stance towards the President, C4A seems to some extent to have lost the unity and internal consensus that had characterised support for President Obama's policies. Although my interviewees always stressed the bipartisan character of the network, official documents seem to reveal a different picture. In fact, the amicus briefs and the letters and petitions taking positions against Trump measures appear to have been supported by a more limited number of mayors than before, and primarily by mayors sharing a progressive approach to migration and in most cases affiliated with the Democratic party. In other words, in the context of the troublesome Trump years C4A seems to have acted as an organisation of 'like-minded' cities articulating a progressive political agenda on migration based on a combination of humanitarian principles and pragmatic considerations on the contribution of immigrants to local economies as workers and taxpayers.

Regarding the more technical agenda developed by City Commissioners and senior officials, the aim has always been to provide data and evidence on city models and best practices to support mayors' political advocacy. Through the organisation of annual conferences and regular meetings, and of more informal relations on a workaday basis, a peer-to-peer networking mode of policymaking emerged. In other words, municipal migration offices in different cities, actively coordinated by New York City's MOIA, have been able to develop regular routines for exchanging best practices and sharing expertise on local migration policy, creating a sort of community of practice (see Sect. 2.2.2).

Thus, overall, C4A engagement in policymaking on migration seems to have been characterised by a persistent pattern of contentious hierarchical relations, in which cities perceive themselves as subject to federal and state jurisdictions yet not totally subordinated, which enables them to articulate a distinct vision of migration policy as grounded in local practices and grassroots knowledge of what 'really works.' This perception is supported by intense peer-to-peer networking between local officials. Non-public stakeholders, while acknowledged as important actors in official reports and best practice collections, appear at the margins of C4A policy relationships. In this context, no traces of MLG policymaking have been found. The recent involvement of C4A in the Mayoral Migration Forum seems instead to signal an interest in engaging in global migration policymaking, and therefore to raise the voices of cities beyond US-centred and contentious intergovernmental relations.

5.4 Comparative Insights

WA and C4A are considered by US scholars on local migration policies to be part of the broader welcoming movement that started to take hold in the early 2010s through the mobilisation of grassroots organisations and municipalities on immigrant inclusion issues. However, as the in-depth analyses above show, the two organisations could not be more different. Whereas WA arose from civil society mobilisation in local communities, to engage only in a second step with municipalities, C4A is an expression of mayoral leadership and reflects the system of contentious intergovernmental relationships underlying migration enforcement in the US.

It therefore comes as no surprise that the two CNs are characterised by very different policy agendas and modes of engaging in policymaking processes. WA has clearly privileged mobilisation on the horizontal dimension to establish broad partnerships between public actors, non-profit organisations, immigrant groups and the like in order to build a movement of welcoming communities able to change perceptions and migration policies from the bottom up. In contrast, C4A has mobilised primarily on the vertical dimension to articulate mayoral leadership and vision on migration enforcement and integration policy vis-à-vis the White House and state governors. In other words, C4A can be better characterised as an organisation engaged in various forms of political advocacy, from raising awareness of the role of local authorities in facing the consequences of federal migration policies to lobbying on specific legislation such as DACA, the removal of the National Security Entry-Exit Registration System and Temporary Protection Status etc.

MLG, understood as the establishment of collaborative relations on both the vertical and horizontal dimensions, does not seem to feature in the agendas of the two CN organisations. However, as my reconstruction above highlighted, WA has been engaged in instances of intergovernmental cooperation and MLG initiated by national-level authorities, i.e. the ORR and the Task Force for New Americans respectively. Both initiatives were promoted by the Obama administration, which indeed showed considerable interest in coordinating policies on immigrant inclusion across various levels of government and collaborating with NGOs. The task force report *Strengthening Communities by Welcoming all Residents*, published in April 2015 (WA_doc6), provides interesting details on the consultations carried out between January and March 2015 to draft the *Federal Strategic Action Plan on Immigrant and Refugee Integration*. WA, defined in the report as a "national, grassroots-driven collaborative fostering mutual respect and cooperation between foreign-born and native-born Americans," was involved in at least two meetings, while no specific mention is made of C4A (pp. 55–57). Cities were indeed part of the process, as is shown by the mention in the report of meetings with the executive of Montgomery County and with the mayors of Los Angeles, Boise (Idhao) and Beaverton (Oregon) to discuss the efforts of these local authorities "to integrate New Americans and ways that national service programs can contribute" (p. 57). Furthermore, as C4A stated, contributions to the plan were provided by New York City, Boston and Seattle (C4A_doc4). However, whereas WA participated in MLG coordination around the implementation of the Federal Plan actions, C4A was not involved in this process.

Thus, MLG and intergovernmental collaborative relations in the US emerge essentially as moves from above, and more specifically from the White House, to which a grassroots organisation like WA seems to have responded more pro-actively than the mayor-led C4A network. Furthermore, as is clear, these attempts were carried out during the Obama period, when the President clearly expressed his willingness to establish a governance structure on the highly pitched migration issue. This was certainly not the case during the Trump administration, as our analysis has shown. To this changed political context, marked by the closure of any communication channels between local authorities and the White House on migration policy, the two networks reacted in different manners. On the one hand, WA strengthened even more its engagement with local communities and its grassroots work while avoiding taking an explicit position on federal migration policy, with the exception of critical statements on President Trump's more controversial initiatives (see above). C4A, in contrast, continued to vocally advocate for political reforms and pro-immigrant policies, often taking a highly confrontational stance vis-à-vis the White House, even at the risk of losing some of the enlarged consensus and bipartisan membership that had characterised the network in the previous years.

Notwithstanding the different strategies undertaken by the two networks in the face of the new political climate, a common development can be pointed out, i.e. internationalisation. In fact, between 2017 and 2018 both networks started to go international, although in different ways: WA by supporting the building of new city-to-city relations in different countries under the aegis of the so-called Welcoming International programme; C4A by deploying, under the leadership of New York City, US mayors' global activism in the Mayoral Migration Forum. These international developments seem to have reconfigured the field of city networking in the US, from being centred on domestic horizontal and vertical relations towards a more outward-oriented governance.

References

Bauder, H. (2017). Sanctuary cities: Policies and practices in international perspective. *International Migration, 55*, 174–187. https://doi.org/10.1111/imig.12308

Bloemraad, I., & de Graauw, E. (2013). Diversity and Laissez-Faire integration in the United States. In P. Spoonley & E. Tolley (Eds.), *Diverse nations, diverse responses: Approaches to social cohesion in immigrant societies* (pp. 35–57). McGill-Queen's University Press.

Colbern, A., & Ramakrishnan, S. K. (2018). Citizens of California: How the golden state went from worst to first on immigrant rights. *New Political Science, 40*, 353–367. https://doi.org/10.1080/07393148.2018.1449065

de Graauw, E. (2019). City immigrant affairs offices in the United States: Taking local control of immigrant integration. In T. Caponio, P. Scholten, & R. Zapata-Barrero (Eds.), *The Routledge handbook of the governance of migration and diversity in cities* (pp. 169–181). Routledge.

Filomeno, F. A. (2017). *Theories of local immigration policy*. Palgrave Macmillan.

Gulasekaram, P., & Ramakrishnan, S. K. (2015). *The new immigration federalism*. Cambridge University Press.

Huang, X., & Liu, C. Y. (2018). Welcoming cities: Immigration policy at the local government level. *Urban Affairs Review, 54*, 3–32. https://doi.org/10.1177/1078087416678999

Kuge, J. (2020). Countering illiberal geographies through local policy? The political effects of sanctuary cities. *Territory, Politics, Governance, 8*, 43–59. https://doi.org/10.1080/21622671.2019.1604255

McDaniel, P. (2014). *Revitalization in the heartlanf of America: Welcoming immigrant entrepreneurs for economic development*. American Immigration Council, Immigration Policy Center, Washington, D.C.

McDaniel, P. N., Rodriguez, D. X., & Wang, Q. (2019). Immigrant integration and receptivity policy formation in welcoming cities. *Journal of Urban Affairs, 41*, 1142–1166. https://doi.org/10.1080/07352166.2019.1572456

Peri, G. (2010). *The impact of immigrants in recession and economic expansion*. Migration Policy Institute.

Ridgley, J. (2008). Cities of refuge: Immigration enforcement, police, and the insurgent genealogies of citizenship in U.S. Sanctuary Cities. *Urban Geography, 29*, 53–77. https://doi.org/10.2747/0272-3638.29.1.53

Rodriguez, D. X., McDaniel, P. N., & Ahebee, M.-D. (2018). Welcoming America: A case study of municipal immigrant integration, receptivity, and community practice. *Journal of Community Practice, 26*, 348–357. https://doi.org/10.1080/10705422.2018.1477081

Varsanyi, M. W., Lewis, P., Provine, D. M., & Decker, S. (2017). Immigration policing practices in new destinations. In S. Chambers, D. Evans, A. M. Messina, & A. F. Williamson (Eds.), *The politics of new immigrant destinations: Translatantic perspectives* (pp. 225–247). Temple University Press.

Williamson, A. F. (2018). *Welcoming new Americans? local governments and immigrant incorporation*. University of Chicago Press.

CHAPTER 6

City Networks, Migration and Multilevel Governance. Making Sense of a (Missing) Nexus

Abstract In this chapter, I present the results of the transatlantic cross-case comparison carried out in the previous chapters with the aim of assessing the validity of the interpretations presented in the literature, and I draw conclusions on the explanatory leverage of the actor-centred and relational interpretative framework for the CN-MLG nexus. On this basis, I discuss the contribution of my study to ongoing debates on MLG (6.3) and on the role of CNs in the governance of global challenges and migration more specifically (6.4). I finally identify perspectives and venues for possible future developments in research on MLG, cities and migration in the context of the (post-) COVID-19 pandemic and new emerging challenges for policymakers.

6.1 The CN-MLG Nexus. Towards a Comparative Synthesis

In a context like that in which this book has been written, i.e. that of the pandemic crisis, an attempt to overcome the nation-state thinking of old times might seem all the more urgent and necessary. Not only have national governments shown their incapacity to deal with a continually changing and fluid epidemic situation, but also supranational and international institutions like the EU and WHO, which were established by states to deal with complex regional and global coordination problems, seem to have fallen short in providing credible solutions. The temptation could

T. Caponio, *Making Sense of the Multilevel Governance of Migration*, https://doi.org/10.1007/978-3-030-82551-5_6

be to turn to cities and to their international and global connections as a possible way out, as scholars have suggested with respect to the environmental (Kemmerzell, 2019) and refugee crises (Oomen, 2020; Thouez, 2020).

If it is undeniable that cities have hands-on knowledge that might help craft sound pragmatic solutions in different local situations, from the analysis carried out in this book the political implications of city engagement in national and international network organisations should not be overlooked. Migration and mobility are 'wicked' policy issues suitable to be interpreted and framed in very different ways by the multiple actors interacting in local decision-making processes. Not only is the city far from being a unitary actor, and power is as conterminous with local policymaking as it is at the national level, but also the networks that articulate the voices of cities are complex arenas where different actors and agendas are at play. By problematizing the role of cities and their networks in policymaking processes on the highly politicised migration issue, in this book I have engaged in unravelling concrete modes of policymaking. In other words, beyond discourses emphasising collaboration and consensus-building, I have attempted to delve in more depth into the practices concretely put in place by CNs to affirm their role as policymakers in the multilevel political dynamics on migration and mobility.

More specifically, three questions have underlain this study. Why do cities get together to coordinate their efforts and policies on typical matters of state sovereignty such as migration and mobility? Are these coordination efforts from below leading to the emergence of a new multilevel governance of migration? And, in the affirmative, which are the key factors and mechanisms accounting for the emergence of a CN-MLG nexus?

To answer, I have proposed a conceptualisation of MLG as an *instance* or mode of policymaking (Alcantara et al., 2016) in which CNs can be involved, along with other possible modes, i.e. intergovernmental collaboration, network governance and hierarchical relations. In this perspective, the distinctiveness of MLG lies in the simultaneous occurrence of three conditions: (1) different levels of government are simultaneously involved; (2) non-government actors at different levels are also involved; (3) relationships defy existing hierarchies and take the form of non-hierarchical networks (Piattoni, 2010; see also Caponio & Jones-Correa, 2018). This conceptualisation enables us to avoid vague definitions of MLG such as dispersion of power across multiple levels while at the same time it moves beyond approaches that constrain the concept to the boundaries of a specific multilevel system like the EU. As was argued in Chapter 2, the instances approach finally allows for a meaningful comparison of MLG policymaking across different multilevel political systems.

It is against this background that in this book I have proposed an original comparative study of CN engagement in policymaking on migration in two different multi-layered institutional contexts, i.e. the EU supranational polity and the US federal system, to throw light on the concrete relations established on the vertical and horizontal dimensions from their founding up to 2019. More specifically, the study has pursued the double aim of: (1) assessing the validity of the hypotheses on the nexus between migration CNs and MLG that can be derived from existing literature; and (2) unravelling under-explored causal factors and mechanisms underlying the emergence of this nexus in different multilevel institutional contexts. To this end, I have used a theory-building process-tracing method, understood as a creative iterative process of moving back and forth between empirical probing and theorisation in which inference is based on cross-case comparison of within-case causal mechanisms and configurations of factors (Beach & Pedersen, 2019).

As was argued in Sect. 3.4, whereas existing literature on the CN-MLG nexus in migration policymaking tends to emphasise the EU opportunity structure or alternatively problem pressure, it is my contention that the key mechanisms linking CNs to MLG are primarily of a political kind. These regard: (1) CN internal migration policy agendas; and (2) the political approach of national governments to the sensitive migration issue. In other words, MLG is not a politics-free mode of governing migration but is instead highly politics-dependent. CNs engagement in MLG on the highly topical migration issue is the result of a contingent process of converging interests and views between political actors, both within network organisations and with respect to national governments, which play a key gatekeeping role. International and supranational organisations can provide important resources. However, MLG policymaking does not take place simply in the "shadow of the hierarchy" (Börzel, 2010) but first and foremost at the will of national governments.

Below, in Sect. 6.2, I start by considering the explanatory leverage of propositions drawn from the literature, and then—in Sect. 6.3—I turn to an assessment of the actor-centred and relational interpretative framework proposed in Chapter 3 and to throwing new light on the 'political work' underlying the emergence of a CN-MLG nexus in the migration policy field. In Sect. 6.4 I elaborate on the implications of this study for the MLG literature, while in Sect. 6.5 I explore its possible contribution to studies on CNs. Section 6.6 delves into future research paths and open questions on cities, MLG and migration.

6.2 Prevailing Explanations: The EU Opportunity Structure and Problem Pressure

As was discussed in Chapter 3, the few available studies on the nexus between CNs and MLG in the migration policy field take either a top-down or a bottom-up perspective and emphasise the importance of two different explanatory factors. The top-down approach stresses the importance of the EU opportunity structure while the bottom-up approach suggests that MLG policymaking reflects efforts by local governments to establish collaborative relations and coordinate policy solutions on particularly worrisome migration-related challenges. Table 6.1 unpacks and specifies the expected causal process observations for the two hypotheses

Table 6.1 Research hypotheses, expected causal process observations and research evidence

Hypothesis	*Expected causal process observations*	*Research evidence*
H1. EU opportunity structure	1. EU-based CNs involved in MLG 2. No engagement of US CNs in MLG	1. Prevailing intergovernmental cooperation + very recent engagement in MLG (after 2015) 2. WA also involved in MLG in 2015–2016
H2. Problem pressure	1. CNs directly established by cities, i.e. WGM&I and C4A, will exert pressure to set up MLG venues and initiatives 2. CNs established by NGOs like WA will show a moderate mobilisation in MLG policymaking 3. No MLG engagement in the case of ICC	1. No. This reflects in part the case of the WGM&I but does not apply to C4A 2. Yes, but MLG was not an initiative from below 3. No, ICC has promoted a MLG agenda since 2016

(see also Table 3.2) and shows the main research findings regarding each expected observation.

H1 looks at MLG as a specific outcome of the EU sui-generis political system in which the European Commission attempts to strengthen its legitimacy on migration-related issues by establishing direct relations with city governments that bypass national governments. Thus, the key causal factors identified by these accounts are EU programmes and funding for migrant integration policies and the reception and integration of refugees like the INTI (Integration of Third Country Nationals) programme from 2004 to 2006, the EIF (European Integration Fund) and the ERF (European Refugee Fund) from 2007 to 2013. According to Penninx (2015, p. 107), "For the European Commission as a policymaker, these funds are important, since they create direct relations between the EU and local and regional authorities (and their policies) on the one hand, and non-governmental society partners at all levels on the other." Against the background of this constellation, the argument goes, new networks of European cities came into existence after 2004.

Building on these premises, we should expect to find CNs in the EU to be engaged in lively MLG-like policymaking venues and initiatives since 2004, while on the contrary these types of relationships should be almost absent in the US. However, my results as shown in Table 6.1 are more mixed. In fact, my reconstruction of migration CN modes of policymaking in the EU shows a prevailing pattern of intergovernmental relations taking the form of partnerships between supranational authorities—and more specifically the EC and in the case of ICC also the Council of Europe—and CNs. This partnership does not extend to non-governmental organisations, which are eventually included only in the implementation phase at a local level. Some instances of MLG-like policymaking seem to have taken place much later than 2004. In fact, this was the case in 2015 of the Partnership for the Integration of Migrants and Refugees with respect to the WGM&I, which was established by the City of Amsterdam and the EC in the context of the Urban Agenda for the EU, while in the case of ICC, MLG policymaking started to take place in 2016 with the launch of the Policy Labs. At about the same time, in 2015 an instance of MLG policymaking also took place in the US, as is indicated by the extensive process of consultation and collaborative decision-making undertaken by President Obama's Task Force for New Americans.

As is clear, the thesis of a particular MLG mode of policymaking characterising the EU system as opposed to the US does not seem to hold. The timing of the emergence of MLG policymaking in both the EU and the US, i.e. around 2015, might signal a greater explanatory leverage of H2. These were the years of the refugee crisis in Europe, while in the US scholars have emphasised the crisis caused by the stalemate of migration reforms in a deadlocked Congress (Newton, 2018; Williamson, 2018), with cities having to respond to an increasing number of undocumented immigrants residing within their jurisdictions. According to H2, to face such challenges cities will start to collaborate with each other and with NGOs to exchange best practices and promote mutual learning. In a second step, following the process described by Scholten et al. (2018), CNs and non-governmental actors will put pressure on other government authorities to coordinate policy efforts and find effective collaborative solutions. MLG-like instances of policymaking will arise as a consequence of interactions established by CNs through conferences, consultation processes, open letters and the like.

As is shown in Table 6.1, the expectation is that engagement in bottom-up MLG processes should be particularly intense in the case of the WGM&I in Europe and C4A in the US, since these are networks directly established by cities and for cities, and therefore reflect their interests, concerns and efforts to search for effective solutions. Some attempts to establish MLG interactions might also be expected in the case of a CN promoted by an NGO like WA, given its roots in local communities and engagement with municipalities. ICC, instead, represents a least likely case for MLG in the context of H2, since this CN was promoted top-down by an international organisation and its agenda can be expected to reflect priorities that are not linked with municipalities' grassroots work on migration issues.

Again, the evidence is mixed and does not fully support the bottom-up interpretation of CN engagement in MLG policymaking. More specifically, as was reported in Sect. 4.3, C4A does not seem to have been particularly active in pursuing policy collaboration either on the vertical or the horizontal dimension. On the vertical dimension, C4A's agenda has pursued mayoral leadership rather than collaboration with states and/or the federal government, leading to an intense engagement in political advocacy and, in the Trump period, contentious mobilisation. On the horizontal dimension, peer-to-peer networking among city officials, while feeding city-to-city policy-learning exercises, had primarily the aim of legitimising the mayors' agenda and their claims for a city-centred approach to migration, while collaboration with non governmental actors appears on the overall limited.

As for the WGM&I, on the other hand, the refugee crisis indeed spurred city mobilisation, as evidenced by the Solidarity Cities initiative, yet this took a highly contentious tone and, similarly to C4A, put mayoral leadership to the fore. More specifically, mayors pursued a strategy of political advocacy rather than seeking collaboration on the horizontal and vertical dimensions of MLG policymaking. The collaboration of the city of Amsterdam in setting up and coordinating the Partnership for the Integration of Migrants and Refugees, as mentioned above, might be regarded as testifying to the emergence of a city-led multilevel cooperative agenda. However, my in-depth reconstruction in Sect. 4.3 revealed that the Urban Agenda initiative was essentially promoted by the Dutch government in the context of its presidency of the European Council. The city of Amsterdam indeed represented an important policy broker bringing cities' representatives to the table. However, looking in more depth at the mode of engagement of the WGM&I within the Partnership, lobbying prevailed. More specifically, collaboration was sought with DG Home on the introduction of the so-called conditionality principle, which required national governments to coordinate with local authorities in order for them to benefit from AMIF funding. NGOs were not involved at all in this process.

Last but not least, H2 does not seem to hold for the two control cases, i.e. WA and ICC. First of all, WA engagement in MLG policymaking took place in the context of a top-down government initiative, since the Task Force for New Americans was promoted by the White House. As for ICC, which according to the bottom-up approach should represent a least likely case of MLG, on the contrary, as mentioned above, this CN turns out to have been particularly active in promoting specific venues for MLG cooperation, i.e. the Policy Labs. The MLG agenda crafted by the CoE Secretariat and experts in the aftermath of the refugee crisis seems, however, to have only been mildly welcomed by cities, which were more interested in engaging in political advocacy vis-à-vis national governments.

Hence, a preliminary conclusion that can be drawn from the discussion so far is that MLG is more of a top-down move which CNs are invited to take part in, as in the cases of the Urban Agenda for the EU and the Task Force for New Americans (on these two cases see also: Caponio, 2021), than the result of city and CN bottom-up mobilisation. Furthermore, as is shown by the case of ICC, MLG can be pursued by a specific category of actors within the network, i.e. the CoE Secretariat and experts, without necessarily reflecting cities' priorities. A more complex mechanism of interaction between the demand and supply sides of MLG seems to be at play.

6.3 An Actor-Centred and Relational Interpretative Framework for the CNs-MLG Link

As has been argued throughout this book and in more detail in Chapter 3, to make sense of the CN-MLG nexus I build on a pluralistic approach to cities and CNs as arenas rather than monolithic entities. In other words, following Payre (2010) and others (see Bassens et al., 2019) who take an urban sociology approach to the study of city network mobilisation, I look at the 'political work' taking place within CN organisations and how it interacts with the 'political work' of other key policymakers and stakeholders operating in a given institutional context and vis-à-vis specific migration challenges. Table 6.2 presents a first assessment of the expectations of the causal factors and mechanisms leading to the emergence of a CN-MLG nexus in the actor-centred and relational interpretative framework (see also Table 3.3) based on the findings of the structured narratives presented in Chapters 4 and 5.

First of all, it might seem quite obvious that the emergence of a CN-MLG nexus implies that there are CNs actively mobilised in the migration policy field. However, the mere presence of CNs is not a sufficient condition for MLG to take place. In fact, the analyses conducted in Chapters 4 and 5 show that CNs are not necessarily oriented to promoting MLG policymaking but instead can pursue very different policy agendas. Meaningful MLG relations will emerge when a CN's agenda aimed at establishing multiple collaborative relations encounters a 'window of opportunity' provided by gatekeepers having the political willingness to engage in MLG on the politically sensitive migration issue. National governments have a key role in this respect, even though supranational institutions like the European Commission and the Council of Europe can provide relevant symbolic and material support for setting up MLG-like venues.

More specifically, with respect to the demand side, my research shows the emergence of three agendas: (1) a primarily

Table 6.2 The actor-centred and relational framework. Expected causal process observations and research evidence

	Causal factors and mechanisms	*Expected causal process observations*	*Research evidence*
Demand side	CNs articulating agendas aimed at establishing collaborative relations on the vertical and horizontal dimensions of multilevel policymaking processes	1. CN leaders as brokers (rather than contenders) 2. Policy actions actively promoting multiple collaborations	1. WA and ICC 2. More in the case of WA and ICC than WGM&I; not at all in the case of C4A
Supply side or gatekeepers	Gatekeepers' interest in establishing MLG policymaking on migration-related issues, i.e – Supportive supranational/international organisations AND/OR – Supportive national governments or at least interest and willingness to engage	1. Discourses explicitly endorsing MLG policymaking 2. Actions, like platforms, consultation processes etc., to put MLG into effect 3. Participation in cooperative venues on migration policy established by other institutions	1. CoE in Europe; Obama Administration in the US 2. Policy Labs (CoE); Task Force for New Americans (White House – Obama administration); Urban Agenda (Dutch Government) 3. Participation by (a few) national government representatives in the Partnership and the Policy Labs

vertical/intergovernmental agenda underlying the mobilisation of the WGM&I and C4A as local-government-based organisations; (2) a prevalently horizontal agenda, characterising WA as a civil society-led organisation; and (3) a more MLG-oriented agenda promoted by the ICC network at least since 2016, although skewed in the direction of the vertical dimension. Whereas the first agenda reflects cities' engagement in political advocacy and lobbying, the second and third agendas seem to reveal more collaborative modes of policymaking.

The first agenda is grounded on the idea that cities should participate and be represented in policymaking processes that touch on issues of relevance to urban policy. Mayors, and sometimes their deputies are the key leaders articulating cities' interests and voices, even though city officers play an important role in providing policy inputs. In any case, this type of political mobilisation takes place almost exclusively on the vertical/intergovernmental dimension and leads to modes of policymaking like lobbying and venue-shopping, whereby cities attempt to establish collaborative relations only with those institutional venues that are more open to accommodating their requests (Scholten, 2013). With respect to this study, this is certainly the case of the European Commission for the WGM&I and of the White House during the Obama administration for C4A. This type of CN agenda appears particularly suited to paving the way to intergovernmental partnerships but is not necessarily conducive for MLG.

In a similar vein, the grassroots community mobilisation agenda pursued by WA also appears distant from MLG, since it promotes a networking mode of policymaking that privileges relations with NGOs. However, the overall collaborative attitude underlying the WA agenda seems to have also favoured collaboration on the vertical dimension, as indicated by the partnership with the US Office for Refugee Resettlement (ORR) on the integration of refugees. A similar approach favouring the establishment of multiple collaborative relations has always underpinned the intercultural model of immigrant integration proposed in the ICC agenda, even though representatives of municipalities have at times expressed dissatisfaction with the scarce engagement of the network in political advocacy.

Hence, on the demand side, my research shows that, unlike what is observed by the bottom-up approach, cities understood as municipalities are not the main drivers of MLG policymaking. In fact, the political advocacy agenda pursued by networks of municipalities like the WGM&I and C4A is aimed first and foremost at promoting cities' interests and views vis-à-vis national governments and does not seem particularly keen to engage with NGOs. On the contrary, when CN leaders act as policy brokers between different actors and work to build multiple vertical and horizontal relations, then the premises for establishing MLG instances of policymaking on the demand side seem to be in place.

However, these premises, while important, are by no means sufficient conditions for the emergence of MLG policymaking. To establish an effective nexus, gatekeepers on the supply side have a fundamental role. Gatekeepers have to show clear willingness and interest in pursuing collaborative policymaking engaging both municipalities and non-public organisations. MLG policymaking, therefore, reflects a political will to go beyond bilateral partnerships and pursue cooperation with all the relevant actors and stakeholders in a specific policy field.

As is indicated by the evidence presented in Chapters 4 and 5 and summarised in Table 6.2, the gatekeepers which have more consistently pursued MLG are the Obama administration in the US from 2015 and the Council of Europe in the EU context from 2016. These institutional actors deployed discourses and actions that aimed to bring together policymakers and stakeholders dealing with migration-related issues at different territorial scales. More specifically, in the first case, the discourse underlying the establishment of the Task Force for New Americans and, with respect to actions, the extensive consultations carried out by the Task Force and the Building Welcoming Communities Campaign are clear cases in point. As for the Council of Europe, discourses emphasising the importance of establishing relationships with multiple public and non-public actors characterised the intercultural model of integration policy from the very beginning, even though it was only with the *Medium-term strategy 2016–2019* (see Sect. 4.3.4) that concrete actions such as the Policy Labs started to be put in place.

On the other hand, my findings show a less clear orientation of the European Commission, and more specifically of the Barroso II and Junker executives (see Sect. 4.2). The Barroso II Commission, while officially presenting a discourse on MLG, actually pursued the establishment of a system of intergovernmental relations centred on the Committee of the Regions. As for the Junker Commission, on the other hand, this showed at least at the beginning a lack of interest in local authorities and focused its action on establishing relations with Member states. It was only in the context of the refugee crisis that, according to my interviewees, the Junker Commission attempted to start a dialogue with local authorities. Overall, if in the past the European Commission was certainly engaged in providing opportunities for the mobilisation of migration CNs (Penninx, 2015), this does not seem to have necessarily been the case in more recent years.

With respect to national governments in the EU context, even if their role in establishing MLG policymaking venues seems quite limited, they still remain key gatekeepers when it comes to considering the functioning and impact of these venues. The Partnership for the Inclusion of Migrants and Refugees is a good case in point. Even though the initiative was launched by the Dutch Government, the venue was concretely organised and coordinated by the City of Amsterdam that acted as a policy broker in engaging the EC and CNs. Furthermore, national government representatives participated only occasionally and did not show a particular interest in the venue. This lack of effective participation seems to reveal an ambiguous attitude of national governments to the partnership, the results of which were not fully accepted. In fact, the EU Council of Home Affairs Ministers did not approve the adoption of the conditionality principle in the revision of the AMIF funding regulations. With respect to the Policy Labs, national governments seem to have played a similar gatekeeping role. Some representatives did participate in the meetings but these venues do not appear to have been able to propose the kind of 'coherent and coordinated intercultural integration policy model' that was in the original ambitions of the CoE secretariat.

Hence, if in the US MLG policymaking clearly emerges from a top-down government-led initiative, in the EU supranational system my research shows, at least *prima facie*, a greater dispersion of power, in particular regarding the initial mobilisation of MLG venues and initiatives. However, this does not rule out the capacity of national governments to act as veto players, i.e. as decision-makers whose agreement is required in order to change the status quo (Tsebelis, 2000, p. 442). As is clear from my analysis, in the EU context the interest of national governments in promoting policy change through collaborative policymaking seems overall uncertain. The only exception is represented by the Portuguese Government, which in 2018 engaged in a national Policy Lab together with representatives of ICC cities and various NGOs, leading to the adoption of a series of collaborative programmes for the intercultural integration of migrants (see Sect. 3.4.3).

In other words, in the supranational EU context government authorities seem to play a key gatekeeping role not unlike that of the federal government in the US. Participation in MLG-like instances of policymaking does not imply a real willingness to share power. This reluctance does not come as a surprise given the high political sensitiveness of the migration issue and its key symbolic relevance to state sovereignty. Not only hierarchy but also national power stands out as alive and kicking in instances of MLG migration policymaking.

By employing an actor-centred and relational interpretative framework, this study has clearly shown how the emergence of MLG policymaking cannot be simply linked to a top-down opportunity structure or a bottom-up local government move but is the result of a more complex mechanism of matching between the demand and supply sides of migration policy-making. On the demand side, MLG is more likely to emerge when CNs articulate a collaborative agenda, i.e. an agenda that is oriented to establishing multiple collaborations rather than simply to putting pressure on national authorities. On the supply side, the willingness and interest of national governments in promoting and engaging in collaborative relations with a broad spectrum of actors is similarly crucial. Without a real interest in being part of a process of policy change, power is likely to prevail, as seems to be the case in the EU context and in the US during the Trump administration. Whereas in the EU, however, there can still be space for intergovernmental partnership between local authorities and EU institutions, and more specifically the EC, this opportunity is certainly lacking in the US federal system. The recent engagement of WA and C4A in the international and global sphere described in Chapter 5 seems to testify to a search for alternative and more open venues for migration policymaking, which, however, as shown in this study, does not imply that MLG can be effectively put in place by simply going beyond the nation state.

6.4 Implications for an MLG Research Agenda. Towards a Reconciliation of Systems and Instances Approaches

As was pointed out in Chapters 1 and 2, debates on MLG have been characterised by the concomitant presence of different and not always explicit definitions of the concept. More specifically, at least four definitions emerge from the existing literature: as dispersion of power; as the mode of functioning of the—sui generis—EU polity; as a more general—and optimal—system of allocation of state power; and as a specific instance or mode of policymaking characterised by an orientation to collaborative problem-solving. A common trait in all these variants is the emphasis on MLG as antithetical to hierarchy, implying more or less explicitly that MLG is a more efficient and more legitimate mode of allocating values in contemporary multi-layered political systems (Piattoni, 2010). However, the different conceptual approaches underlying studies on MLG as a *system* and MLG as an *instance* of policymaking (Alcantara & Nelles, 2014; Alcantara et al., 2016) so far seem to have impeded the development of proper cumulative research, and most of all of causal explanations.

In this study, I have attempted to contribute to the ongoing debate not by proposing yet another different and more sophisticated definition of MLG, but instead by taking a clear position vis-à-vis the variants of the concept deployed in the literature. More specifically, I have taken a middle-range or meso-level perspective on MLG policymaking by focusing on migration CNs, which are regarded in the literature as new emerging policymakers the legitimacy of which builds on cities' direct and grassroots experience in dealing with migration and mobility issues (Penninx, 2015; Thouez, 2020). As was argued in Sect. 2.2, such a perspective is not only relevant in order to contribute to a better understanding of processes of decision-making and implementation but can also provide relevant insights for theorisation on how the emergence of CN organisations can actually contribute to macro-processes of redefinition of state authority on the highly state-sensitive issue of cross-border mobility.

The adoption of a meso-level *instances* approach has the merit of enabling the building of typologies that help to differentiate MLG from other modes or configurations of policymaking and to better identify cases of its concrete occurrence (for a similar approach, see Alcantara & Nelles, 2014; Alcantara et al., 2016; Scholten, 2013; Scholten et al., 2018). To this end, I emphasise the importance of looking at the type of relations linking the different actors that participate in specific policymaking processes. These relations can be more or less inclusive, in the sense that they can be limited to relevant policy actors on the vertical or on the horizontal dimension of policymaking processes or include both, as in ideal-type MLG (see Fig. 2.1). Furthermore, policymaking relationships can be underpinned by different degrees of collaboration. Hence, unlike other typologies that link the occurrence of MLG to the notion of negotiated governance (Alcantara & Nelles, 2014; Alcantara et al., 2016) or policy convergence (Scholten, 2013), I have taken a descriptive and analytical approach that enables the identification of possible gaps between official discourses emphasising cooperation with all relevant policymakers and stakeholders, on the one hand, and concrete practices of MLG policymaking, on the other.

Following this framework, in Fig. 6.1 I show the cases of MLG-like policymaking arrangements identified in this study in the typology of modes of policymaking discussed in Sect. 2.2. The cases are the Partnership for the Inclusion of Migrants and Refugees, the Policy Labs

		Horizontal dimension – Collaboration with stakeholders	
		+ High	Low -
Vertical dimension – Intergovernmental collaboration	+ High	MLG **PIMR** **Task force for NA** **BWCC**	**Policy Lab** IGR Coop *Venue shopping*
	- Low	Network governance	*Lobbying* *Peer-to-peer network* Hierarchical relations

Fig. 6.1 Venues of MLG of migration

and the Task Force for New Americans. All these venues of migration policymaking were characterised by a discourse that emphasised the importance of establishing extended multilevel collaborative relations in order to reach more legitimate and efficient public policy on migration-related issues, with particular attention to the role of cities. However, their concrete functioning seems to reveal different practices of MLG policymaking more or less coherent with official discourses.

More specifically, whereas the Partnership for the Inclusion of Migrants and Refugees (PIMR in the above figure) established in the context of the Urban Agenda for the EU and the Policy Labs promoted by the CoE reveal a greater prominence of the vertical dimension, since intergovernmental relations prevail over collaboration with non-public actors, the Task Force for New Americans and the resulting Building Welcoming Communities Campaign (BWCC) reveal the opposite pattern. Under the profile of intergovernmental relations, the Task Force undertook consultations with cities, counties and a few states, while regarding civil society there were hearings with representatives of various NGOs, national and local coalitions for immigrant rights and immigrant groups. The BWCC initiative was one of the outcomes of this extensive consultative work which, as was reported in Sect. 5.2.3, was carried out by a more restricted partnership among WA, the Corporation of National Community Service (AmeriCorps), the YMCA, Catholic charities and national refugee resettlement organisations.

Hence, at a descriptive level, my research findings show not only that instances of MLG policymaking are quite rare (see also Scholten et al., 2018 on the Dutch case) but also that they are characterised by a non-negligible degree of inconsistency between official discourses and concrete implementation. At a more explanatory level, and more specifically with respect to the identification of the causal factors and mechanisms leading to the emergence of different patterns of MLG policymaking, a main result of this study highlighted above is that MLG is characterised essentially as a 'move from above,' i.e. by the Dutch government in the case of the PIMR, by the CoE in that of ICC and by the White House with respect to the Task Force for New Americans. In fact, in none of these cases did CNs play a decisive role in the initial phase but they became involved as representatives of cities once MLG venues were established. In other words, following the actor-centred and relational approach presented in Sect. 2.4, the presence of CNs mobilised on the migration policy issue is neither a sufficient nor a necessary condition for the emergence of MLG. More important is the supply side, i.e. the interest and willingness of policymakers with a gatekeeping role to engage in this type of collaboration.

However, again, the openness of gatekeeper institutions alone is neither a sufficient nor necessary condition for MLG. First of all, CNs have to present what might be called a 'connective' policy agenda, i.e. an agenda that seeks to establish multiple networks, especially with civil society organisations, as in the case of WA. At first sight, this was also the case of ICC, even though my in-depth reconstruction actually showed that the municipalities involved in the network had a greater interest in political advocacy than in establishing new collaborations with NGOs, which they perceived as partners already mobilised at the local level in providing services to migrants. In fact, when the CN agenda is centred on mayoral leadership or local government interests, as in the cases of C4A and WGM&I respectively, political advocacy—rather than MLG—is more likely to prevail. Second, another key condition already mentioned above is that no gatekeepers on the supply side act as veto players. If this is quite obvious in the US, where the federal government represents the key gatekeeper, it is also a necessary condition for MLG to consolidate as a mode of policymaking and produce some policy impact in the EU supranational system, where power is *prima facie* more dispersed. Nevertheless, as was shown above, the intermittent participation of national governments in the PIMR and the lack of strong support for the Policy

Labs promoted by ICC seem to unravel a veto-player strategy of national governments that reduces the effective possibility of pursuing policy change. Hence, it follows that, notwithstanding the different institutional structures characterising the EU supranational and the US federal systems, MLG policymaking on migration is still highly dependent on national governments' political will. The influence of anti-immigrant parties on government positions is certainly a factor making collaboration more difficult, as was reported in the case of the PIMR, if not simply impossible, as during the Trump administration in the US.

The meso-level perspective adopted in this study brings to light the very political pre-conditions of MLG policymaking. On the one hand, CN leaderships and agendas should be of an outward-looking kind, promoting connectivity and collaboration rather than being guided by cities' specific interests. On the other hand, national governments should not act as gatekeepers but instead engage to find common ground and/or consensus on specific multi-actor policy programmes, as shown by the BWCC initiative in the US and by the Policy Lab promoted by ICC in Portugal. In other words, rather than representing a way out from politics, governance, and even more MLG, when analysed empirically, reveals its deep political intricacies.

Scholars taking a critical approach to governance have already shown how collaborative forms of policymaking, while at first glance promising in terms of inclusiveness and pluralism, can nevertheless have negative consequences in terms of democratic accountability. Papadopoulos (2010) identifies four properties of MLG that can produce a democratic accountability deficit: the lack of visibility of governance networks, which deliberately operate in an informal and opaque way in order to facilitate compromise; the uncoupling from representative institutions, in the sense that decisions prepared and implemented by networks clearly show a weakening of parliaments' legislative and control functions; the composition of networks, which does not necessarily reflect all possible relevant social interests but only those that are able to organise in powerful organisations listened to by decision-makers; and the multi-levelness itself, which especially for local authorities can create a double accountability dilemma, to their electoral constituencies on the one hand and vis-à-vis the partners in a specific MLG venue on the other hand. As is clear, these dilemmas and contradictions are likely to be all the more relevant when highly pitched migration issues are stake and in political contexts characterised by the rise of populist parties, which openly challenge the thinking behind the governance paradigm (Stoker, 2019).

Hence, the study of MLG policymaking, rather than just contributing to middle-range theorisation on public policy and implementation, offers a valuable window to explore processes of state power (non) transformation. The lack of a clear nexus between migration CNs and MLG, or at least its subordination to 'the shadow of the hierarchy' and the will of national governments, certainly does not reflect a process of weakening of traditional nation states, but rather testifies of their persistent capacity to act as gatekeepers in the emergence of MLG policymaking.

6.5 Implications for Research on City Networks

The results of this study not only cast doubts on MLG as an alternative to hierarchical and top-down modes of policymaking but also help to put in perspective the enthusiasm for migration CNs as *agents* of a new wave of international mobilisation countering the restrictiveness of nation states' migration policies with the open-mindedness and cosmopolitan ethos of cities. By adopting the *city as arena* analytical lens and applying it to the analysis of CN mobilisation, my research reveals the different agendas or, using the terminology of Payre (2010), the 'political work' underlying CN organisations. This is a fundamental step in order to answer key questions regarding why cities get together to coordinate their efforts and policies on typical matters of state sovereignty such as migration and mobility.

Processes of agenda-setting within CNs seem to have been overlooked by scholars taking a *city as agent* perspective. In this literature, cities, implicitly conceptualised as local governments or sometimes identified with mayors, strategically mobilise in the international and/or European sphere to take advantage of new opportunities and to articulate their perspectives on global challenges. However, if local governments and/or mayors indeed represent key players in the CN arena, the role of other policy actors should not be completely overlooked. First of all, political élites are usually flanked by city administrative officers who have a more direct knowledge of the situation on the ground. Second, CNs are often supported by secretariats and staff officers who can pursue more general organisational goals like accreditation of the network at the EU level as in the case of the WGM&I or realising the vision of an international organisation like the CoE in the case of ICC. Last but not least, CN leaderships can have different backgrounds, as is shown in the case of NGO activists in WA, and therefore a different vision of the network's role and initiatives to that of city government officials. The structured narratives presented in Chapters 4 and 5 clearly show that various categories of actors are engaged in articulating different agendas in terms of CN aims and modes of policymaking on migration. Table 6.3 provides an overview of the key research findings in this respect.

Table 6.3 Policy actors' agendas and modes of policymaking

	Agenda	*Mode of policymaking*	*Examples*
Mayors and deputies	City leadership	Political advocacy	1. Mayor of Rotterdam and the IC process 2. Solidarity Cities 3. C4A mayors' statements
City officers	Technical exchange and policy learning	Peer-to-peer networking (Support for) political advocacy	1. WGM&I periodic meetings 2. C4A Steering Board 3. ICC coordinators meetings 4. WA convenings
Secretariats and staff officers	Support for achievement of the organisation's goals	Different depending on the aims of the organisation	1. WGM&I policy officers' support in the IC partnership 2. ICC Secretariat's support and promotion of MLG
CN (external) leaders with an NGO background	Connecting public and non-public actors	Network governance	WA Welcoming Standards and Certified Communities Programme

First of all, mayors and other political actors like deputy mayors engage in CNs primarily to affirm their leadership and articulate their—political—vision of migration and mobility. In other words, these actors have a prevalently political agenda based on narratives which are usually built to contrast the narratives of other higher-ranking government authorities. A clear case in point is C4A discourse on the contribution of immigrants to the local economy and the wealth of the city as opposed to the securitisation agenda of the federal government primarily during the Trump administration but also in some respects during the Obama years (see, e.g. the mobilisation in support of Sanctuary Cities and against deportation). In a similar vein, mayors emerged as key actors in the launch of the Solidarity Cities initiative in the context of the WGM&I. As is shown in Table 6.3, this political agenda privileged engagement in political advocacy aimed at positioning cities vis-à-vis higher levels of government, to obtain political recognition and claim a seat in decision-making processes.

City administrative officers, instead, have a more technical agenda focused on policy learning and exchange of best practices, and engage primarily in a peer-to-peer networking mode of policymaking. However, this does not seem to necessarily lead to the emergence of 'communities of practice' along the lines specified by Wenger (2000, see also Chapter 2). The type of network is important in this respect. In city-government-led organisations like the WGM&I and C4A, city officers work somewhat in connection with their political principals: peer-to-peer networking and policy learning are often 'used' to build consensus around a city's or a group of cities' specific political agenda. In the case of C4A, this is clearly reflected in the leading role played by the main cities sitting in the Steering Board. As for the WGM&I, the minutes of the periodic meetings (see also the analysis in Flamant, 2017 on the period 2010–2014) clearly reveal how cities bring to the table the different priorities of their political leaders. In 2012–2013, for instance, as we saw in Chapter 4, whereas central European cities like Amsterdam and Vienna stressed their intention to take action on the topic of the pitfalls of intra-EU mobility, southern European cities like, but not only, Barcelona and Milan raised concerns about irregular migration. On the contrary, the emergence of a community of practice seems more pronounced in the case of externally founded migration CNs like ICC and WA. These networks, in fact, are structured around specific visions or policy models, i.e. intercultural integration in the first case and the welcoming approach in the second. Discussions and policy exchanges usually have a more technical content and focus on how to concretely implement these specific visions or models. However, in the case of ICC, the minutes of the Annual Meetings of the Coordinators, which gather together city officers and the CoE Secretariat, reveal a certain discontent among cities with the scarce impact of technical work on cities' political élites.

This observation brings us to consider more closely the role played by the fourth group of actors underlying CN mobilisation, i.e. CN internal officers and secretariats. In fact, with the only exception of C4A where coordination is carried out by New York City MOIA officers, all the networks analysed have dedicated support staff. In general, the agendas of CN internal officers are centred on pursuing the organisational goals of the networks, which are of course different and therefore lead to privileging different modes of policymaking. Regarding Eurocities project managers, the ambition of the organisation to represent (second) European cities vis-à-vis EU institutions is reflected in their work to institutionalise a partnership with DG Home through the Integrating Cities project and collaboration in the activities of the PIMR. Therefore, intergovernmental collaboration appears as the privileged mode of policymaking. The ICC Secretariat and the WA Board of Directors, on the other hand, have backgrounds that link to the external sponsors of the networks. The ICC Secretariat is formed of staff from the CoE Directorate General on Democracy, who are engaged in implementing the intercultural model of immigrant integration as set out in various CoE official documents. To this end, the Secretariat appears to have been constantly engaged in peer-to-peer networking with experts from outside the organisation, primarily from academia and independent research institutes, to craft the network's concrete agenda and strategies. Also WA staff members are external to local government institutions, and more specifically present backgrounds linked to civil society activism. Coherently with their backgrounds, they seem to have been constantly engaged in promoting network governance and partnership between public and non-public actors.

Hence, the actor-centred and relational interpretative framework underlying this study clearly shows that migration CNs represent a complex and diversified phenomenon which cannot be simply interpreted in the abstract terms of *city agency*. Different categories of actors are at play in internal processes of agenda-setting, and these processes actively shape CN mobilisation on migration and mobility, or in other words the 'demand side' of migration policymaking processes. Accounts that identify migration CN aims with the promotion of new alliances in migration policymaking (Penninx, 2015) or challenging national restrictive approaches (Oomen, 2020) reflect primarily official discourses and narratives. However, by engaging in in-depth analysis of policy actions and internal agenda-setting processes, it is possible to flesh out the political work that underpins CNs' engagement in policymaking on migration as in other policy fields. In other words, normative expectations of CNs as conveying pragmatic and enlightened approaches to migration and mobility issues risk overlooking the inevitably different agendas that deeply characterise these organisations as a result of their internal 'political work.'

6.6 Postscript. Looking Ahead at Cities, Local Communities and MLG in Pandemic Times

At the end of this journey one might be disappointed to discover that what was expected to be a promising new development in migration policy, the CNs-MLG nexus, is actually a missing link. CNs do not necessarily pursue engagement in MLG. This mode of policymaking usually takes place in the shadow of the hierarchy and is highly dependent on the will of national governments. At the very end, everything is politics as usual and, even worse, top-down politics. In an age of populism, this does not sound like good news.

However, as a scholar in political science, I am used to thinking of politics in a rather different way to the popular images of top-down commands from an unaccountable élite. Politics is also all the mundane processes that take place within CNs to shape a vision, identify priorities and act accordingly. In this case too, as we have seen, leadership is important and yet, depending on CNs' histories and foundation trajectories, there is room for negotiation, adaptation and revision. Politics is a process of 'allocation of values' in the words of Easton (1965), which certainly implies interests and power but also vision and ideas.

In this perspective, I think we should not be too concerned about the fact that an organisation, a CN in this study, articulates a particular vision of migration and mobility grounded on specific interests and ideas. What seems more concerning is that some ideas and interests might not have the capacity to organise and get access to the venues where policies are discussed. This is likely to be even more the case when considering the multi-layered global and international arena. Many places and localities where migrants live and work, especially the smaller ones, are certainly not there. If big cities have room for choice in this respect, and therefore can decide to engage or not on the basis of their vision and approach to the issue (see, e.g. Fourot et al., 2021), for smaller cities and rural areas this is simply not a choice. Organisational costs are likely to be too high and the gains uncertain. Yet small localities are no less important in the shaping of bigger national and supranational visions and policies on migration.

Research has already shown that these areas can play a key role in national elections and debates on migration and diversity, leading to the emergence of an urban/rural political divide, as was indicated by the vote for Brexit in the UK and the electoral victory of Donald Trump in 2016 (Brooks, 2020; Rodden, 2020). In Europe, many small localities have only become contexts of migrant settlement in the last decade because of redistribution plans put in place by national governments in order to deal with inflows of asylum-seekers and refugees from areas of humanitarian crisis. Superdiversity is not necessarily welcomed in contexts struggling with economic decline, austerity policies and political polarisation. Such unfavourable conditions are likely to be exacerbated in the context of the post-COVID-19 recovery. Economic sectors of vital relevance, like agriculture and food processing, and sectors hit hard by the pandemic like tourism are characterised by both a high prevalence of migrant workers and a high territorial concentration in small towns and rural areas. While it is certainly too early to say anything definitive on this point, it does not seem too far-fetched to expect that migration will represent a main challenge for the social cohesion of these areas in the years to come.

Hence, if CNs reflect the mobilisation of an élite of mainly big—but not necessarily global—progressive cities, scholars are starting to realise that there are intrinsic limits to the capacity of these organisations to represent the extreme plurality of local migration contexts (Oomen & Baumgärtel, 2018). From a scientific point of view, these developments call for scholars to pay greater attention to the complex political realities where migrants' daily interactions with the receiving society concretely take place. Various actors at the local level, such as local authorities, non-profit organisations and/or private businesses, can either provide different types of support for migrant workers or simply ignore them and maybe even contribute to segregating them. These processes will impact on how migrants and local residents engage with each other and experience processes of local community (re)making. As a result of these local interactions, communities will either become more cohesive and welcoming towards migration and diversity in general or more fragmented and unwelcoming.

Existing research on party politics and the politicisation of migration tends to focus on the national level (for a recent overview, see Hadj-Abdou et al., 2021), yet to go local appears of the utmost importance in order to explain processes of political change in contemporary multilevel systems triggered by the emergence of pro/anti-migration stances within local communities. For political scientists, this shift of focus implies a greater engagement with non-standard methodologies, or at least with non-canonical comparative research. The most similar and most different systems designs, which still dominate debates in comparative politics, cannot be easily applied to local-level research, where a presence of very dissimilar systems in terms of institutions, organisations and relevant local actors is the rule (see, e.g. Magnusson, 2014). In this context, the only option is a solid theory-driven case selection based on carefully crafted typologies with the aim of assessing hypotheses and/or building new interpretative theoretical frameworks.

From the perspective of policymakers, dealing with the extreme variation of local situations is a challenge that cannot be easily met in the context of MLG policymaking venues. As is argued in the literature (Bache et al., 2004; Papadopoulos, 2007, 2010) and shown in this study, MLG policymaking inevitably implies the (auto)selection of a limited number of partners, and this cannot but be an extremely difficult task given the variegated plethora of local realities. There are no quick fixes that can solve this dilemma in a satisfactory manner. Reconciling governance with politics and problem-solving objectives with participation and the representation of societies' different voices, immigrants included, emerge as urgent challenges that require politics to think outside the box of fixed social categories and established interests. City Networks, as this book has shown, can certainly provide a different perspective on migration to that of nation states and yet they do not exhaust the many facets and voices of local politics.

References

Alcantara, C., Broschek, J., & Nelles, J. (2016). Rethinking multilevel governance as an instance of multilevel politics: A conceptual strategy. *Territory,*

Politics, Governance, 4, 33–51. https://doi.org/10.1080/21622671.2015.1047897

Alcantara, C., & Nelles, J. (2014). Indigenous peoples and the state in settler societies: Toward a more robust definition of multilevel governance. *Publius, 44*, 183–204. https://doi.org/10.1093/publius/pjt013

Bassens, D., Beeckmans, L., Derudder, B., & Oosterlynck, S. (2019). An urban studies take on global urban political agency. In S. Oosterlynck, L. Beeckmans, & D. Bassens et al. (Eds.), *The city as a global political actor*. Routledge.

Beach, D., & Pedersen, R. B. (2019). *Process-tracing methods: Foundations and guidelines*. University of Michigan Press.

Börzel, T. (2010). European governance: Negotiation and competition in the shadow of hierarchy. *JCMS: Journal of Common Market Studies, 48*,191–219. https://doi.org/10.1111/j.1468-5965.2009.02049.x

Brooks, S. (2020). Brexit and the politics of the rural. *Sociologia Ruralis, 60*, 790–809. https://doi.org/10.1111/soru.12281

Caponio, T. (2021). Governing migration through multilevel governance? City networks in Europe and in the United States. *JCMS: Journal of Common Market Studies*. https://doi.org/10.1111/jcms.13214

Caponio, T., & Jones-Correa, M. (2018). Theorising migration policy in multilevel states: The multilevel governance perspective. *Journal of Ethnic and Migration Studies, 44*, 1995–2010. https://doi.org/10.1080/1369183X.2017.1341705

Easton, D. (1965). *A systems analysis of political life*. John Wiley.

Flamant, A. (2017). Les cadres de l'action publique locale en charge des politiques d'intégration des étrangers. *Politique Europeenne, 57*, 84–115.

Fourot, A.-C., Healy, A., & Flamant, A. (2021). French participation in transnational migration networks: Understanding city (dis)involvement and "passivism." *Local Government Studies*. https://doi.org/10.1080/03003930.2020.1857246

Hadj-Abdou, L., Bale, T., & Geddes, A. P. (2021). Centre-right parties and immigration in an era of politicisation. *Journal of Ethnic and Migration Studies*. https://doi.org/10.1080/1369183X.2020.1853901

Kemmerzell, J. (2019). Bridging the gap between the local and the global scale? Taming the wicked problem of climate change through trans-local governance. In N. Behnke, J. Broschek, & J. Sonnicksen (Eds.), *Configurations, dynamics and mechanisms of multilevel governance* (pp. 155–172). Palgrave Macmillan.

Magnusson, W. (2014). The symbiosis of the urban and the political. *International Journal of Urban and Regional Research, 38*, 1561–1575. https://doi.org/10.1111/1468-2427.12144

Newton, L. (2018). Immigration politics by proxy: State agency in an era of national reluctance. *Journal of Ethnic and Migration Studies, 44*, 2086–2105. https://doi.org/10.1080/1369183X.2017.1341714

Oomen, B. (2020). Decoupling and teaming up: The rise and proliferation of transnational municipal networks in the field of migration. *International Migration Review, 54*, 913–939. https://doi.org/10.1177/019791831988 1118

Oomen, B., & Baumgärtel, M. (2018). Frontier cities: The rise of local authorities as an opportunity for international human rights law. *European Journal of International Law, 29*, 607–630. https://doi.org/10.1093/ejil/chy021

Papadopoulos, Y. (2007). Problems of democratic accountability in network and multilevel governance. *European Law Journal, 13*, 469–486. https://doi.org/10.1111/j.1468-0386.2007.00379.x

Papadopoulos, Y. (2010). Accountability and multi-level governance: More accountability, less democracy? *West European Politics, 33*, 1030–1049. https://doi.org/10.1080/01402382.2010.486126

Payre, R. (2010). The importance of being connected. City networks and urban government: Lyon and eurocities (1990–2005). *International Journal of Urban and Regional Research, 34*, 260–280. https://doi.org/10.1111/j.1468-2427.2010.00937.x

Penninx, R. (2015). European cities in search of knowledge for their integration policies. In P. Scholten, H. Entzinger, R. Penninx, & S. Verbeek (Eds.), *Integrating immigrants in Europe: Research-policy dialogues* (pp. 99–115). Springer International Publishing.

Peters, G. B., & Pierre, J. (2004). Multi-level governance and democracy: A Faustian bargain? In I. Bache & M. Flinders (Eds.) *Multi-level governance* (pp. 75–89). Oxford University Press.

Piattoni, S. (2010). *The theory of multi-level governance: Conceptual, empirical, and normative challenges*. Oxford University Press.

Rodden, J. A. (2020). *Why cities lose: The deep roots of the urban-rural political divide*. Basic Books.

Scholten, P. W. A. (2013). Agenda dynamics and the multi-level governance of intractable policy controversies: The case of migrant integration policies in the Netherlands. *Policy Sciences, 46*, 217–236. https://doi.org/10.1007/s11 077-012-9170-x

Scholten, P., Engbersen, G., Ostaijen, M. van, & Snel, E. (2018). Multilevel governance from below: How Dutch cities respond to intra-EU mobility. *Journal of Ethnic and Migration Studies 44*, 2011–2033. https://doi.org/10.1080/1369183X.2017.1341707

Stoker, G. (2019). Can the governance paradigm survive the rise of populism? *Policy & Politics, 47*, 3–18. https://doi.org/10.1332/030557318X15333 033030897

Thouez, C. (2020). Cities as emergent international actors in the field of migration: Evidence from the lead-up and adoption of the UN global compacts on migration and refugees. *Global Governance: A Review of Multilateralism and International Organizations, 26*, 650–672. https://doi.org/10.1163/19426720-02604007

Tsebelis, G. (2000). Veto players and institutional analysis. *Governance: An International Journal of Policy and Administration, 13*, 441–474. https://doi.org/10.1111/0952-1895.00141

Wenger, E. (2000). Communities of practice and social learning systems. *Organization, 7*, 225–246. https://doi.org/10.1177/135050840072002

Williamson, A. F. (2018). *Welcoming new Americans? Local governments and immigrant incorporation*. University of Chicago Press.

Appendix

General Note
Official documents and web pages were downloaded in different time periods, i.e. in November–December 2018 for the first time and then in the spring and autumn of 2019 to check for new documents and updates. The links provided below have been accessed for the last time between March and July 2020.

Working Group on Migration and Integration (WGM&I)

List of Documents

WGM&I_doc1 (2003). Proceedings of the Conference: Foreigners' integration and participation in European Cities, Stuttgart, 15–16 September 2003, Council of Europe. https://rm.coe.int/168071aeb6.

WGM&I_doc2 (2004). Immigration and integration at the local level. Political recommendations to national governments and the EU institutions, Eurocities, Brussels. available at https://ec.europa.eu/employment_social/social_situation/responses/a15568_en_2.pdf.

WGM&I_doc3 (2007). Milan Declaration, Comune di Milano—Press release, 5–6 November 2007.

WGM&I_doc4 (2008). Benchmarking Integration Governance in Europe's Cities. Lessons from the INTI-CITIES project, Eurocities, Brussels. https://nws.eurocities.eu/MediaShell/media/Inticities_english.pdf.

T. Caponio, *Making Sense of the Multilevel Governance of Migration*,
https://doi.org/10.1007/978-3-030-82551-5

WGM&I_doc5 (2012). Minutes WG Migration Integration—Brussels, 1–2 October 2012, available at: http://backend.eurocities.eu/v2/documents/WG-Migration-Integration-meeting-October-2012-outputs-WSPO-92LT7M.

WGM&I_doc6 (2015). EUROCITIES statement on asylum in cities, Eurocities. https://nws.eurocities.eu/MediaShell/media/Final%20EUROCITIES%20statement%20on%20asylum.pdf.

WGM&I_doc7 (2016). Refugee Reception and Integration in cities, Eurocities, Brussels. https://solidaritycities.eu/images/RefugeeReport_final.pdf.

WGM&I_doc8 (2017). Delvino, N. European Cities and Migrants with Irregular Status: Municipal initiatives for the inclusion of irregular migrants in the provision of services. Report for the 'City Initiative on Migrants with Irregular Status in Europe' (C-MISE). https://www.compas.ox.ac.uk/wp-content/uploads/City-Initiative-on-Migrants-with-Irregular-Status-in-Europe-CMISE-report-November-2017-FINAL.pdf.

WGM&I_doc9 (2017). Action Plan. Partnership on Inclusion of migrants and refugees, Urban Agenda for the EU. https://ec.europa.eu/futurium/en/system/files/ged/action_plan_inclusion_of_migrants_and_refugees.pdf

WGM&I_doc10 (2018). Recommendations for improving cities' use of and access to EU funds for integration of migrants and refugees in the new programming period, Urban Agenda for the EU. https://ec.europa.eu/futurium/en/system/files/ged/uaeu-inclusion-recommendations-funding.pdf.

WGM&I_doc11 (2018). Cities and Migrants III: Implementing the Integrating Cities Charter, Eurocities, Brussels. https://nws.eurocities.eu/MediaShell/media/3rd_Integrating_Cities_Report_October_2018_FINAL.pdf.

WGM&I_doc12 (2018). EUROCITIES Working Group on Migration and Integration meeting, 8–9/11/2018, Milan, Meeting report. https://nws.eurocities.eu/MediaShell/media/Report_WG_meeting_and_policy_learning_Milan_8-9_November_2018_FINAL.pdf.

WGM&I_doc13 (2019). European Parliament legislative resolution of 13 March 2019 on the proposal for a regulation of the European Parliament and of the Council establishing the Asylum and Migration Fund (COM(2018)0471—C8-0271/2018—2018/0248(COD), available at https://www.europarl.europa.eu/doceo/document/TA-8-2019-0175_EN.pdf.

WGM&I_doc14 (2019). 5th European Migration Forum, 'From Global to Local Governance of Migration: The Role of Local Authorities in Managing Migration and Ensuring Safe and Regular Pathways to the EU', 3-4th April 2019, Brussels, Summery Report. https://www.eesc.europa.eu/sites/default/files/files/2019-04-03_04_5th_meeting_emf_from_global_to_local_governance_of_migration.pdf.

List of Websites

WGM&I_web1, https://ec.europa.eu/migrant-integration/, European Website on Integration.

WGM&I_web2, http://www.eurocities.eu/integrating-cities, Integrating Cities.

WGM&I_web3, https://www.eukn.eu/news/detail/european-commission-and-eurocities-sign-milan-declaration-on-integration/, Milan Declaration.

WGM&I_web4, http://www.integratingcities.eu/integrating-cities/projects/inti-cities. INTI-Cities Project.

WGM&I_web5, http://www.integratingcities.eu/integrating-cities/projects/dive. Dive Project.

WGM&I_web6, http://www.integratingcities.eu/integrating-cities/charter. Integrating Cities Charter.

WGM&I_web7, http://www.integratingcities.eu/integrating-cities/projects/implementoring. ImpleMentoring Project.

WGM&I_web8, http://www.integratingcities.eu/integrating-cities/events/Integrating-Cities-VI-European-cities-shaping-the-future-of-integration-WSWE-ARLBVD. Sixth Integrating Cities Conference, Tampere 9–10 September 2013.

WGM&I_web9, http://www.integratingcities.eu/integrating-cities/events/Barcelona-roundtable-City-Responses-to-Irregular-Migrants-WSWE-9SJFET. Roundtable 'City responses to irregular migrants', Barcelona, 16–17 October 2014.

WGM&I_web10, http://wsdomino.eurocities.eu/eurocities/working_groups/Migration-and-integration-&tpl=home. Working Group on Migration and Integration.

WGM&I_web11a, http://wsdomino.eurocities.eu/v2/news/Cities-welcome-refugees-Vienna-WSPO-A28C8C. Cities Welcome Refugees: Vienna.

WGM&I_web11b, http://wsdomino.eurocities.eu/v2/allcontent/Cities-welcome-refugees-Gdansk-WSPO-A2FALT. Cities Welcome Refugees: Gdansk.

WGM&I_web11c, http://wsdomino.eurocities.eu/v2/allcontent/Cities-welcome-refugees-Munich-WSPO-A2CMD5. Cities Welcome Refugees: Munich.

WGM&I_web12, 'Cities are at the forefront of the asylum crisis': https://www.euractiv.com/section/social-europe-jobs/opinion/cities-are-at-the-forefront-of-the-asylum-crisis/. Article by Secretary General of Eurocities Annalisa Boni.

WGM&I_web13, http://www.integratingcities.eu/integrating-cities/projects/cities-grow. Cities Grow Project.

WGM&I_web14, http://wsdomino.eurocities.eu/v2/news/EUROCITIES-joins-asylum-discussions-with-MEPs-WSPO-9XRJ7J, Eurocities join asylum discussion with MEPs, 23 June 2015.

WGM&I_web15, http://wsdomino.eurocities.eu/v2/news/EUROCITIES-calls-for-direct-access-to-EU-migration-funds-WSPO-A2VKGU. 'EUROCITIES calls for direct access to EU migration funds', news, 1 October 2015.

WGM&I_web16, https://solidaritycities.eu/about, Solidarity Cities.

WGM&I_web17, http://wsdomino.eurocities.eu/v2/news/Resettlement-lessons-through-SHARE-WSPO-9GQAP9. Resettlement lessons through SHARE, news, 26 February 2014.

WGM&I_web18, https://ec.europa.eu/migrant-integration/about-european-integration-forum?page=2. European Website on Integration.

WGM&I_web19, https://ec.europa.eu/futurium/, Urban Agenda for the EU.

WGM&I_web20, https://ec.europa.eu/futurium/en/inclusion-migrants-and-refugees/urban-academy-integration, Urban Academy.

WGM&I_web21, https://www.eesc.europa.eu/en/agenda/our-events/events/european-migration-forum-5th-meeting, European Integration Forum, 5th Meeting.

WGM&I_web22, http://www.integratingcities.eu/integrating-cities/projects/values, Project Values.

Interviews

WGM&I_int1, Past Officer at Eurocities, 26 July 2019.

WGM&I_int2, Project Manager, Eurocities Forum for Social Affairs, 10 July 2019, Brussels.

WGM&I_int3, Officer WGM&I, 4 April 2019, Brussels.

WGM&I_int4, Officer DG HOME, 4 April 2019, Brussels.

WGM&I_int5, Representative local authorities in the Partnership for the Inclusion of Migrants and Refugees, Urban Agenda for the EU, 4 April 2019, Brussels.

WGM&I_int6, vice-Mayor of a city member of the WGM&I, 23 July 2020, skype interview.

WGM&I_int7, city officer, member city of the WGM&I, 24 August 2020, skype interview.

WGM&I_int8, city officer, member city of the WGM&I and representative of cities in the Urban Agenda for the EU, 7 September 2020, skype interview.

Intercultural Cities (ICC)

ICC_doc1 (2008). Highlights of the European Year of Intercultural Dialogue 2008, European Communities, Directorate General for Education, Youth, Sport and Culture, Luxembourg, Office for Official Publications of the European Commission. https://op.europa.eu/en/publication-detail/-/publication/3e89f8d6-6ac9-4f33-b00a-89cfc5fcec85.

ICC_doc2 (2009). Intercultural Cities. Towards a model for intercultural integration. Insights from Intercultural cities, joint action of the Council of Europe and the European Commission. Edited by Phil Wood, Strasbourg, Council of Europe Publishing. https://rm.coe.int/16802ff5ef.

ICC_doc3 (2013). The Intercultural City Index 2013. A methodological overview (updated version: The Intercultural City Index 2019. A methodological overview. https://rm.coe.int/the-intercultural-city-index-2019-a-methodological-overview/16809074ab).

ICC_doc4 (2013). The intercultural city step by step. Practical guide for applying the urban model of intercultural integration, Council of Europe, Strasbourg, Council of Europe Publishing. https://book.coe.int/en/cultural-policies/5051-the-intercultural-city-step-by-step-practical-guide-for-applying-the-urban-model-of-intercultural-integration.html.

ICC_doc5 (2014). Council of Europe. Mexico City: Results of the Intercultural Cities Index—Date: May 2014—A comparison between more than 50 cities. https://rm.coe.int/16802ff6d2.

ICC_doc6 (2015). De Torres, D., Baglai, C., Ó Siochrú, S., & Khovanova-Rubicondo, K. Cities free of rumours: How to build an anti-rumour strategy in my city, Council of Europe. https://pjp-eu.coe.int/c4i/images/prems%20079615%20gbrfinal%202587%20citiesfreerumours%20web%2021x21.pdf.

ICC_doc7 (2015). Recommendation CM/Rec(2015)1 of the Committee of Ministers to member States on intercultural integration. https://search.coe.int/cm/Pages/result_details.aspx?ObjectID=09000016805c471f.

ICC_doc8 (2015). Intercultural Cities Programme. Medium-term strategy 2016–2019. https://rm.coe.int/16806a5e96.

ICC_doc9 (2016). Council of Europe. Time for Europe to get migrant integration right, Issue paper. https://rm.coe.int/16806da596.

ICC_doc10 (2016). Council of Europe. Sharing our cities, sharing the future. Intercultural Cities—Annual report. Available at. https://rm.coe.int/16806c9674.

ICC_doc11 (2016). Meeting of Intercultural Cities' Coordinators, Reykjavik 15–16 September 2016, Conclusions. Available at: https://www.coe.int/en/web/interculturalcities/documents.

ICC_doc12 (2017). Council of Europe. Intercultural Cities—Annual report. https://rm.coe.int/intercultural-cities-annual-report-2017/1680775ee7.

ICC_doc13 (2017). The Squared Circle. Inclusive Integration Policy Lab—Concept Paper, 3 April 2017.

ICC_doc14 (2017), Incontro Città del Dialogo, 25 May 2017. Report available at https://www.coe.int/en/web/interculturalcities/-/coordination-meeting-of-the-italian-intercultural-cities-network.

ICC_doc15 (2017). ICC Milestone Event. 10 Years of Inclusive Integration—Urban Policies for Immigrant Integration and Diversity Advantage—Main

Conclusions. Available at: https://www.coe.int/en/web/interculturalcities/documents.

ICC_doc16 (2017). Policy Lab for Inclusive Migrant Integration, Lisbon, 28 November 2017, Conclusions. https://rm.coe.int/policy-lab-for-inclusive-migrant-integration-lisbon-28-november-2017-c/1680780451

ICC_doc17 (2017) Declaration of the Intercultural Cities Milestone Event—Urban Policies for Inclusive Migrant Integration and Diversity Advantage. Lisbon, 28–29 November 2017. Available at: https://www.coe.int/en/web/interculturalcities/documents.

ICC_doc18 (2017), Meeting of Intercultural Cities' Coordinators, Lisbon 30 November 2017, Conclusions. Available at: https://www.coe.int/en/web/interculturalcities/documents.

ICC_doc19 (2018). Policy Lab Strasbourg 26 June 2018. Report available at: https://www.coe.int/en/web/interculturalcities/international-policy-labs.

ICC_doc20 (2018). Meeting of Intercultural Cities' Coordinators, Rijeka, 26–27 September 2018, Conclusions. https://rm.coe.int/meeting-of-intercultural-cities-coordinators-rijeka-26-27-september-20/16808eca6c

ICC_doc21 (2018). RPCI Coordination Meeting and first Portuguese Policy Lab, Lisbon Portugal 9–10 October. https://rm.coe.int/conclusion-of-the-1st-portuguese-policy-lab-lisbon-9-10-october-2018/16809232bb.

ICC_doc22 (2018). Council of Europe. Intercultural Cities – Annual report. https://rm.coe.int/intercultural-cities-annual-report-2018/1680930b43.

ICC_doc23 (2019). Policy Lab Helsinky, 28–29 May 2019, https://www.coe.int/en/web/interculturalcities/-/inclusive-integration-policy-lab-meeting.

ICC_doc24 (2019). Meeting of Intercultural Cities Coordinators, Odessa 25–26 September 2019. https://rm.coe.int/meeting-of-intercultural-cities-coordinators-odessa-25-26-september-20/168098ab5e.

ICC_doc25 (2019). 4th Meeting of the Inclusive Policy Lab, Limassol, Cyprus, 13–14 November 2019, Meeting report. https://rm.coe.int/4th-meeting-of-the-inclusive-integration-policy-lab-limassol-cyprus-13/1680992bad.

ICC_doc26 (2019). Council of Europe. Intercultural Cities—Annual report. https://rm.coe.int/intercultural-cities-annual-report-2019/16809983c4.

List of Websites

ICC_web1, https://www.coe.int/en/web/interculturalcities/origins-of-the-intercultural-concept. Intercultural concept.

ICC_web2, https://www.coe.int/en/web/interculturalcities/about-the-index. Intercultural Index.

ICC_web3, https://www.coe.int/en/web/interculturalcities/italy. Network Città del Dialogo.

ICC_web4, https://www.coe.int/en/web/interculturalcities/norway. Intercultural Cities Norway.

ICC_web5, https://www.coe.int/en/web/interculturalcities/spain. Reci Spanish Intercultural Cities Network.
ICC_web6, https://www.coe.int/en/web/interculturalcities/portugal. Portuguese Intercultural Cities Network.
ICC_web7, https://www.coe.int/en/web/interculturalcities/-/melitopol-forum-2015-launches-its-intercultural-city-strategy-2015-2020-and-marks-a-new-era-in-the-development-of-national-icc-ua-network. Melitopol Intercultural Strategy.
ICC_web8, https://www.coe.int/en/web/interculturalcities/international-net work. International Network.
ICC_web9, https://www.coe.int/en/web/interculturalcities/about. Intercultural Cities history.
ICC_web10, https://www.coe.int/en/web/interculturalcities/business-and-div ersity. Deli Project.
ICC_web11, https://pjp-eu.coe.int/en/web/c4i/. C4i Project.
ICC_web12, https://www.coe.int/en/web/interculturalcities/icc-experts. ICC list of experts.
ICC_web13, https://www.coe.int/en/web/interculturalcities/australia. Australian Intercultural Cities Network.
ICC_web14, https://www.coe.int/en/web/interculturalcities/-/brainstor ming-meeting-on-the-setting-up-of-an-intercultural-integration-academy. Brainstorming meeting on the setting up of an intercultural integration accademy, Florence, 26th May 2016.
ICC_web15, https://www.coe.int/en/web/interculturalcities/-/towards-a-new-inclusive-integration-policy-lab. Towards a new inclusive Integration policy lab, Florence, 23rd May 2016.

List of Interviews

ICC_int1, Officer ICC-CoE, 30 March 2019, online interview.
ICC_int2, Officer ICC-CoE, 30 March 2019, online interview.
ICC_int3, Academic expert, 30 October 2018, Rotterdam.
ICC_int4, City Officer, 19 June 2019, Turin.
ICC_int5, Expert, 19 June 2019, Turin.
ICC_int6, City Officer, 19 June 2019, Turin.

Welcoming America (WA)

List of Documents

WA_doc1 (2011). Lubell, David. Foreword. In M. Jones-Correa, *All Immigration Is Local. Receiving Communities and Their Role In Successful Immigrant Integration*, Center for American Progress. https://www.welcomingamerica.

org/sites/default/files/wp-content/uploads/2011/09/All-Immigration-is-Local.pdf.

WA_doc2 (2011). Downs-Karkos, Susan. *The Receiving Communities Toolkit: A Guide for Engaging Mainstream America in Immigrant Integration.* https://www.welcomingamerica.org/sites/default/files/Receiving-Communities-Toolkit_FINAL1.pdf.

WA_doc3 (2012). *Welcoming Cities: Framing the Conversation, written by Welcoming America*, supported by The German Marshall Fund of the United States. https://www.welcomingamerica.org/sites/default/files/Welcoming-Cities-Framing-Paper-Updated.pdf.

WA_doc4 (2015). WE Global Network, Leading Rust Belt Immigrant Innovation. Third Annual Convening—Dayton (OH), July 9th 2015. https://www.weglobalnetwork.org/wp-content/uploads/2015/07/WE-2015-Program.pdf.

WA_doc5 (2015). *Strengthening Communities by Welcoming All Residents. A Federal Strategic Action Plan on Immigrant & Refugee Integration*, The White House Task Force on New Americans. https://www.welcomingamerica.org/sites/default/files/final_tf_newamericans_report_4-14-15_clean.pdf.

WA_doc6 (2015). White House Task Force on New Americans, *One Year Progress Report*, The White House. https://obamawhitehouse.archives.gov/sites/default/files/image/tfna_progress_report_final_12_15_15.pdf.

WA_doc7 (2015). Reeves, J.A. *Community Planning Process Guide for Fostering Greater Refugee Welcome.* https://www.welcomingamerica.org/sites/default/files/WA%20Community%20Planning%20Process%20Guide.pdf.

WA_doc8 (no date). Building Welcoming Communities, *Building Welcoming Communities Campaign: Roadmap to Success.* https://obamawhitehouse.archives.gov/sites/default/files/docs/bwcc_campaign_roadmap.pdf.

WA_doc9 (2016). Hassan M. *Neighbors Together: Community-Based Practices to Strengthen Relations with Refugees and Muslim Communities and Counter Backlash.* Atlanta, GA: Welcoming America.

WA_doc10 (2016). The Welcoming Standards & Certified Welcoming, Welcoming America. https://www.welcomingamerica.org/sites/default/files/Welcoming%20Standard%20%2B%20Certified%20Welcoming.pdf.

WA_doc11 (2016) Welcoming America, *2016 in Review—Annual Report 2016*, https://welcomingamerica.org/wp-content/uploads/2021/04/2016-Annual-Report.pdf.

WA_doc12 (2018). Welcoming America, Welcoming Refugees + Global Detroit, *Welcoming Economies Playbook. Strategies for Building an Inclusive Local Economy*. https://www.welcomingrefugees.org/sites/default/files/documents/resources/Playbook_v4.pdf.

WA_doc13 (2018). Welcoming America/Welcoming Refugees. *Harnessing Volunteer Energy to Support and Welcome Refugees in Your Community. Five Tips for Success*. https://welcomingamerica.org/wp-content/uploads/2021/01/WA_Volunteer-Toolkit_FINAL.pdf.

WA_doc14 (2019). 2019 Annual Report. 10 Years of Welcoming, Welcoming America. https://www.welcomingamerica.org/sites/default/files/2019_Welcoming_America_Annual_Report_High_Res.pdf.

List of Websites

WA_web1, https://www.welcomingamerica.org/news/national-welcoming-week-2012. Welcoming Weeks 2012.

WA_web2, https://www.welcomingamerica.org/news/announcing-welcoming-cities-and-counties-initiative. Welcoming Cities and Counties.

WA_web3, https://www.weglobalnetwork.org/about/. Global Detroit.

WA_web4, https://www.welcomingamerica.org/programs/we-global. Global Detroit.

WA_web5, https://www.weglobalnetwork.org/2013-detroit/. Global Detroit.

WA_web6, https://obamawhitehouse.archives.gov/champions/welcoming-america. Champions of Change: Welcoming America.

WA_web7, https://www.welcomingrefugees.org. Welcoming Refugees.

WA_web8, https://obamawhitehouse.archives.gov/the-press-office/2014/11/21/presidential-memorandum-creating-welcoming-communities-and-fully-integra. White House Memorandum, 21 November 2014.

WA_web9, https://www.welcomingamerica.org/news/white-house-launches-building-welcoming-communities-campaign. White House Launches the Building Welcoming Communities Campaign, press release.

WA_web10, https://www.welcomingamerica.org/programs/certification. WA Certification Programme.

WA_web11, https://certifiedwelcoming.org/become-certified/#costs. Certification Programme.

WA_web12, https://www.welcomingamerica.org/programs/welcoming-international. Welcoming International.

WA_web13, https://welcominginternational.org/about/. Welcoming International.

WA_web14, https://culturalvistas.org/programs/specialty/welcoming-communities-transatlantic-exchange/. Welcoming Communities Transatlantic Exchange.

WA_web15, https://welcomingamerica.org/welcoming-economies-program. Welcoming Economies.

WA_web16, https://welcomingamerica.org/gateways-for-growth. Gateways for Growth programme.

WA_web17, https://welcomingamerica.org/belonging-begins-with-us. National Welcoming Campaign.

List of Interviews

WA_int1, Deputy Director, 24 July 2019, Washington, Welcoming America local office.

WA_int2, Deputy Director, 27 May 2019, Berlin, Welcoming America (Skype interview).

WA_int3, City Officer, Rust Belt area, 16 May 2019, Pittsburgh.

WA_int4, National NGO member of WA, 16 May 2019, Pittsburgh.

WA_int5, Local Coalition, 17 May 2019, Pittsburgh.

WA_int6, County Officer member of WA, Migration Unit, 17 May 2019, Pittsburgh.

WA_int7, external expert engaged in WA activities between 2008 and 2010, 24 July 2020, skype interview.

WA_int8, external expert, academic, 16 May 2019, Pittsburgh.

Cities for Action (C4A)

List of Documents

C4A_doc1. 'Statement from 34 mayors & groups on Federal Judge's temporary order delaying President Obama's immigration actions', 2015/02/17, press release. https://www.citiesforaction.us/2015_02_17_statement_from_34_mayors_groups_on_federal_judge_s_temporary_order_delaying_president_obama_s_immigration_actions.

C4A_doc2. 'Statement from Cities United for Immigration Action on DOJ seeking court order to implement President's executive actions', 2015/02/20, press release. https://www.citiesforaction.us/2015_02_20_statement_from_cities_united_for_immigration_action_on_doj_seeking_court_order_to_implement_president_s_executive_actions.

C4A_doc3. 'Mayors De Blasio and Garcetti announce expanded coalition to take legal action in support of immigration reforms', 2015/04/06, press release. https://www.citiesforaction.us/2015_04_06_mayors_de_blasio_and_garcetti_announce_expanded_coalition_to_take_legal_action_in_support_of_immigration_reforms.

C4A_doc4. 'U.S. cities hail White House recommendations on integration of new Americans', 2015/04/14, press release. https://www.citiesforaction.us/

2015_04_14_u_s_cities_hail_white_house_recommendations_on_integration_of_new_americans.

C4A_doc5. ‘As Court hears arguments today on Obama’s immigration reforms, cities nationwide announce new actions’, 2015/04/17, press release. https://www.citiesforaction.us/2015_04_17_as_court_hears_arguments_today_on_obama_s_immigration_reforms_cities_nationwide_announce_new_actions.

C4A_doc6. ‘Cities announce nationwide day of action to advance President’s immigration reforms’, 2015/05/19, press release. https://www.citiesforaction.us/2015_05_19_cities_announce_nationwide_day_of_action_to_advance_president_s_immigration_reforms.

C4A_doc7. ‘On Citizenship Day, cities announce nationwide action on immigration-related initiatives’, 2015/09/17, press release. https://www.citiesforaction.us/2015_09_17_on_citizenship_day_cities_announce_nationwide_action_on_immigration_related_initiatives.

C4A_doc8. ‘As Pope Francis visits U.S., 18 mayors join forces to commend Obama Administration, and call on them to accept more refugees amid Syrian crisis’, 2015/09/23, press release. https://www.citiesforaction.us/2015_09_23_as_pope_francis_visits_u_s_18_mayors_join_forces_to_commend_obama_administration_and_call_on_them_to_accept_more_refugees_amid_syrian_crisis.

C4A_doc9. ‘Cities to U.S. Senate: oppose legislation that threatens critical funding for so-called ‘Sanctuary Cities’’, 2015/10/19, press release. https://www.citiesforaction.us/2015_10_19_cities_to_u_s_senate_oppose_legislation_that_threatens_critical_funding_for_so_called_sanctuary_cities.

C4A_doc10. ‘Cities United for Immigration Action statement on Governors’ refusal to allow refugees in their states’, 2015/11/17, press release. https://www.citiesforaction.us/2015_11_17_cities_united_for_immigration_action_statement_on_governors_refusal_to_allow_refugees_in_their_states.

C4A_doc11. ‘Cities commemorate one-year anniversary of President Obama’s executive action on immigration’, 2015/11/19, press release. https://www.citiesforaction.us/2015_11_19_cities_commemorate_one_year_anniversary_of_president_obama_s_executive_action_on_immigration.

C4A_doc12. ‘Cities and counties file legal brief urging U.S. Supreme Court action on immigration reforms’, 2015/12/03, press release. https://www.citiesforaction.us/cities_and_counties_file_legal_brief_urging_u_s_supreme_court_action_on_immigration_reforms.

C4A_doc13. ‘Statement from Cities United for Immigration Action on recent reports of Federal ICE raids’, 2016/01/07, press release. https://www.citiesforaction.us/statement_ice_raids.

C4A_doc14. 'Cities and counties file amicus brief in United States v. Texas urging U.S. Supreme Court to permit President Obama's executive action on immigration to move forward', 2016/03/08, press release. https://www.citiesforaction.us/2016_03_08_statement.

C4A_doc15. 'Statement from Cities for Action on reports of future ICE raids', 2016/05/12, press release. https://www.citiesforaction.us/2016_05_12_statement.

C4A_doc16. 'Cities and counties commit to fighting for immigration reforms as the U.S. Supreme Court rules against President Obama's executive actions on immigration', 2016/06/23, press release. https://www.citiesforaction.us/release_2016_06_23.

C4A_doc17. 'Cities for Action urges party leaders to commit to immigration reform', 2016/07/26, press release. https://www.citiesforaction.us/release_2016_07_26.

C4A_doc18. 'Municipal ID Program Toolkit', 2016/10/31, report. https://d3n8a8pro7vhmx.cloudfront.net/citiesforaction/pages/59/attachments/original/1469627290/Municipal_ID_Program_Toolkit_-_Cities_for_Action.pdf?1469627290.

C4A_doc19. 'Cities for Action calls upon President Obama to continue his Administration's support for immigrant communities as he leaves office', 2016/12/29, press release. https://www.citiesforaction.us/release_2016_12_23.

C4A_doc20. 'Statement from mayors and county executives on our commitment to immigrant communities', 2017/01/19, press release. https://www.citiesforaction.us/statement_2017_01_19.

C4A_doc21. 'Statement from Cities for Action on the President's executive actions', 2017/01/25, press release. https://www.citiesforaction.us/statement_2017_01_25.

C4A_doc22. 'Brief for Amici Curiae the Cities of New York, NY; Albany, NY; Austin, TX; Buffalo, NY; Chicago, IL; Gary, IN; Ithaca, NY; Jersey City, NJ; Los Angeles, CA; Madison, WI; Minneapolis, MN; Nashville, TN; New Haven, CT; Oakland, CA; Paterson, NJ; Philadelphia, PA; Plainfield, NJ; Portland, OR; Providence, RI; Rochester, NY; Santa Monica, CA; Seattle, WA; Schenectady, NY; Somerville, MA; South Bend, IN; Syracuse, NY; Trenton, NJ; West Hollywood, CA; and Yonkers, NY; the City and County of San Francisco, CA; the Town of Carrboro, NC; the Boroughs of Haledon, NJ and Princeton, NJ; and the Village of Skokie, IL in support of petitioners', 2017/02/17, press release. https://d3n8a8pro7vhmx.cloudfront.net/citiesforaction/pages/250/attachments/original/1487357289/Darweesh_-_Cities_Amicus.pdf?1487357289.

C4A_doc23. 'Cities and counties file amicus brief challenging President's travel ban', 2017/02/17, press release. https://www.citiesforaction.us/release_2017_02_17.

C4A_doc24. 'Statement from Cities for Action on the President's new travel ban executive order', 2017/03/06, press release. https://www.citiesforaction.us/statement_2017_03_06.

C4A_doc25. 'Cities for Action shares lessons learned from first travel ban', 2017/03/17, press release. https://www.citiesforaction.us/release_2017_03_17.

C4A_doc26. 'Cities for Action. Case Studies of Cities' Responses to Travel Ban Executive Order's Impact at US Airports 1/27–1/29', 2017/03/17, report. https://d3n8a8pro7vhmx.cloudfront.net/citiesforaction/pages/48/attachments/original/1489755829/C4A_Airport_Response_Case_Studies_Report.pdf?1489755829.

C4A_doc27. 'Statement from Cities for Action on the Federal Court's ruling', 2017/04/26, press release. https://www.citiesforaction.us/statement_2017_04_26.

C4A_doc28. 'Mayors issue letter urging the Administration to extend TPS for Haitians', 2017/05/17, press release. https://www.citiesforaction.us/release_2017_05_17.

C4A_doc29. 'Statement from Cities for Action on DHS rescission of DAPA and expanded DACA', 2017/06/16. https://www.citiesforaction.us/statement_2017_06_16.

C4A_doc30. 'Cities to House Leadership: oppose anti-immigrant bills H.R. 3003 & H.R. 3004', 2017/06/28, press release. https://www.citiesforaction.us/release_2017_06_28.

C4A_doc31. 'Statement from Cities for Action on anti-immigrant House bills', 2017/06/29, press release. https://www.citiesforaction.us/statement_2017_06_29.

C4A_doc32. 'Mayors & county officials call on President to continue DACA and support America's Dreamers', 2017/08/15, press release. https://www.citiesforaction.us/release_2017_08_14.

C4A_doc33. 'Mayors & county officials denounce President Trump's decision to end Deferred Action for Childhood Arrivals', 2017/09/05, press release. https://www.citiesforaction.us/statement_2017_09_05.

C4A_doc34. 'Mayors issue letter urging the Administration to extend TPS for Hondurans and Nicaraguans', 2017/11/02, press release. https://www.citiesforaction.us/release_11_2_17.

C4A_doc35. 'Cities for Action declares TPS phase-out for Nicaragua "Inhumane", Calls on Congress to protect TPS recipients', 2017/11/08, press release. https://www.citiesforaction.us/statement_2017_11_08.

C4A_doc36. 'Cities for Action: Trump Administration's decision to end TPS for Haiti is abhorrent, Congress must find a permanent solution', 2017/11/22, press release. https://www.citiesforaction.us/statement_2017_11_22.

C4A_doc37. 'Cities for Action: it's cruel and counter-productive for Trump Administration to terminate TPS for Salvadorans', 2018/01/08, press release. https://www.citiesforaction.us/statement_2018_01_08.

C4A_doc38. 'NYC and Chicago author joint op-ed urging Trump Administration to extend TPS for Syrians', 2018/01/30, press release. https://www.citiesforaction.us/release_2018_01_30.

C4A_doc39. 'Statement from Cities for Action on Senate immigration negotiations', 2018/02/15, press release. https://www.citiesforaction.us/statement_2018_02_15.

C4A_doc40. 'Statement from Cities for Action on termination of Temporary Protected Status for Hondurans', 2018/05/04, press release. https://www.citiesforaction.us/statement_2018_05_04.

C4A_doc41. 'Mayors & county officials urge Congress to bring the DREAM Act up for a vote', 2018/06/05, press release. https://www.citiesforaction.us/release_2018_06_05.

C4A_doc42. 'Statement from Cities for Action on travel ban ruling', 2018/06/26, press release. https://www.citiesforaction.us/18_06_26_statement_from_cities_for_action_on_travel_ban_ruling.

C4A_doc43.'Cities for Action urges Trump Administration to re-designate and extend Temporary Protected Status for Yemen', 2018/06/29, press release. https://www.citiesforaction.us/release_2018_06_29.

C4A_doc44. 'Statement from Cities for Action on the extension of Temporary Protected Status for Somalia', 2018/07/24, press release. https://www.citiesforaction.us/release_2018_07_24.

C4A_doc45. 'Statement from Cities for Action on Trump Administration's decision to slash U.S. refugee admissions', 2018/09/19, press release. https://www.citiesforaction.us/release_2018_09_19.

C4A_doc46.'Cities for Action and Lumos Foundation launch Critical Report on Confronting Family Separation', 2018/09/24, press release. https://www.citiesforaction.us/release_2018_09_24a.

C4A_doc47. 'On the Frontlines of the Family Separation Crisis: City Response and Best Practice for Assisting Families', 2018/09/24, report. https://d3n8a8pro7vhmx.cloudfront.net/citiesforaction/pages/29/attachments/original/1537804683/Family_Separation_Crisis_Report_WEB-SINGLES_21SEP18.pdf?1537804683.

C4A_doc48. 'Statement from Cities for Action on Trump Administration's Proposed "public Charge" Rule Change', 2018/09/24, Press Release. https://www.citiesforaction.us/release_2018_09_24b.

C4A_doc49. 'Statement from Cities for Action on the House Passage of H.R. 6, the American Dream and Promise Act of 2019', 2019/06/04, press release. https://www.citiesforaction.us/release_2019_06_04.

C4A_doc50. 'Statement from Cities for Action on Trump Administration's "public charge" rule change', 2019/08/13, press release. https://www.citiesforaction.us/19_08_13_-statement_from_cities_for_action_on_trump_administration_s_public_charge_rule_change.

C4A_doc51. 'Cities for Action Statement in Support of Refugees and the U.S. Refugee Administration Program', 2019/10/31, press release. https://www.citiesforaction.us/19_10_31_statement_from_c4a_in_support_of_refugees_and_u_s_refugee_admissions_program.

C4A_doc52. 'Cities for DACA—Resource Guide for DACA Recipients and Impacted Communities', no date, report/toolkit. https://d3n8a8pro7vhmx.cloudfront.net/citiesforaction/pages/494/attachments/original/1612818352/Cities_for_DACA_Resource_Guide_2.8.2021_-_pdf_%281%29.pdf?1612818352.

List of Websites

C4A_web1, https://www.citiesforaction.us/mission. C4A homepage.

C4A_web2, https://www.citiesforaction.us/mayors_form_coalition_to_support_obama_s_immigration_action. News.

C4A_web3, https://citiesofmigration.ca/ezine_stories/cities-united-for-immigration-action/ Cities of Migration, News.

C4A_web4, https://medium.com/@globalnyc/local-advocacy-on-immigration-a-conversation-with-niti-suchdeve-cities-for-action-program-f9d61aed5995. Interview with MOIA Officer Niti Suchdeve.

C4A_web5, http://www.atlantaloop.com/pro-immigration-policy-coalition-to-meet-in-atlanta/. Atlanta Meeting.

C4A_web6, https://seattlechannel.org/videos?videoid=x107398. Seattle Meeting.

List of interviews

C4A_int1, Officer C4A, 22 July 2019, New York.

C4A_int2, Officer C4A, 22 July 2019, New York.

C4A_int3, Officer foundation, 21 July 2019, New York.

C4A_int4, City Officer, 19 May 2019, Pittsburgh.

Index

T. Caponio, *Making Sense of the Multilevel Governance of Migration*,
https://doi.org/10.1007/978-3-030-82551-5

S

T

U

V

W

Y

CPSIA information can be obtained
at www.ICGtesting.com
Printed in the USA
LVHW110854030422
715181LV00003B/33